In the Shadow
of the
United States

In the Shadow
of the United States:
Democracy
and
Regional Order
in the Latin Caribbean

Giancarlo Soler Torrijos

BrownWalker Press
Boca Raton

In the Shadow of the United States:
Democracy and Regional Order in the Latin Caribbean

BrownWalker Press
Boca Raton, Florida ♦ USA
2008

ISBN-10: 1-59942-439-8 *(paper)*
ISBN-13: 978-1-59942-993-9 *(paper)*

ISBN-10: 1-59942-440-1 *(ebook)*
ISBN-13: 978-159942-440-8 *(ebook)*

www.brownwalker.com

Library of Congress Cataloging-in-Publication Data

Soler, Giancarlo.
  [A la sombra de los Estados Unidos. English]
  In the shadow of the United States : democracy and regional order in the Latin
Caribbean / Giancarlo Soler Torrijos.
      p. cm.
  Includes bibliographical references.
  ISBN-13: 978-1-59942-439-2 (pbk. : alk. paper)
  ISBN-10: 1-59942-439-8 (pbk. : alk. paper)
  1. Caribbean Area--Foreign relations--United States. 2. United States--Foreign
relations--Caribbean Area. 3. Democratization--Caribbean Area. 4. Caribbean Area--
Politics and government--1945- I. Title.
  F2178.U6S6713 2008
  327.73072909'04--dc22
                                        2008003216

TABLE OF CONTENTS

ACKNOWLEDGEMENTS

This work is the culmination of a study that started as an interest with explaining political processes in my home country, Panama. Meanwhile, democratic transitions were taking place in Central America, the region to which I have devoted most of my professional life. I became interested in democratisation studies because the local, the regional and the global seemed to converge on the issue of regime transitions but then couldn't quite formulate a way to understand it. Thus all of these issues became part of a research project that took this form, first as a thesis submitted in fulfilment of the requirements for the DPhil in International Relations at Oxford University, from where I received the academic training and advice that allowed me to give a coherent shape to these concerns.

The project began life in Oxford, continued in Quito, Panama and Mexico City, but not without having the opportunity to visit, undertake interviews and do archival and periodical research in London, Washington DC, Panama City, Managua and Santo Domingo. I could not have reached this point without the support of numerous institutions and persons who backed my efforts to complete my research and writing. I am indebted to the Ford and MacArthur Foundations' Program for Central American and Mexican students and the Institute of International Education, US Department of State; Wolfson College (Oxford); the Carlos Emilio de Sola Wright Fund, the Norman Chester Fund, the Mellon Fund, the Inter-faculty Committee for Latin American Studies; the Cyril Foster Fund, and the Committee for Graduate Studies, all of them at Oxford; the Simón Bolívar Andean University (Quito), and the Monterrey Institute of Technology (ITESM), State of Mexico Campus. I am particularly thankful to Laurence Whitehead and Andrew Hurrell of Nuffield College, Oxford, for their invaluable support in this endeavour. Needless to say, the text here is my own.

No words can express my gratitude to my parents, whose value orientation at one point in time led them to trade their house for a smaller place to live in support of their son's aspiration for a first-class education; and to my daughter, from whom I took most of the time that as a father I could have spent rearing her during the first years of her life.

Giancarlo Soler Torrijos

Introduction

Understanding and Explaining Latin Caribbean Regime Transitions

I t is now a familiar story that, in the post-Cold War era, transitions to democracy in the Latin Caribbean have progressed well and farther ahead
than in many other parts of the world. In the eighties, countries in the
area formerly under authoritarian or dictatorial regimes adopted liberal democratic institutions and procedures. At first, beneath the veil of political openings,'exclusionary democracies' emerged: political competition and the exercise
of political rights remained restricted, while (most notably in Nicaragua, El
Salvador and Guatemala) armed conflicts prevailed. Despite this tormented
past, with the end of East-West rivalries these societies took steps towards
strengthening their incipient democracies and now seem to be way past that
situation. In spite of possible shortcomings, these events provide the basis for
claiming that present prospects for democratic consolidation in the sub-region
have no parallel in history. How did this happen? How can we explain it? What
can we learn from it?

These advances have been taking place in a global setting that has stirred
regime changes worldwide. As post-Cold War political developments, we may
be tempted to group them together as deferred repercussions of the 1989 revolution, said to be caused by "the collapse of authoritarian alternatives to liberal-
ism and the decline of brutality in both internal and international affairs."[1] To
an extent, this is true of regime transitions in the Latin Caribbean, because authoritarian forces lost strength as post-1989 events behind the Iron Curtain and
the sub-region unfolded. Yet, democratisation in these states cannot be depicted
simply as a process mirroring international trends.[2] In the eighties, for example,

---

1. John Lewis Gaddis, *The United States and the End of the Cold War Implications, Reconsiderations, Provocations*, (New York and Oxford: Oxford University Press, 1992), p. 156.

2. Karen L. Remmer, "Democratization in Latin America." In Robert O. Slater, Barry M. Schutz,
and Steven R. Dorr (eds.), *Global Transformation and the Third World*, (Boulder and London:
Lynne Rienner Publishers and Adamantine Press, 1993), p. 97.

Right-wing authoritarianism had ceased to be a creditable political option elsewhere, while in the area it remained as an alternative.

In contrast to most of Latin America, these transitions are rather late by western world standards. The waves of democratic transitions began in Southern Europe with Portugal's military-led 'Revolution of Carnations' in 1974, followed later by similar developments in Greece, Spain and South America. By the end of the eighties, all South American nations had undergone transitions from authoritarian rule, and most had sworn in a second president-elect. During this interval, however, prevailing conditions in the Latin Caribbean gave way to the belief that the sub-region was far from this achievement. Compared in terms of the nature of the political regimes in place during most of the sixties and seventies, the Latin Caribbean was generally not too different from its South American counterparts. In the seventies, authoritarian regimes throughout Latin America were beleaguered by mass popular movements demanding democracy and human rights. Latin Caribbean political activists, like their South American counterparts, struggled for democratisation.

Then why did the Latin Caribbean not follow the democratising trend of its neighbours to the south? What distinguishes Latin Caribbean regime changes from transitions elsewhere? Relying on both comparative political and international relations perspectives, this book argues that different geo-strategic conditions account for the sub-region's atypical trajectory. There were regime conditions such as the existence of formal democratic institutions and previous or concurrent experiences with pluralism that were country-specific but not totally out of line with Latin America. The book argues that the Latin Caribbean's different trajectory resulted from the continuous exertion of US power that, through time, projected itself and solidified into the political character of these states.

The United States has the oldest democracy in the world, and it has been the world power that has most intervened or influenced Latin American and Caribbean affairs. Why did these influences not translate themselves into earlier or less traumatic democratisations in the Latin Caribbean, compared to other parts of the continent, and the world? If it were for being so close to the United States and for the declared intention of US foreign policies, the Latin Caribbean should have been one of the first and not one of the last regions to democratise. Evidently, US involvement or resolve does not always translate into desired changes, no matter how powerful the regional hegemon is vis-à-vis the states in the area. Witness the direction taken by the Cuban revolution in the sixties, in the midst of the Cold War. Yet, whereas transitions in the Latin Caribbean cannot be explained as direct results of US influence, neither can they be understood without appraising the role of the United States. Throughout the twentieth century, the United States imbued the Latin Caribbean's economical, political and cultural affairs and, as such, it is imperative to incorporate the role of the United States into the explanation: US influence should be seen in the context of the regional construction that historically permeated political change in the area.

This book presents answers to these questions by examining the following comparative hypothesis. First, that the exercise of US power distorted regime transitions, without being sufficient to determine outcomes. But hegemonic patterns are not static. Depending on the sum of local and external circumstances, US influence aided or impaired democratic prospects. Second, domestic actors altered their calculations and strategies to take into account the likely reactions of the hegemon. Having to cope with a regional order structured from without, actors engaged in cost-benefit analysis of regime change based on the opportunities and constraints offered by the external environment. Third, that the set of domestic-international interactions propelling each regime transition is also conditioned by the broader regional order and by the sequence of political events in neighbouring countries.

To provide the background for that discussion and for the case studies that follow, heretofore this introductory chapter addresses the following propositions. Firstly, whereas the existing comparative literature on democratisation—including that stressing its international aspects—helps us understand the interplay of forces leading the change from one regime to the next, a geo-strategic dimension needs to be incorporated. But geo-strategic conditions are country- and region-specific and this book is dealing with processes that seem to be taking place on a regional basis. Thus, secondly we need to understand what is meant by the Latin Caribbean and why such differentiation matters for the study of regime transitions in the area. The United States has been the sub-region's hegemonic power and has conducted a great deal of its relations with these states under the banner of promoting democracy. Then, thirdly we delve into the US democracy-promotion policies in general and in relation to this sub-region in particular. Fourthly, all this brings us to realise that, to fully comprehend the political evolution of the Latin Caribbean, we must pay attention to the interlocking of regime transitions and regional orders and to the shadow that the US projected. Finally, a section on research methods expands on the complexities of addressing the scope of this study.

Democratisation and its international aspects

So far, research on democratisation has gone through three generations, each of which has attempted to explain what brings forward and sustains democracy. The perception that full democracy existed only in Western (and Westernised) industrial countries conditioned the first generation. The second drew out comparisons from the transitions in Southern Europe and South America. The flourishing third generation, to which this study aims to contribute, strives to incorporate transitions' external environment, as both Eastern and Central Europe manifested at the end of the Cold War.

The first studies on democratisation assumed that some combination of social and economic conditions would steer democratic political transformations. Seen from this perspective, democratisation required a "suitable" distribution of land, wealth and income, high levels of education and economic development, and cultural homogeneity.[3] These writings grew out of the generalisation that, since

---

3. See, primarily, the oft-cited works of Seymour Martin Lipset, "Some Social Requisites of

most industrialised, capitalist economies were democracies, the Third World would become democratic only if it increasingly resembled those of the First, socially and culturally. Reality added weight to this belief since, by mid-1970, there were relatively few democracies in the world.

In the social sciences, this perception took ground within the "modernisation school" of political development. It argues that socio-economic development affects the prospects for democracy at all layers of society. At the individual level, a higher level of income, education and social or occupational status would buttress democratic norms, values and behaviours. However, transitions have taken place and are underway despite many setbacks in social and economic indicators. As Remmer has stated regarding Latin America, the sub-region's political development does not conform to the notion that modernisation promotes democracy. Changes in social status, education and income have not lessened individuals' propensity to support authoritarianism. At the societal level, democratisation has not mirrored socio-economic development. "The most modernized countries in Latin America have not necessarily been the most democratic, nor have gains in literacy, per capita income, or popular organisational capacity been predictably translated through time into democratisation." For instance, the democratic advances of the eighties were concurrent with economic crisis, de-industrialization, and abrupt falls in standards of living.[4]

In tracing the causality of political processes, this perspective has given way to explorations of the linkages between economic reform and political change. Research on this topic points out the ways in which economic reforms affect political developments but, contrary to the requisites-of-democracy argument, these are non-deterministic.[5] As such, it is a step forward towards comprehending the engines of political liberalisation and democratisation.

The second generation of the literature on democratisation does not reject the possible effect that "structural" factors may have in the long term on the prospects for democracy. Rather, it asserts that democratisation is grounded on politi-

---

Democracy," *American Political Science Review*, Vol. 53, 1959, pp. 69-105; Seymour Martin Lipset, *Political Man: The Social Bases of Politics*, expanded edition, (Baltimore: The John Hopkins University Press, 1981), pp. 27-63; Seymour Martin Lipset, "The Centrality of Political Culture," *Journal of Democracy* 1 (Fall 1990), pp. 88-91; Robert A. Dahl, *Polyarchy: Participation and Opposition*, (New Haven: Yale University Press, 1971), pp. 48-188; and Dankart Rustow, "Transitions to Democracy: Towards a Dynamic Model," *Comparative Politics* 2 (April 1970), pp. 358-361.

4. Karen L. Remmer, "Democratisation in Latin America." In Slater, Schutz, and Dorr (1993), *op. cit.*, pp. 97-98.

5. See Adam Przeworski, *Democracy and the Market: Political and Economic Reform in Eastern Europe and Latin America*, (New York: Cambridge University Press, 1991), and Laurence Whitehead, *Economic Liberalization and Democratisation: Exploration of the Linkages*, (New York: Pergamon Press, 1993). For an earlier discussion, see George A. Lopez and Michael Stohl (eds.), *Liberalization and Redemocratisation in Latin America*, (Westport, Connecticut: Greenwood Press, 1987). For an analysis of the political impact of the transition to market economies in Socialist societies, see Yanqi Tong, "Economic Reform and Political Change in Reforming Socialist Societies: The Cases of China and Hungary," Ph.D. Dissertation, The Johns Hopkins University, 1992.

cal choices, not necessarily on social and economic conditions. Works along these lines began with the emergence of democratic transitions in Southern Europe in the seventies, and in South America in the eighties. The emerging democracies triggered comparative and country studies pointing out a number of intervening variables, mostly domestic in nature, which could be identified at distinct conjunctures of the transient period from the breakdown of authoritarianism to the onset of constitutional rule. A fundamental tenet of the second generation is that the sequence of actions/choices is essential for the outcome of transitions. In examining the transitions in Southern Europe and South America, we learned what sparks democratic transitions, that these factors may vary and that they might end in regimes that take different institutional shapes.[6] Actors of various kinds, in pursuing their interests, coalesce or clash to affect government policies or the composition of regimes. However, outcomes depend on the sequence of choices made at every phase of the process. The probability of later transitional circumstances pushing towards a democratic outcome "rests on earlier transitional choices and events that set the stage for a democratic scenario-a scenario that becomes more progressively difficult to deflect or reverse as it plays itself out."[7] As such, it provides a process-driven explanation, for sequences of interactions create scenarios upon which later political activity takes place.

The degree to which second-generation works accepted the weight of external actors varied from total non-recognition to acknowledging certain influences that nevertheless remained secondary to understanding democratisation. As in most comparative political studies, the evaluation of regime change grew from the assumption that political processes occur within national boundaries and, as a result, causality must be traced in the domestic realm. Whenever an external aspect was taken into consideration, the norm was to consider it as a one-off input with repercussions limited to the moment in which it intrudes in a country's political process. Baloyra (1987), for instance, made no room for foreign actors in formulating a framework aimed at identifying the initial stages of transitions.[8] Similarly, Vanhanen (1990, 1992) mentioned no external linkages to democratisation in an initial comparative study of 147 states, and later in developing a model in which specific domestic strategies determined the success of the struggles for democracy.[9] Likewise, Diamond imputed political changes to the domestic interplay of political forces, though conceded that domestic politi-

6. The pioneering studies are contained in the four volumes edited by Guillermo O'Donnell, Philip C. Schmitter and Laurence Whitehead, *Transitions from Authoritarian Rule*, (Baltimore: John Hopkins University Press, 1986).

7. Giuseppe Di Palma, "The European and the Central American Experience." In Giuseppe Di Palma and Laurence Whitehead (eds.), *The Central American Impasse*, (London and Sidney: Croom Helm and the Friedrich Naumann Foundation, 1986), pp. 30-31.

8. Enrique Baloyra, "Democratic Transitions in Comparative Perspective." In Enrique Baloyra (ed.), *Comparing New Democracies*, (Boulder and London: Westview Press, 1987), pp. 9-52.

9. Tatu Vanhanen, *The Process of Democratisation: A Comparative Study of 147 States, 1980-1988*, (Washington, Philadelphia and London: Crane Russak, 1990); and Tatu Vanhanen, "Introduction." In *Strategies of Democratisation*, (Washington, Philadelphia and London: Crane Russak, 1992), pp. 1-29.

cal structures in the Third World have a substantial foreign component, rooted in colonial legacies.[10]

Regional studies followed the same line of thought. In appraising the role of the United States over Latin American transitions, for instance, Lowenthal called US influence "of secondary or tertiary importance." Lowenthal also noted the exception of rare cases when external influence could "tip the scale," such as in the Dominican Republic's elections in 1978, or in highly penetrated countries that are vulnerable to the United States.[11] Overall, social scientists agreed that international actors played at best an indirect role, excepting countries occupied by foreign powers.[12]

The largely peaceful changes that took place in the former Communist block in 1989-1990 challenged the assumptions laid out by prior models of democratisation. The only foreign aspect systematically studied thus far was the influence of the European Economic Community, especially in terms of the attractiveness it posed to the élites of its Southern European neighbours.[13] Transitions to democracy in Southern Europe and the Southern Cone had occurred in peacetime, from regimes of the Right, in developing or newly industrializing countries within the Western alliance system. However, in Central and Eastern Europe they took place from regimes "of the Left," in countries with command economies and with little historical experience with liberal democracy-factors which were not present in previous cases.

---

10. Larry Diamond, "Introduction: Persistence, Erosion, Breakdown and Renewal," in Larry Diamond, Juan Linz and Seymour Martin Lipset. (eds.), *Democracy in Developing Countries: Asia*, (Boulder, Colorado: Lynne Rienner Publishers, 1989), pp. 1-53. In later writings, Diamond incorporated external variables to his theoretical framework.

11. Abraham Lowenthal, "The United States and Latin American Democracy: Learning from History." In Abraham Lowenthal (ed.), *Exporting Democracy: The United States and Latin America*, (Baltimore and London: The Johns Hopkins University Press, 1991), p. 400.

12. Laurence Whitehead, "International Aspects of Democratisation." In Guillermo O'Donnell, Philippe C. Schmitter and Laurence Whitehead (eds.), *Transitions from Authoritarian Rule: Comparative Perspectives*, Vol. 3, (Baltimore and London: The Johns Hopkins University Press, 1986), p. 45; Philippe Schmitter, "Una introducción a las transiciones desde la dominación autoritaria en Europa meridional: Italia, Grecia, Portugal, España y Turquía." In Guillermo O'Donnell, Philippe C. Schmitter and Laurence Whitehead (eds.), *Transiciones desde un gobierno autoritario: Europa Meridional*, Vol. 1, (Buenos Aires, Barcelona, Mexico: Paidós, 1989 [1986]).

13. See Geoffrey Pridham, "Comparative Perspectives on the New Mediterranean Democracies: A Model of Regime Transition?" In Geoffrey Pridham (ed.), *The New Mediterranean Democracies: Regime Transition in Spain, Greece and Portugal*, (London: Frank Cass and Co., 1984), p. 22. The influence of the EEC was not incorporated systematically in an interpretative framework until the early nineties, when events in Eastern Europe made evident its importance. See, among others, Bassilios Tsingos, "Underwriting Democracy, Not Exporting It." M.Phil. Thesis, Oxford University, 1994. See also John Pinder, "The European Community and Democracy in Central and Eastern Europe." In Geoffrey Pridham, Eric Herring, and George Sanford (eds.), *Building Democracy? The International Dimension of Democratisation in Eastern Europe*, (London: Leicester University Press, 1994), pp. 119-143; and Susannah Verney, "To be or not to be within the European Community: the party debate and democratic consolidation in Greece." In Geoffrey Pridham (ed.), *Securing democracy: political parties and democratic consolidation in Southern Europe*, (London and New York: Routledge, 1990), pp. 203-223.

The third generation of the literature on democratisation, an offspring of the second, begins with the assumption that transitions must be studied in relation to the international context. The new international circumstances laid out the impetus for systematising the external environment of democratization processes. The political transformations in Eastern Europe showed the overall importance of the international context, specially the end of the Cold War, but had to be incorporated into the analytical framework. Pridham, for instance, a pioneer in the study of the international aspects of democratisation, in a 1984 study underrated the external environment of Southern European transitions. But the new situation demanded reconsideration, "The international context is the forgotten dimension in the study of democratic transition... whether [it] is secondary to domestic development is less clear-cut than [...] suggested in the theoretical or comparative literature."[14] Previously a few studies had regarded external factors, but they had usually taken it for granted, precisely because -at least in relation to Southern Europe in the 1970's and South America in the 1980's- it "seldom intruded too conspicuously on an essentially domestic drama."[15] The notion that external factors may significantly influence the outcome of regime change has increasingly served as the basis for comparative studies on democratisation.[16]

In this sense, the Latin Caribbean's democratic advances—as post 1989 developments—indicate that they have incorporated an 'international dimension.' However, the area's international context has been substantially different from that experienced by states elsewhere. For international politics is played within particular regional contexts, "marked by a distinctive pattern of powers and agen-

---

14. Geoffrey Pridham, "International Influences and Democratic Transition: Problems of Theory and Practice in Linkage Politics." In Geoffrey Pridham (ed.), *Encouraging Democracy: The International Context of Regime Transition in Southern Europe*, (London: Leicester University Press, 1991), pp. 1, 26. This is a reversal from Pridham, "Comparative Perspectives on the New Mediterranean Democracies: A Model of Regime Transition?," pp. 1-29.

15. Whitehead, "International Aspects of Democratisation," p. 5. Other pioneering works in this aspect are: Alfred Tovias (1984), "The International Context of Democratic Transition." In Pridham, *The New Mediterranean Democracies*, pp. 158-171; and Terry Karl, "Imposing Consent? Electoralism vs. Democratisation in El Salvador." In Paul W. Drake and Eduardo Silva (eds.), *Elections and Democratisation in Latin America, 1980-1985*, (San Diego, California: University of California, San Diego, 1986), pp. 9-36.

16. See Laurence Whitehead, "The Imposition of Democracy." In Abraham Lowenthal (ed.), *Exporting Democracy: The United States and Latin America*, (Baltimore and London: The Johns Hopkins University Press, 1991), pp. 356-382; a revision of the transitions in Southern Europe to consider the external aspects is in Pridham, "International Influences and Democratic Transition: Problems of Theory and Practice in Linkage Politics;" on Eastern Europe, see Geoffrey Pridham and Tatu Vanhanen (eds.), *Democratisation in Eastern Europe: Domestic and International Perspectives*, (London and New York: Routledge, 1994), and the volume edited by Pridham, Herring, and Sanford, *Building Democracy? The International Dimension of Democratisation in Eastern Europe*; Tony Smith, *America's Mission: The United States and the Worldwide Struggle for Democracy*, (Princeton: Princeton University Press, 1994), an ambitious attempt to cover the history of democratic development as a by-product of American influence in the world. The most comprehensive work on this subject to date is Laurence Whitehead (ed.), *The international dimension of democratisation: Europe and the Americas*, (Oxford: Oxford University Press, 1997).

da of concerns."[17] South America and Mediterranean Europe are regions located in the outer layers of the US-dominated system of alliances. The Latin Caribbean is located within the innermost layer of the US sphere-of-influence.[18] This variation denoted the Western hegemonic power's lesser involvement and commitment in the democratisation processes of Southern Europe and South America in the seventies and eighties; transitions in those regions went on with a large degree of autonomy from the international environment and took place without forceful foreign pressures. Excepting, briefly, Portugal's military-led 'Carnation Revolution' in 1974, overall their transitions did not threaten the world's balance of power.

The external dimension of regime change in the Latin Caribbean may have long been apparent, as decades of US involvement in the sub-region's conflicts attest. Yet, the extent to which geo-strategic circumstances influence the outcome of transitions has until recently been not been incorporated into the analytical framework of democratisation, though so far it has concentrated on Eastern Europe. Post-Cold War studies on the Eastern European transitions naturally take into account the impact of geo-strategic conditions: the effect of the Soviet Union's effective withdrawal from Eastern European affairs in 1989 and the stabilizing force of European democracies. As such, they could not have occurred the way they did without the Soviet Union's lifting of its "veto power" over the sub-region's political developments.[19] East-Central European states experienced, however, a different form of 'subordination:' they went from a Moscow-based, direct form of domination, to a more loose relationship with multi-centred European powers.[20] The Latin Caribbean has intermittently experienced both direct and indirect forms of hegemonic control by Washington, but under a substantially more relaxed atmosphere than that of the monolithic Soviet Union, an environment pertaining to the complexities of American political institutions and culture. Latin Caribbean political developments evidence that there is a geo-strategic dimension at play. Yet, the analytical framework of democratisation has not adequately dealt with the extent to which regional circumstances have conditioned democratic transitions in this area of the world.[21]

---

17. Robert H. Jackson and Alan James, "The Character of Independent Statehood." In Robert Jackson and Alan James (eds.), *States in a Changing World: A Contemporary Analysis*, (Oxford: Clarendon Press, 1993), p. 12.

18. Similar considerations regarding this subregion are in Thomas G. Weiss and James G. Blight (ed.), *The suffering grass: Superpowers and regional conflict in Southern Africa and the Caribbean*, (Boulder and London: Lynne Rienner Publishers, 1992).

19. Laurence Whitehead, "East-Central Europe in Comparative Perspective." In Pridham, Herring, and Sanford (eds.), *Building Democracy? The International Dimension of Democratisation in Eastern Europe*, pp. 32–59. See also Gary Goertz and Jon Solem, "Eastern Europe, 1945–1989." In Gary Goertz, *Contexts of International Politics*, (Cambridge: Cambridge University Press, 1994), pp. 137–170; Laurence Whitehead, "Geography and democratic destiny," *Journal of Democracy*, (January 1999), pp. 74.

20. For a plausible comparison between the USSR and the United States vis-à-vis their respective spheres-of-influence, see Jan Triska (ed.), *Dominant Powers and Subordinate States: The United States in Latin America and the Soviet Union in Eastern Europe*, (Durnham: Duke University Press, 1986).

21. On Central America, two works deal with the notion of an hegemonic impediment to democratisation: One, briefly, by Giuseppe Di Palma, *To Craft Democracies*, (Berkeley,

Geo-strategic conditions are relevant because political-geographic circumstances influence a state's political configuration and foreign relations.[22] The condition of vicinity entails intense interactions with adjacent political, economic and cultural influences. As geographically-based entities, states can hardly renounce having relations with their neighbours. Despite a Head of State's will to isolate his nation from outside influences (as was the case of Albania under Enver Hoxha) or another's attempt to isolate a pariah state (as the United States and Cuba under Fidel Castro), it is practically impossible to avoid the totality of interactions with the surroundings.

As players in the international arena, states find constraints derived from the world system's (and its regional counterpart's) distribution of power. For less developed countries and, therefore, subordinate players in the international arena, geo-strategic circumstances mean that their actions are constrained by rules and norms established by dominant hegemons. Latin Caribbean states' proximity to the United States was often viewed in Washington as possible sources of threat to its national security while their weakness was interpreted as a justification to dictate them rules and control their behaviour. For more developed and, consequently, dominant players, it means that their world-wide exertion of authority is not homogeneous. Considerations about their relations with each region are also influenced by their geographical proximity (the closer states within these regions are, the greater the potential danger to its national security) and by their power capabilities (the weaker the states within these regions are, the easier it may be to dictate rules and force behaviour). In this sense, though America's sphere-of-influence extends to the whole Western Hemisphere—if not beyond—weaker states located within its 'shadow'—as in the Caribbean Basin—have endured substantial and greater US tutelage over their affairs.

Costa Rica's 'exceptionality' throws light into the framework proposed here.[23] The Cold War had been launched with the enunciation of the Truman 'doctrine' in 1947 but, by 1948, as the Costa Rican Revolution started, Washington had not yet overturned its aim of promoting democracy in the Americas. For example, at this point in time, Washington had not yet fully come to terms with Nicaragua's dictator Anastasio Somoza García who, as head of the National Guard, had deposed the President, breaking the constitutional scheme fostered by the

---

Los Angeles, Oxford: University of California Press, 1990), p. 192; and the other also by Giuseppe Di Palma "The Central American and the European Experience." In Giuseppe Di Palma and Laurence Whitehead (eds.), *The Central American Impasse*, (London and Sydney: Croom Helm and the Friedrich Naumann Foundation, 1986), pp. 3031.

22. This argument is developed thoroughly in Jackson and James, "The Character of Independent Statehood," *Op. cit.*

23. Most of the keys to Costa Rican exceptionalism have been searched for in the domestic realm. See Kirk S. Bowman, "New scholarship on Costa Rican Exceptionalism," *Journal of Interamerican Studies and World Affairs*, vol. 41, no. 2 (Summer 1999), pp. 123–130. The fact that the post-revolution governments implemented foreign policies aimed at maintaining a close relationship with the United States has been found to have contributed to the consoliudation of Costa Rican democracy. See Cynthia Chalker Franklyn, "Riding the wave: the domestic and international sources of Costa Rican democracy," PhD Dissertation, University of Pittsburgh, 1998, p. 195.

State Department at the end of the War. The new and subsequent Costa Rican regimes' adaptive behaviour—banning Communist party activity (made easier by the latter's active participation in the defeated government) and allying with Washington, though pursuing left-of-centre government policies—allowed the country to evolve into democratic consolidation, because it did not endure US influences contrary to this outcome.[24]

Guatemala's transition (1944–1954), despite taking place at similar historical conjunctures, followed a dissimilar path. It seems to have ended differently because of Washington's greater opposition to leftist influence in the government of Col. Jacobo Arbenz in Guatemala in the first half of the fifties than to that in San José (whose Communists opposed and fought against Costa Rica's Revolution). Guatemala faced US hostility: by 1954, McCarthist paranoia at home and zero-sum Cold War logic abroad propelled Washington to overturn Guatemala's brief democratic trajectory, destroying what might have been the second (though historically it would have been the first) pillar of democracy in the Latin Caribbean.[25]

The Latin Caribbean

The Caribbean is traditionally known as the area made up by the heterogeneous group of the smallest states in the Americas with coasts in the Caribbean Sea; these states share a variety of cultural and climatic elements, and maybe similar problems, in view of their dual condition as being lesser-developed and the most vulnerable states. Those states bordering the Caribbean whose formation as nation-states led them on a different course—due to their size, strength, history or ties to other Latin American countries—are not normally deemed part of this sub-region. Among them are the United States, Mexico, Panama (whose sub-regional identity is pending), Venezuela and Colombia (the latter two have stronger ties to the Andean region). Due to historical and geographic circumstances, Central American states have developed few links with the Caribbean, and one of them, El Salvador, borders only the Pacific Ocean. In this picture, the Caribbean is formed by the island-states in the Caribbean Sea and the mainland countries (Guyana, Surinam and Belize) that belong to the Caribbean Economic Community (CARICOM), plus Cuba, Haiti and the Dominican Republic. Non-sovereign entities such as the Commonwealth of Puerto Rico are excluded, though their actors sometimes partake in the sub-region's cultural and political interactions.

As a politically constructed sub-region, the definition of the Caribbean is undergoing change. The United States, with its geo-strategic vision of the area, has continually referred to the region as the Caribbean Basin, to include the Central American States and Panama in this aggregation. Given its condition as a transit route for a significant portion of its trade, differences in culture, history or any other condition separating the countries in the area has mattered little for

---

24. US attitudes toward the Costa Rican revolution are in Jacobo Shifter, *Costa Rica, 1948: Análisis de documentos confidenciales del Departamento de Estado*, (San José, Costa Rica: Editorial Universitaria Centroamericana, 1982).

25. This story is best narrated by Piero Gleijeses, *Shattered Hopes: The Guatemalan Revolution and the United States, 1944–1954*, (Princeton: Princeton University Press, 1991).

the US vision of the Caribbean. Nonetheless, since the nineties, political actors from within the area have sought to set up their own definition and put it into practice. These formed the Association of Caribbean States (ACE) to foster the integration of its members, in aspects such as transportation and the environment, among others. ACE includes the countries of Central America, the member states of CARICOM, Panama, Cuba, the Dominican Republic, Mexico, Colombia and Venezuela. In this regard, since the mid-nineties CARICOM and Central America have increased their contacts through periodical bi-regional meetings.

From the point of view of the Caribbean's history of foreign relations, there is a sub-region differentiated from the rest of the Caribbean and Latin America: the Latin Caribbean. The political evolution of the states in this area have endured the constant intervention of the United States and are characterised by their subordinate relationship with the northern hegemon; they have developed a political configuration that differentiates them from the rest of the Caribbean and Latin America. This definition leaves out Belize and the Anglo-Dutch Caribbean, as well as Guyana and Surinam, which for historical circumstances evolved under the umbrella of European powers even after their independence. Though these countries have not been free from US intervention (as the 1983 US invasion of Grenada suggests), the exercise of US influence took into consideration Europe's ascendancy over them, for which reason its impact was less overwhelming. Due to their distinct history (not free from US intervention, but with stronger institutions that allowed them to overcome it), Mexico, Venezuela and Colombia are not part of this area. The five Central American countries, Panama, the Dominican Republic and Haiti, thus make up the Latin Caribbean. Cuba before the revolution in 1959 and Puerto Rico before it acquired the Commonwealth status could be included in this definition and, if the criteria that have set them apart from their neighbours changes (as could be the case for Cuba), in the future they might be included.

The different pattern of foreign relations between the United States and Mexico, on the one hand, and the United States and Latin Caribbean states, on the other, illustrates the importance of location, power and history in the construction of this asymmetric relationship. At the same time that the United States has forcefully intervened, occupied or otherwise attempted to exert control over matters of smaller states in the Latin Caribbean, towards post-revolutionary Mexico the US government has not only abstained from intervening to any significant degree, but has generally refrained from expressing statements that might awake suspicions of interventionism in its southern neighbour. To put it another way: while post-revolutionary Mexican political evolution enjoyed a fair degree of stability and evolved with a substantial degree of autonomy from external influences, hardly any regime change in Latin Caribbean states has occurred without a substantial degree of US involvement.

What is so different between Mexico and the Latin Caribbean states? Being in the shadow of the United States does not carry the same meaning for each of the states in the area. One dissimilarity lies in its larger size, which has generally meant a larger capacity of the Mexican government to dispose of resources to defend its relative autonomy in international affairs. This condition also made it difficult for foreign powers to attempt direct control over its entire territory. Another is that Mexico—aside the 1910 Revolution and its aftermath—has generally enjoyed greater political stability than its Latin Caribbean neighbours, precisely a condition which allowed the United States to immerse itself in their domestic affairs. It must also be noted the regrouping effect that, since the nineteenth century, foreign interventions had on Mexican national consciousness.

Seen from a power-political point of view, the Latin Caribbean is composed of the states whose political trajectory was for many decades carefully observed by the United States. The subordinate relationship with Washington and what this condition implied for their domestic political development (they were not colonies, but neither were they completely sovereign nor did enjoy any benefits from this condition) can also be applied to states such as Liberia in Africa and the Philippines in the Pacific. Nonetheless, it is a sine-qua-non stipulation for this definition that they are close to each other and to the United States. This last peculiarity, as explained later in this chapter, has had important implications for the political evolution of the states in this sub-region.

The Caribbean Basin represents the most important international environment for the states of the Latin Caribbean. This sub-region is made of mainly small states whose history of unfinished state formation led them to develop poor institutional foundations and become easier prey of foreign pressures. As the largest and most powerful state in the area, the United States cast an unavoidable shadow that pervaded the Latin Caribbean economically, culturally and politically. Once it became a world power, the US took advantage of this asymmetry to secure the sub-region's capabilities and make sure that it did not become the site for other power's encroachments. This fact of political geography meant that throughout their independent history, but most importantly, since the late nineteenth century, the United States was the Latin Caribbean states' most important source of external influence. Other international or regional powers did try to exert their ascendancy in the area, such as France, Great Britain and Mexico, but particularly after the Spanish-American War and the construction of the Panama Canal, their reach was never so profound and their impact was not so continuous and overwhelming.

The huge asymmetries between the United States and Latin Caribbean states created the conditions for the latter to establish a subordinate relationship with the regional hegemon.[26] First, there has been a large degree of interaction between them, usually across a broad range of issue areas of concern to one or both. Second, this interaction has had historical roots and functional breadth. Patterns of action and reaction, of the exercise and the receipt of influence, may be discernible over the history of United States-Latin Caribbean relations. Third, interaction between the dominant one and subordinates has been more significant for the latter. Customarily, the larger effect has occured on the domestic and

---

26. David B. Abernethy, "Dominant-Subordinate Relationships: How Shall We Define Them? How Shall We Compare Them?" In Triska, *Dominant Powers and Subordinate States*, pp. 103–123.

foreign policies of the subordinate states. Fourth, the United States, as the dominant power, has had many more objectively measured, mutually acknowledged and mutually valued attributes of power than have had Latin Caribbean nations. The United States not only possesses the capacity to gain compliance from the subordinate states, it has also displayed the will to gain compliance. Fifth, the capacity for autonomous action of Latin Caribbean countries, the subordinate states, has been severely limited by the sheer fact of the dominant state's existence. Seventh, representatives of institutions based in the United States sometimes have penetrated the territory of the subordinate states, playing a direct and visible role as domestic actors in the latter's political life.[27]

Facing a regional order structured from without, the Caribbean Basin became the most important environment for Latin Caribbean leaders; in it, they found most of the opportunities and constraints for their political activity. To confront domestic or external dangers, imminent or potential, actors have struggled to influence policy in Washington.[28] To take advantage of or avert situations found within the sub-region, actors form coalitions with other actors in the area or in the United States. Their interaction generates the environment in which they must live. Accordingly, the behaviour of any one of them has been an obligatory factor in the calculation of others. In this scenario, the nature of the regime and the domestic struggles to change them also alter the regional environment. This has had circularity implications, for not only the regional order has affected regime transitions, but also regime transitions have altered the cohesiveness and unity of the regional order. Political processes within it partake in the strengthening or challenging of the sub region's construction as the US inner sphere-of-influence. In this sense, they have 'forward effects:' Episodes such as the Cuban and Nicaraguan revolutions, the negotiations for new treaties regarding the ownership and sovereignty over the Panama Canal and, fundamentally, regime transitions themselves, altered the face of the regional order.

This book argues that being in the 'shadow' of the United States has been crucial for the political trajectory of Latin Caribbean states. This location implied that the sub-region experienced a form of external involvement different from that experienced by neighbouring countries. For practical purposes the world's— and the region's—distribution of power is fixed; that is, the United States is and has been the power with the willingness and capacity to influence the destinies

---

27. This situation fits Rosenau's definition of 'penetrated systems.' See James Rosenau, "Pre-theories and theories of foreign policy." In R. B. Farrell (ed.), *Approaches to Comparative and International Politics*, (Evanston, Illinois Northwestern University Press, 1966), pp. 65. See also James N. Rosenau, "Toward the Study of National-International Linkages." In James Rosenau (ed.), *Linkage Politics: Essays on the Convergence of National and International Systems*, (New York and London: The Free Press and Collier-Macmillan, 1969), pp. 44–63.

28. On the effect these small nations have had on the formulation of policy in the United States, see Robert A. Pastor, "The United States and Central America Interlocking Debates." In Peter B. Evans, Harold K. Jacobson, and Robert Putnam (eds.), *Double-Edged Diplomacy: International Bargaining and Domestic Politics*, (Berkeley, Los Angeles, London: University of California Press, 1993), p. 303. On the Panamanian case see also Robert A. Pastor, "The Lessons and the Legacy of Omar Torrijos." In *Whirlpool: US Foreign Policy Towards Latin America and the Caribbean*, (Princeton: Princeton University Press, 1993).

of the states in its orbit, even when other powers of lesser status, such as Mexico and Venezuela, did attempt to exert their ascendancy in the area. The exercise of power is laden with meaning. Due to historical circumstances—European state's self-perception as having a 'civilised' role in world affairs emerging from their history as colonial powers—European governments and the United States have differed in their perception of threats from abroad, and have not had the same availability of means or the national will to engage overtly or covertly in activities to promote specific political arrangements overseas. Washington has been less reluctant to use military force in this sub-region, because it could do so with little defiance from other powers. The United States has paid more attention to the regime break-down phases of transitions because of their underlying uncertainties and potential for realignments. On the other hand, Europe has placed a major emphasis on political and economic instruments in dealing with nations undergoing regime change. When they did make efforts at fostering democratic institutions, European powers usually did it while they were extricating themselves as colonial powers but also to make sure that the new institutions took root before they left. The result of these two emphases is self-evident: Those Caribbean states maintaining ties with their former English and Dutch metropolis have undergone different forms of influence and have experienced a more favourable environment for democratisation.[29] The stability of Jamaica and Trinidad and Tobago's democracies, while their Latin sisters in the Caribbean Basin evolved under autocratic or dictatorial rule, illustrates the point.

The United States and the promotion of democracy

The primary purpose of any country's foreign policy is the establishment of a favourable international environment. Unlike other powers in that quest, the United States has frequently endeavoured to alter the political regimes of other nations. Depending on the means at its disposal, perceptions of threats from the international order and Washington's willingness to engage in that transformation, the United States has oscillated between bolstering client regimes and forcing them to change the premises upon which they base their relations with the governed. During the Cold War, Washington often aided non-democratic governments or groups in procuring to avoid losses or to provoke them in the camp of an adversary with which it had engaged in a zero-sum game worldwide. More often than not, however, Washington went beyond the minimum efforts for a stable order, fostering political, social and economic changes in the nations to which it committed itself.

The call to protect and promote democracy is a persistent feature of the history of American foreign relations. During the course of the twentieth century, authorities in Washington often encouraged and expected other nations to become democratic and invoked the cause of democracy when pursuing its rela-

---

29. See Jorge I. Dominguez, "The Caribbean Question: Why Has Liberal Democracy (Surprisingly) Flourished?" In Jorge I. Dominguez, Robert A. Pastor, and R. De Lisle Worrell (eds.), *Democracy in the Caribbean: Political, Economic and Social Perspectives*, (Baltimore and London: The Johns Hopkins University Press, 1993), pp. 1–25.

tions with the rest of the world. The process whereby the United States emerged and consolidated itself as a world power in the international arena was accompanied by attempts to formulate policies consistent with conceptions of its national interests. In that process, promoting democracy took the shape of a policy objective implemented with varying combinations of military, economic and political resources, along with other aims that sometimes took precedence over the first.

Why would the United States want other nations to become democratic and commit political, military and economic resources to that end? How can we best understand the impact Washington has had over the nature and characteristics of the political regimes of the countries to which it has directed its policies? An explanation to the former question is not an answer to the latter, but the second cannot be understood without having an answer to the first. To be sure, the relationship between the two is more complex than that between desiring and being able to encourage democracy, because both impinge upon factors pertaining to US domestic politics, the nature of the international order, and the characteristics of the regimes and societies with which Washington gets involved. It could be argued that the answer to the first lies in the realm of foreign policy analysis and the second in the realm of comparative politics. But, inasmuch as each of these factors affect specific features of the policy and its ability to induce regime change, they must be studied together, that is, as an aspect of the international relations field. To answer the first I will explore the sources of US foreign policy and their influence on the policy to protect and promote democracy. To answer the second, I present a model that builds upon previous inquiries into the history of US foreign relations and incorporates new elements of analysis.

For those engaged in the domestic roots of American foreign relations, the answer to the first question springs out of the specificities of the American political system. The school of historical interpretation known as "American Exceptionalism" points out that the United States experienced a different development path that affected the way its population perceived itself in relation to the rest of the world. Alexis de Tocqueville, nineteenth-century French student of American democracy, stated that Americans "arrived at a state of democracy without having to endure a democratic revolution... [they] are born equal, instead of becoming so." Founded by immigrants who fled class and religious conflicts in Europe, American society was embedded with ideas of equality of opportunity and individual liberty. These ideas took form in a political system designed to defuse power rather than accumulate it. The observation of the nation's uniqueness justified a foreign policy aimed at maintaining an external environment advantageous to the durability and prosperity of the nation's domestic institutions. Throughout the nineteenth century, this aim brought about an isolationist foreign policy meant to take advantage of its geographic position—far from Europe's perennial quarrels and close to lands which would nurture its territorial expansion—to channel the national stamina toward the construction of a homeland. "As the Union does not meddle in the affairs of Europe it has, so to say, no external interests at stake, for as yet it has no powerful neighbors in America."[30] The United States believed itself to possess exemplary political standards and regard the rest of the world as corrupt, for which it would extend its ways of life to the rest of the world. Under the philosophy of Manifest Destiny, the United States extended itself westwards, reaching California, and southwards, incorporating the area from Texas to Florida. Once its natural frontiers reached its limits and it got stronger, the United States took small but firm steps toward becoming an international power. Washington's isolationism gradually gave place to an active foreign policy often wrapped around the defence of democracy.

The first area in which it projected its power abroad was precisely the Caribbean Basin where, after defeating Spain in 1898, the US took over the island of Puerto Rico and established itself to arbitrate political developments in the Caribbean. US uniqueness was also interpreted as a mandate whereby the US could not totally overrule the sovereignty of these countries, as had European powers. Thus Washington adopted hybrid methods for exerting its power: Caribbean nations that became object of US interests remained nominally independent, yet they were forced to adopt Constitutional amendments sanctioning US rights to intervene in their internal affairs—as Cuba in 1902 and Panama in 1904. Before the Russian Revolution and the onset of the Cold War, the United States frequently intervened in the area to foster political stability, exclude the encroachment of foreign powers and teach Caribbean leaders, including Mexicans, to "elect good men" and establish constitutional rule.

Yet the relationship between the American domestic political structure and its commitment to the democratisation of other countries is partial at best. There is no necessary causality between a democratic domestic structure and a foreign policy aiming to enhance democracy. In fact, it can be the case that a democratic nation engages in actions threatening the democratic governance of another nation or in actions causing the overthrow of a democratic regime. Through direct and indirect means, for example, the US government provoked the overthrow of democratically elected governments in Guatemala in 1954 and in Chile in 1973, and often helped to polarize political conditions in countries undergoing regime transitions. The opposite can also take place. The record of the Soviet Union regarding the states under its sphere of influence in Northern and Eastern Europe between the end of World War II and the enunciation of the Truman doctrine in 1947, shows that a nation with a dictatorial political system may tolerate and establish working relationships with democratic governments.

The domestic structure issue may not respond to the question but it does explain why democracy is so central to the discourse of American foreign relations. It helps explain why American policymakers often recur to democratic values when promoting their decisions—ranging from intervening militarily in a Third World country or signing arm sales agreements with non-democratic nations—to the public. The theme 'democracy' appeals to the basic emotions of Americans who see their country as a force for good in the world. This implies that US ex-

---

30. Alexis de Tocqueville, *Democracy in America*, (New York and London: Harper and Row, 1969), p. 228.

ecutives "cannot totally dismiss for very long periods the humanitarian values in foreign policy without provoking adverse reactions from various important domestic governmental and non-governmental sectors."[31] The oscillation between active and passive postures in the world may be due, in large part, to Washington's attempts to close the gaps between aspects of the American ideology and its participation in foreign affairs. In this sense, the underlying ideology that accompanies the American domestic political structure could thus account for specific features of US foreign policy. The Carter administration's human rights policy, for instance, originated in the belief by Congress and wide segments of the public that the massive human rights violations in Latin America were caused by regimes the United States buttressed with military aid. Similarly, the Reagan administration's move to support the establishment of constitutional regimes in Central America—partially shying away from the bolstering approach—can be understood as a way to lessen public opinion and Congressional opposition to his policies in support of the Contras in Nicaragua and in support of its allies in this area.[32]

To be sure, though not a determinant of a foreign policy in support of democracy, the domestic political environment does affect specific features of the policy.[33] Public Opinion, Congressional-Executive relations, bureaucratic politics and the beliefs of the foreign policy elite act together or in isolation to influence targets, means and ends of American foreign relations. For an effective foreign policy, the Executive requires support from the public and Congress, as well as a consensus among the relevant bureaucratic structures of the administration that a chosen policy is the most suitable for the established ends. Public opinion—through the power of the vote—and Congress—through the power of the purse—may alter Washington's foreign policy means and objectives. American ideology—the universal web in which public leaders are entangled—and specific beliefs held by policymakers in Washington also affect what and how a given objective is persecuted and implemented. Domestic political patterns, such as a new administration viewing the previous administration's performance as having failed, influences the way in which Washington executes a particular foreign policy. This recurrently occurs every four or eight years when, following US constitutional practices, a new President gets into or is re-elected to the White House.

In these terms, domestic variables do elucidate why Washington maintains an interest in promoting democracy, but it does not fully explain why it gets involved in the transformation of other nations' regimes. Establishing the promo-

---

31. Heraldo Muñoz, "Chile: The Limits of Success," in Abraham Lowenthal (ed.), *Exporting Democracy: The US and Latin America*, (Baltimore, MD: The Hohns Hopkins University Press, 1991), p. 152.

32. This period is examined by Thomas Carothers, *In the Name of Democracy: US Policy toward Latin America in the Reagan years*, (Berkeley, Los Angeles and London: University of California Press, 1991).

33. According to Mark Peceny, *Democracy at the Point of Bayonets*, (University Park, PA: Pennsylvania University Press, 1999), p. 45, reviewing six case studies, realist concerns account for the initial decisions to intervene of US Presidents, while Congressional partisan dynamics explain their final choices.

tion of democracy as in the national interest of the United States does not carry a necessary drive to implement it. Thus, to elucidate the first question we need to comprehend what drives US intervention, which can be ascertained only by references to the international order.

This discussion about the causes of Washington's democracy policy began with the observation that all nations are likely to seek a congenial international environment. America's drive to involve itself in foreign lands comes from the challenges and opportunities the United States has perceived in the outside world. It may have been able to remain—and enjoy—being isolationist throughout its first century and a half as an independent state, but once it emerged as an international power—particularly after the 1898 war with Spain—it could not have avoided getting increasingly involved in international affairs without losing its status as such.

The first major opportunity came at the end of World War I, but this was not taken advantage of because, despite President Wilson's willingness to participate in the new post-war order, the isolationist majority in Congress blocked his initiatives. However, throughout the inter-war years, the United States continued to project its power primarily toward the Caribbean Basin, occupying Cuba, the Dominican Republic, Nicaragua and Haiti. The Great Depression increased the cost of intervention; thus Washington withdrew US Marines from the Dominican Republic, Haiti and—aided by Sandino's struggle against the occupying forces—Nicaragua. The Good Neighbour Policy was born in response to the need to secure the cooperation of Latin America as the conflagration in Europe approached. Then Washington rescinded the Constitutional amendments sanctioning US intervention in Panama and Cuba and adopted the principle of non-intervention in the internal affairs of other countries. As it extricated itself, it created constabularies that were given the task of maintaining order, out of which emerged lasting dictatorships that remained vivid proofs of the legacy of US involvement.

The next major opportunity to affect the international environment came with the culmination of World War II, which left devastated Europe behind in the race for supremacy and left the United States and the Soviet Union in much better economic and military positions to assume a world leadership role. However, the type of interaction that would emerge from its position in the world system was not a predetermined result. Rather, domestic variables influenced the way in which Washington behaved in what it perceived a world full of promises but also full of threats. The international post World War II order posed situations that the United States chose to deal with when it perceived threats to its national security. The reaction depended on the political and military objectives, the means at its disposal, the perceived levels of threat and the analytical tools to understand them. Matters involving the normal state of affairs between the United States and other countries have been dealt with through established national and international organizational channels. Matters involving greater perceived levels of threat have been deemed to require a greater amount of involvement, both politically and militarily. When Washington has had the willingness and the resources to carry out an extensive intervention to cope with a threat abroad, it has also engaged in the reformulation of political regimes, sometimes forcing democratic forms of government. In any given situation, global and domestic concerns have then shaped the relative weight accrued to the promotion of democracy among other foreign policy goals.

This overview brings us closer to answering the first question, namely, why would the United States desire that other nations become democratic and commit resources to that end? The United States wants other nations to become democratic, and sometimes commits political, economic and military resources to that end, because doing so allows it to foster an international order compatible with its domestic political system. Nevertheless, this is only half the problem. Washington has not always been successful in the promotion of democracy. To respond to the second question I will return to two characteristics of the international order and its effects on the policy of supporting democracy.

First, the complexities of perceived threats makes it difficult for policymakers to isolate the problems associated with the nature of a political regime. When Washington engages in regime transformations it usually does so as part of a package involving the perceived need to protect its strategic concerns or as a way to gain domestic and international support for its policies. Historically, the United States has promoted democracy when doing so it fosters political stability, creates profitable business opportunities and excludes rival powers (or their allies) from having the possibility of exerting influence in a country. The more a region has been considered vital to US national interests, the more Washington has tried to assure that no situation actually or even potentially damaging to US security has a chance to develop, as has been the case of the Latin Caribbean. Then, the more the relative weight of aims unrelated to the quality of democratic governance, the more has it been difficult for the United States to foster democratic forms of government. When it has been successful, it has been under conditions that are difficult, if not impossible, to replicate. There are trade-offs between both objectives. If true, this observation has obvious normative implications: if a policy in support of democracy is to be successful in the long run, the United States must be willing to leave aside some if not all of its other concerns.

Second, the nature of the international order is fundamental to understanding the impact of Washington's democracy policy because it brings about consequences unintended at its conception. The complexities of the interaction among social, economic and political variables at national and international levels make it difficult to control all the aspects intervening in the formation of a political regime. This is a two-edged condition. On the one hand, this implies that even if the United States acted solely or primarily to foster democracy it cannot simply transform the realities of another country to fit its image of a stable, constitutional government. On the other, it implies that a policy of promoting democracy should be more comprehensive than helping to set up the formal mechanisms of democracy if it is to have a greater impact upon the democratic governance of other societies.

Now we can answer the second question. To best understand the impact of the United States over the political regimes of the nations in which it has become involved, we need to consider the promotion of democracy in relation to the priorities Washington establishes and the complexities of the objective and subjective factors affecting the formation of a particular regime. Democratisation is a complex political process involving domestic and international influences. To understand the impact of the latter, coming from the United States or from the rest of the world, they must be appraised as elements of a dynamic and interactive process having a cumulative historical impact on the countries undergoing regime change.

Interlocking regime transitions and regional order

To understand Latin Caribbean regime transitions we must study them in relation to the state of the international order—and of its regional counterpart, where the United States has behaved as the regional hegemon. Thus, the comparative study of democratisation processes must be linked to the study of changes in the international order. After World War II, these two fields of study evolved from and contributed to the development of Comparative Politics and International Relations, respectively. For the most part, however, they remained virtually separate; one examined what occurred within nations, and the other explored the relationship between states. The first emerged from a concern with the domestic conditions that brought about and sustained democracy, and the second grew out of the theorisation which accompanied the Cold War. To a large extent, democratisation was viewed as an endogenous endeavour; the international order concerns the conditions prevailing among states.

One way to perceive the connection between both concepts is in the conventional power-political conception of regional spheres of influence. It is said that the international system is composed of regions policed by great powers who regulate intra-regional conflicts; thereby providing the structure for international order. Regional order is constructed politically when the great power lays out, for the states within and outside it, rules about acceptable inter-state behaviour. By applying this argument to contemporary international politics we could extend it further: to the extent that the great power is itself a democracy and has the willingness and the resources to foster democracy within its sphere of influence, regional hegemony would provide the background for the construction of a regional community of democratic states. The interlocking of the two notions is paradoxical, for the shared norms and values referred to by the first may be significantly shaped and constrained by the exercise of hegemonic power referred to by the second.

Order refers to relations among the states in a defined area as regards a particular goal or value. It is established when a set of principles guides the behaviour and expectations of the states within it; the arrangement is orderly only in relation to the values espoused by its members. Hence the order prevailing in a region is peaceful insofar as those principles and norms provide the stability and the self-regulating mechanisms with which to transcend conflicts. Democracies by themselves do not create peace; an area made up of democratic states is not necessarily conflict-free. It is the norms and principles they share and their consciousness of a need for regulation that foster the conditions for a peaceful regional order. The maintenance of order presupposes a commonality of interests, but when a hegemonic power establishes itself in a region the norms and principles that guide the relations between states are bound by that state's power structure. The maintenance of hegemonic order is not tantamount to peace if its chief function is to preserve the great power's dominance. For the aim of preserving order invites the hegemonic power to use force and other material incentives to secure the sub-region's alignment with the principles it favours, in disregard of the basic regulations that promote international governance.

Thus hegemonic power and democracy are intertwined features of a regional order. A great deal of a regional order's configuration is shaped during regime transitions in the states located within it. This is because transitions from one form of government to another are periods marked by turmoil and restructuring that may challenge patterns of alliance within and in-between states. Viewed from outside the country undergoing transition, this presents the hegemonic power with an opportunity to facilitate the construction of an order consonant with its own interests, allying itself with individuals or élites they can trust as rulers rather than waiting for the masses to produce their own; within the country, it allows existing élites to exploit opportunities for realignment.

Transitions also have powerful ramifications for the restructuring of regional order: they shape the motivational and objective framework within which later transitions take place. The two most notorious regional examples—the Cuban revolution in 1959 and the Nicaraguan revolution in 1979—illustrate the point. Their impact, among other regional developments, are examined in the case studies included in this book. But we can advance the observation that transitions seem to be 'regional processes'; because they are causally associated over time, each transition is, at least partially, a function of the intersection of choices within which the previous transition unfolded.

The study of democratisation processes in the 'shadow' of the United States affords the opportunity to test the often neglected relationship between regional hegemony, as outlined in the International Relations literature, and democratic transitions, as outlined in the literature on democratisation. But it also allows us to consider how such domestic-international interactions alter the regional order. Regime transitions in this area are episodes in which the US has attempted to maintain a form of order that embodies its preferred values, while the weaker states have sought outlets for political and social change. The regional orders that prevailed during the Cold War were not the product of debate or co-operation, but of struggle; they represented a clash between the norms of international society that the leaders of the hegemonic power publicly subscribed to—democracy and peace—and the norms of order that, in practice, prevailed at the expense of freedom and at substantial cost to regional security. While the US has generally favoured a world based on liberal principles as opposed to one based on great power divisions of the world, regarding the Latin Caribbean it established a sphere-of-influence that remained conflict-prone. During the Cold War, Washington's priority regarding international affairs was to contain the Soviet Union. This aim made most Washington policy-makers to choose their friends not by their democratic credentials but by their loyalty to this cause and their willingness to be led by the US.

Focusing on political processes that coincide with or follow major changes in the international order also offers an opportunity to test the effect of global political restructuring upon democratisation processes. In these times of change, the hegemonic power seeks to adjust to the new constellation of forces and to consolidate its dominant position, while local élites struggle to gain recognition for their efforts to achieve power. Seen the transition from outside the country undergoing political change, the international order seems to be an intervening process blurring the intents of the external influences. Human activities are performed in contexts or scenarios constraining individual choices. As such, the international order is neither the cause nor the effect. Rather, it affects how individuals interact. It provides meaning to human activities in the way they have to take into consideration limits in power, existing norms and past choices before undertaking actions.[34]

This book deals with changing hegemonic patterns and implies a shift to the sub-region as the terrain within which the most important political interactions occur. It means giving integrated consideration to the local, regional and global levels of analysis. To appraise the impact of international influences we need to systematise them so as to expose the mechanisms whereby they influence domestic political processes. The regional subsystem—the Latin Caribbean's regional order—is not just a higher-level factor; it can be active at any level, influencing not only individuals but also societies at large. International influences are mediated by the sub-region's construction, but actors within it may also have the ability to affect the external environment. In this sense, the regional order is not the cause of regime transitions; rather, it affects the way in which actors interact in their pursuit of their goals.

Hegemonic patterns propel regime changes to keep within certain bounds, but they do not determine specific outcomes. As long as local affairs have an external 'dimension' built-in, all international political developments have the potential to affect them. The effect of a superpower's influence rests on the magnitude and form of involvement. This, in turn, is affected by changing international circumstances or by domestic political events. Factors altering the source's ability and willingness to embark upon interfering with another nation's political configuration in turn affect the latter's democratic prospects. For instance, leaders of the hegemonic power may be preoccupied with other matters, such as a Presidential election campaign, or may wish to adopt a more principled foreign policy, such as President Carter's human-rights policy. Maybe it has been recently defeated, such as the United States after Vietnam. Sometimes the influencing power finds itself constrained by domestic opposition to its policies, such as Congressional

---

34. For a discussion on how contexts affect outcomes in international interactions, see Gary Goertz, *Contexts of International Politics*, (Cambridge: Cambridge University Press, 1994).

and public opposition to the use of force in Central America during the Reagan administration. Maybe it lacks effective capabilities to project its military forces, such as the US in Iran in 1978.

Changes may also come from the other side of the equation. The subordinate states may purposely attempt to obtain greater autonomy for themselves, such as Panama under Torrijos (1968–1981). Maybe other powers of comparable (Europe) or lesser status (Mexico, Venezuela and Colombia) might either seek to force or find the means of inducing the dominant power to change the nature of its relationship with the states it influences, such as the efforts to pacify the Central American region in the eighties (Contadora and Esquipulas proposals). When one or a combination of these factors is present, then the prospects for democratisation are enhanced, as there is greater inhibition upon more blatant types of intervention.[35] In any case, the exercise of hegemonic power usually makes the result of regime transitions much more burdensome for all of the actors involved; not only do they have to play the game taking into account domestic actor's interests and strategies, but also those of the hegemonic power. [36]

The interaction between world systemic conditions and its regional counterpart is of utmost importance to understand the operation of hegemonic constraints that actors in pursuit of democratisation may encounter. Because of changing international circumstances, as time has gone by, being in the 'shadow' of the United States has changed meaning. The causal relationship between one and the other is context-specific: depending on the sum of local and external circumstances, US influence has aided or impaired democratic prospects. Washington's agenda of concerns in relation to the rest of the world—and the region—has varied according to different historical contexts. In this century, distinct international eras—the Cold War, the second Cold War and the post-Cold War—affected the pattern of US intervention [altering Washington's priorities], and subsequently (but indirectly), the outcome of regime transitions in the Latin Caribbean.

During the Cold War, American primacy over the Latin Caribbean became a de facto impediment for regime transitions in the area. States in the Latin Caribbean remained locked into a regional security regime characterised by US hegemony and a collection of military authoritarian governments closely identified with Washington's strategic concerns. Domestic attempts at reform were often repressed by overt US military intervention or by other indirect forms of control, with the concourse of military and business élites in the area. In this period, the course of regime transitions depended largely on American dispositions towards this sub-region. This book's working hypothesis is that the late democratisation of Latin Caribbean countries originates in the obstacles deriving from American hegemonic imperatives. Washington encouraged the setting up of democratic

---

35. See Paul Keal, "On Influence and Spheres-of-influence," in Triska, *Dominant Powers and Subordinate States*, p. 138. See also Goertz, *Contexts of International Politics*, where he examines how states interact with their environments, and looks at which contexts are important in understanding international politics.

36. Richard Falk, *The Promise of World Order: Essays in Normative International Relations*, (Brighton, Great Britain Wheatsheaf Books, 1987), pp. 120–121.

institutions and practices only when doing so was deemed convenient to foster political stability and to exclude rival powers from real influence within a given territory. In general, the US undermined the efforts of democratic forces and helped to prolong the permanence of authoritarian regimes.

In the second Cold War (1981–1989), US intervention was also detrimental to democratisation in the Latin Caribbean, but the different context made a difference. As in the Cold War, Washington worked to support authoritarian forces. Still, given the domestic and international concern over the effect and morality of US policies, it did so while fostering some of the formal mechanisms of democracy. As a result, human and political rights remained restricted, but under political frameworks different from the authoritarian past—witness the establishment of electoral processes and civilian—held Presidential offices in Honduras, Guatemala and El Salvador in the eighties. The end of the Cold War has not decreased the likelihood of intervention in the area, as the 1994 intervention in Haiti suggests, but it has altered US attitudes towards the sub-region. The exertion of US power is more likely to be favourable towards democratisation. Prospects for the consolidation of democracy remain largely a function of both the ability of democratic forces to sustain themselves and the permanence of a supportive international environment.[37]

The shadow of the United States

American leaders have long recognised the Caribbean Basin as a distinctive area or 'theatre of operations.' The United States had not reached its first half-century of independence nor completed its territorial expansion when, in 1823, President James Monroe cautioned European powers from intervening in Latin America. The Monroe doctrine marked one of Washington's first steps in gaining ascendancy in hemispheric and world affairs. During the nineteenth century, the United States projected itself primarily towards the Latin Caribbean, particularly concerned with the construction and capitalization of an inter-oceanic waterway.

Historically, the appreciation of the unique character of the sub-region carried prescriptive connotations. President Theodore Roosevelt (1901–1909), for instance, argued that South America's "great and prosperous civilised commonwealths," such as Argentina, Brazil, and Chile, "have advanced so far that they no longer stand in any position of tutelage towards the United States." Accordingly, said Roosevelt, for these countries "there was no more necessity for asserting the Monroe doctrine than there was to assert it for Canada."[38] In similar fashion, Philander C. Knox, Secretary of State under President William Howard Taft (1909–1913), argued that "the logic of political geography and of strategy... make

---

37. [32] According to Giuseppe Di Palma (1990), *To Craft Democracies*, (Berkeley, Los Angeles, Oxford: University of California Press), p. 192, "... no other international agent is and can be more decisive than a al hegemon in removing impediments to al change. One may think of the United States' role in Central America to appreciate the point."

38. Theodore Roosevelt, *The Autobiography of Theodore Roosevelt*, (New York: Charles Scribner's Sons, 1919), p. 270.

the safety, the peace, and the prosperity of Central America and the zone of the Caribbean of paramount importance to the government of the United States."[39] The enforcement of these premises gave the Latin Caribbean identifiable sphere-of-influence attributes: "a determinate region within which a single external power er exerts a predominant influence, which limits the independence and freedom of action of political entities within it, has identifiable geographical limits and there is some degree of exclusion of other powers."[40]

The crucial point here is the way the United States conceived the Caribbean Basin. As Hurrell stated, "It is how political actors perceive and interpret the idea of a region that is critical: all regions are socially constructed and hence politically contested."[41] It was Washington's interpretation—and local actors' adaptive behaviour toward this asymmetrical relationship—that rendered the area its peculiar character. As the regional hegemon, since the late nineteenth century the United States imposed its authority "in the shape of paramountcy in the Central American-Caribbean area, while having to be content with the exercise of mere hegemony—a much less burdensome type of dominion—over South America."[42] Concerning the former, Washington has been keener to employ force and the threat of force, disregarding universal norms of interstate behaviour, but has refrained from such actions regarding the latter. These characteristics differentiate the Latin Caribbean from the rest of the continent, despite their sharing common historical and political legacies. To illustrate the point: The US has intervened in the Caribbean Basin more than 20 times, and no country in the sub-region has escaped substantial US intervention at some point in their history. Yet, no South American country has experienced US military intervention. How different can the character of a state be whose political trajectory has been engaged with off and on by a foreign power?

The continuous projection of US power over the area restructured these states' patterns of political interactions. From the United States' side of the influence equation, Washington acted to exclude other powers from any given influence within the area, to maintain stability, and to use regional capabilities for its own purposes (military bases, interoceanic waterway, and so on). Pushing US strategic concerns as norms for the behaviour of Latin Caribbean states had several implications. First, this meant that American officials often jointly participated— though from highly asymmetrical positions—with members of Latin Caribbean societies, in the allocation of values or the mobilisation of support on behalf of US goals. In this context, movements towards political change deemed contrary to Washington's interests were countered by direct or indirect

---

39. Harold Norman Denny, *Dollars for Bullets: The Story of American Rule in Nicaragua*, (New York: Dial Press, 1929), p. 7.

40. Paul Keal, *Unspoken Rules and Superpower Dominance*, (London: MacMillan Press LTD., 1983), p. 15.

41. See Andrew Hurrell, "Explaining the resurgence of regionalism in world politics." *Review of International Studies*, vol. 21, 1995, p. 334.

42. Fred Parkinson, "Latin America." In Jackson and James, *States in a Changing World: A Contemporary Analysis*, p. 247.

intervention, often involving support and encouragement for ruling or opposition élites or factions. Second, this condition limited the freedom of action of the actors within it. Given the power differentials, and the relatively few alternatives to accommodating the US, local actors found themselves with a constrained range of choices. One, to conform to Washington's wishes by adapting their behaviour to what the US expected from them. Two, to learn the intricacies of politics in Washington as a way to manipulate some of its features for their own purposes; or three, to dissent from them, but at costs directly proportional to US opposition.

Playing 'big brother' in the area's political arena had unintended consequences. In a context where political processes had reached very low levels of institutionalisation, American officials habitually turned to individuals they could entrust with the maintenance of order and keeping the country's allegiance to the United States. Though this custom was carried out many times while fostering constitutional forms, by committing themselves to individuals the United States weakened the political institutions they discursively adhered to—witness the emergence and persistence of one—man rule under constitutional masks throughout the history of the Latin Caribbean. So the United States, through its different government agencies, constructed its own political constituency in every country of the area, whose allegiance sometimes could be counted on when trying to affect the policies or the political arrangement of a regime. In this type of context, the outcome of socio-political conflicts cannot be properly understood in national isolation because they are, largely, dependent on local expectations and interpretations about Washington's "real" intentions and possible courses of action.

This practice also conditioned the framework for the sub-region's political intercourse: local leaders achieved leverage over their countrymen thanks to their apparent or real ties with the United States. In time, being the recipient of US influence became more or as important for gaining and maintaining power than intra-elite negotiations or seeking the support of the masses through elections and constitutional procedures, because more often respecting democratic procedures and practices could be traded for concessions on matters highly regarded by Washington. Evidently, such a habit deformed the elite's and society's political expectations and practices, even if at times Washington shunned from buttressing dictators.

The convoluted effects of this relationship on the institutional character of Latin Caribbean states may be illustrated with the analysis of Her Majesty's Ambassador to the Dominican Republic, who observed the repercussions of this ambiguity before leaving the island in 1965. "For strategic reasons, … the United States has a special interest in the Dominican Republic and the Caribbean," wrote the British diplomat. But this means that this island, "so close to their bases in Puerto Rico, Guantanamo and Panama, and their rocket installations on the coast of Florida," could not fall a prey to Moscow, Peking or Havana. Yet, Washington "cannot, of course, occupy the place again, without a fatal damage to their image all over the world." The murky aspect of this relationship is manifested in the fact that, on the one hand, the Dominicans, "and doubtless the Haitians also, feel that it is only right and logical, therefore, that the Americans should carry the burden of keeping the country afloat." Thus, the diplomat added, the Americans "feel entitled in return to ensure the country is governed by men acceptable to the United States." Consequently, "provided a facade of constitutional legality can be constructed, the Americans will not, I imagine, look too closely at the credentials of any future President, so long as he is able and willing to align the country on the side of the West."[43]

Brandishing US power also had concrete, deep-rooted consequences for the ways in which local élites interacted among themselves and vis-à-vis their societies.[44] The constant search and reception of US influence sometimes produced stronger ties between the actors that became the source and the receivers of influence than between different élite groups within a country. These bonds also created loyalties and expectations not only between those seeking and receiving influence, but also within other sectors in society. What could be the logical conclusion of a Latin Caribbean citizen who has observed the United States exercising its power so often and being so critical for the fortune of their leaders than believing—and expecting—Washington to hold the keys to most of the country's fate? US attitudes towards the Latin Caribbean have been instrumental for the success or failure not only of political leaders, but also for social movements' ability to protest. Between the 1950s and 1980s in Central America, for example, the strength of workers and peasant organisations, and their ability to protest non-violently, occurred when the US encouraged democratic governance in this sub-region. In addition, state repression of workers and peasants was higher when US administrations in Washington were not concerned with democratic governance.[45]

Naturally, recognising the inequalities of power—decisions in Washington may be more important than decisions taken locally—élites in these countries included Washington's agenda of concerns in their calculations. However, having experienced the intricacies of the exercise of US influence, local protagonists 'learned' to play with US interests for their own purposes, working to pull Washington into the area when their rule was threatened. In this scenario, even a temporary hands-off approach by the United States has been a decisive element in

---

43. UK.PRO.FO371/179329. "Mr. Lockhart's Valedictory Despatch." Confidential Correspondence by S. A. Lockhart from the British Embassy in Santo Domingo, dated 2 April 1965.

44. The evaluation of the impact of the United States over the political nature of Third World regimes is an emerging feature in the US foreign policy literature. See Benjamin C. Schwartz, *American Counterinsurgency Doctrine and El Salvador: The Frustrations of Reform and the Illusions of Nation Building*, (Santa Monica, California: Rand, 1991); Morris H. Morley, *Washington, Somoza and the Sandinistas: State and Regime in US Policy Toward Nicaragua, 1969–1981*, (Cambridge: Cambridge University Press, 1994), and Nick Cullather, *Illusions of Influence: The Political Economy of United States-Philippines Relations, 1942–1960*, (Cambridge : Cambridge University Press, 1994).

45. The empirical research was carried out by Rosa Emilia Rodriguez Stein, "Collective Action in Peripheral Nations A comparative analysis of Five Central American countries." Ph.D. Dissertation, University of Arizona, 1989.

the political calculation of the region's protagonists, for it sometimes propelled them to act swiftly against those actors whose fate has depended on US support and intervention for achieving their goals.

With these strands, the United States constructed a regional (sub-systemic) order in the Latin Caribbean. On the one side, the United States was the axis of the sphere-of-influence it secured and linked to its national security concerns; on the other, the area's states gravitate in it, and their political evolution has tended to be constrained by choices defined by the regional hegemon. As such, countries in the area were treated as a tightly linked unit. As has been the case for US-Latin Caribbean relations, movements for political change in one country have customarily been treated as if they had the ability to spill over into other countries in the area and, potentially, the United States itself. Recall Washington's fear that the Cuban revolution be repeated by neighbouring states following Castro's access to power in 1959 and of the Nicaraguan revolution after 1979, both of which propelled US efforts to counteract a possible "domino effect." This 'definition of the situation' had enormous political implications, because what happened in one country (i.e., Cuba) did provoke repercussions, via Washington's policies, in the political configuration of the other states within the area.

Struggles for political change in the Latin Caribbean thus acquired a different meaning. Actors fighting for political and human rights also had to attempt to seek greater international legitimacy for themselves. In time, because of the uncertainties and potential for instability that such a view posed, actors within the area have disputed this definition; this contention is, for example, at the core of the peace proposals put forward by Latin American governments in the eighties.

Research methodology

This book aims to make several contributions to the academic literature. First, it dwells on the international aspects of democratisation, particularly those that underline the relevance of the geo-strategic situation of the country undergoing regime change. In this light, it will present a framework to understand the domestic-international interactions through which regime transitions, that of the Latin Caribbean in particular, may take place. The international dimension refers to the multiplicity of external channels having a cumulative macro-historical impact upon regime transformations, but the most pertinent ones for the Latin Caribbean seem to be those deriving from the sub-region's structure of power. Thus this study will also offer an account of the ways in which the United States influences political processes in the area, an influence that is more complex than has been usually assumed. Prior models of democratic transitions assumed the "existence of a well-defined nation-state in which no major problems of national identity remain pending."[46] Yet, this is not precisely the case of every country in the area. All of these will provide the ground for establishing the links between regime transitions and regional order, and for understanding the Latin Caribbean as a distinct sub-region.

---

46. Whitehead, "The imposition of democracy," p. 356.

The primary focus is on the domestic-international interactions that influenced the course of events from the breakdown of dictatorship to the emergence of a new democracy or to the resumption of authoritarian rule. But these external influences do not operate in one direction only and are not necessarily overwhelming. Rather, they are treated as a two-way linkage in the process of regime transformations that, nonetheless, are exerted under constraints that limit original intentions. The most important source of external influence is US ascendancy, in its political, economic or military forms. What is to be explained and interpreted is how the latter affect the calculations and choices of the actors involved in the process, and how these modify the trajectory of regime transitions.

To understand the impact of external influences on regime trajectories various domestic conditions must be ascertained. For example, the nature of the authoritarian state given the country/ under study, its sources of strength, the interests it serves; what domestic factors seem to unleash the process of regime transformation; the motivations, calculations and mistakes of the main contenders. For example, the meaning of 'democracy' in the political history of the country under study; the difference of the new institutions from previous ones. In addition, the social forces which supported the reinstallation of constitutional rule, and the authoritarian legacies that are present during transitions.

The historical context is ascertained in terms of the terrain laid out by previous and concurrent regime transitions in the area. The regional order is neither the cause nor the effect of regime change. The international context alters the interaction between external and domestic forces when changing regional or international circumstances exert changes in the relation between US influences and domestic actors' choices. The international context may alter the interaction between external and domestic forces when changing regional or international circumstances exerts changes in the relation between US intervention and regime trajectories. Patterns of interaction between the United States and the countries in the area are not static. Change in the power relationships within the regional order may come about in several ways. Sometimes the influencing power modifies its behaviour (a conscious choice) or may be preoccupied with other matters. Maybe the influenced states purposely set out to secure greater autonomy for themselves. Sometimes another power of comparable status seeks to force or find the means of inducing an influencing power to change the nature of its relationship with the states it influences.

The process cannot be plausibly understood by focusing on a single level of analysis. Human factors, for instance, are important because of the low level of institutionalisation of these countries' political processes. Studying regime transitions in the Latin Caribbean requires evaluating how the dominant position of the United States affected the area's political processes. This task may be approached by looking at Washington's specific allocation of resources targeting regimes in the area; by evaluating how domestic élites' structure of incentives towards democratisation is influenced by existing ties with the United States, and by the way actors at both ends of the superpower-regional relationship attempt to influence each other's policy choices. Since the causal relationship between external and internal variables is situation-specific—policies, actions and outcomes influence each other in different ways—these interactions will be viewed in the context of various historical eras.

By focusing on actors' incentive structure, we move the explanatory focus from the regional environment to individuals, their beliefs and preferences. However, since the regional order is not static-regime transitions affect the sub-region's composition—we need to move back and forth. In this sense, regime transitions have embedded an international dimension, but also are expressions of the changing regional order. As well, it is a process embedded in historicity, for it is as important to appraise how the countries under study became immersed in the regional construction to evaluate their prospects for democracy.

Three case studies, the Dominican Republic, Nicaragua and Panama, highlight these issues. The three cases begin with a review of the history and the nature of the dictatorial or authoritarian regime from which a transition was later launched. Particular emphasis is laid on the domestic-international interactions affecting the breakdown of dictatorial rule. The cases end with the inauguration of regimes led by groups that the United States has been conspicuously supporting. Except for Panama, which enjoyed some variant of democracy—though controlled by a small elite—for more than six decades prior to the onset of authoritarian rule, we will be concerned mostly with cases of regime transition that may lead to the resumption of authoritarian rule or to a new democracy.[47]

As well as being political processes in states within the United States' inner sphere of influence, these transitions also share other features that seem possibly causative. First, all three occur against the background of events that prompt Washington to alter the basis of its hegemony. The onset of the transition in the Dominican Republic coincides with and receives input from the unfolding Cuban revolution; in Nicaragua the revolution sparks the regional discord which later helps to shape and constrain its own course; and, in Panama, the transition's trajectory is apparently affected by the same regional conflict, though in different ways (e.g., Panama not directly experiencing a civil war or insurgency). The three transitions were prolonged and contested; in each case, the United States intervened to preserve its regional ascendancy and made the promotion of democracy an explicit foreign policy goal. In addition, there was a legacy of US involvement in each of the three cases; interactions between local and US actors, some of which follow previous patterns of loyalties and expectations, provide the moving force behind the regime breakdown and the earlier transition phases of their democratisation processes. The Dominican Republic and Panama were subject to direct US military intervention (though the United States played a substantially smaller part in the creation of the latter two's political institutions); but US intervention in Nicaragua was by proxy. Washington's involvement also took a more overt form in the Dominican Republic and Nicaragua throughout most of their transition period than it did in Panama.

---

47. According to Weffort, new democracies are cases of democratic transition emerging from authoritarian rule lacking a past, consolidated democracy. Francisco Weffort, "New Democracies, Which Democracies?" (Washington, DC: The Woodrow Wilson International Center for Scholars, 1992), Latin American Program's Working Paper Number 198, p. 1, footnote 3.

To emphasise the impact of various international contexts, one case study, that of the Dominican Republic, is drawn from the Cold War. The Dominican transition is also relevant because of the repercussions that the Cuban Revolution had upon actors' choices on both sides of the hegemonic relationship and in Washington's subsequent political and military strategies towards the sub-region. This case study also serves as a basis for the comparison of two more recent transitions, those in Nicaragua and Panama, which for the most part took place during what has been labelled the 'Second Cold War.' The last phase of these transitions coincided with the end of the Cold War, a major shift in the international order that seems to be causally relevant. The two historical periods were also characterised by different sets of policy choices by the hegemonic power, by a distinctly normative international environment, and by different degrees of willingness on the part of other states to challenge the United States' relationship with the sub-region.

The different nature of the authoritarian regimes and their relations with Washington also provides the occasion for specifying the scene in which the United States can be said to have played a hegemonic role. In the Dominican Republic, the actors constituted themselves within rapidly and sometimes unexpectedly shifting political arenas; the transition began with the dismantling of a severely repressive, three-decades-old dictatorship that had entrenched itself in every aspect of the country's economic, political and social life and that, for most of its lifetime, had enjoyed the support of various influential actors within Washington's political structure. The Dominican transition involved a Civil War in which the United States got itself involved. In Panama and Nicaragua, most of the actors remain clearly identifiable throughout the transition. However, in Panama the authoritarian regime evolved from a military-led populist coalition, which Washington accommodated, to an Army-led, electorally based regime with a strong civilian component, which enjoyed Washington's support most of the time, but also displayed various degrees of independence from the United States. In Nicaragua, the transition began with a revolution that deposed a four-decades-old dynastic dictatorship that received Washington's support while it lasted; the revolutionary regime that ensued was popularly based and acquired an anti-hegemonic character. The transition in Nicaragua also involved a struggle towards peace. These differences allow for a richer discussion of the issues involved, since they pose different options for the élites in both the hegemonic and the subordinate states.

To gather the material needed for this research, both top-down and bottom-up approaches were carried out. Transitions from authoritarian rule and the exercise of hegemony by the United States in this sub-region are treated as a continuum, while the ways in which local, regional and global affairs interact to affect democratisation are evaluated. Information on all official or unofficial US gestures of support or disapproval for the regimes and other main participants in the transitions and the actual allocation and implementation of material incentives (ranging from economic aid to military intervention) were gathered.

From the US side of the equation, it was also reviewed under what set of domestic and international pressures, and based on what security and normative understandings the decisions to intervene were taken. This implied the observation of the extent to which these gestures, normative understandings and networks with Washington constrained the choices of the various strategic actors in the countries undergoing transition.

To develop the regional perspective, this data was analysed against the background of the effects that a previous or concurrent regime transition has on actors' choices. The sequence of interactions between local and external leaders thus provides the domestic and sub-regional setting for the unfolding of regime transformations. The assessment of the regional order is made by determining the impact that the trajectories had upon the power-political and normative integration of the area.

THE DOMINICAN REPUBLIC

From Tyranny
to "Democracy"

The Dominican Republic provides a vivid case study of the interaction between domestic and international factors impinging on transitions toward democracy. From a point of inflexion in Trujillo's tyranny in 1956 to the general elections in 1966 that inaugurated a long period of constitutional rule, Dominican politics basically revolved around the type of regime it was to adopt. But this was far from a purely domestic process.

US influence was particularly crucial. The Kennedy administration used the Dominican Republic to prove that a 'revolution in liberty' was possible, as a test case for the 'Alliance for Progress,' with which it expected to counter the appeal of insurgent movements sparked by the Cuban revolution. From the moment Trujillo disappeared from the scene, the United States guided the Dominican political process, nourishing the little democratic potential there was. It frequently employed the threat of the use of force and actually used it when events seemed to be going out of control. The handling of US influences by Dominicans was important, but not more than US perceptions of reality. It was also a transition in which the regional and international environment (particularly, but not solely the unfolding Cuban revolution) carried much weight on the sequence of choices and events that led from one regime to the next.

The rise of the Trujillo regime

The dictatorship of General Rafael Trujillo Molina (1930–1961) was an unwitting offspring of US' policy in the Caribbean Basin. Sucked in 1916 by a political upheaval that it wanted to placate, the US occupied the Dominican Republic until 1924, paving the way for the emergence of an autocratic dictatorship.[48] The United States set out to organise a stable government that would preserve political and financial stability. The Americans thoroughly stripped the citizenry of arms and replaced the poorly paid and trained municipal police forces with an 'apolitical' constabulary charged with maintaining order. To avoid its use as an instrument of the élites in power, control of the Guard was given to a Commander who was supposed to uphold constitutional rule.[49]

---

48. This period is examined by Bruce J. Calder, *The Impact of Intervention: The Dominican Republic during the U.S. Occupation of 1916–1924*, (Austin: University of Texas Press, 1984).

49. The creation of constabularies by the US following occupations and its consequences is analy-

In effect, the landing of American troops offered Trujillo the chance of his life. Working as a telegrapher, in 1918 he contacted the local head of the American military forces and on January 1919 began to serve as provisional second lieutenant.[50] President Horacio Vásquez, elected in 1924 before the departure of the marines, then promoted Major Trujillo to serve in the Capital and in 1927 appointed him National Guard Commander. In 1930 a crisis erupted after Vásquez attempted re-election, in violation of the Constitution. Following a coup against his former protector, the General arranged his candidacy and became elected President without opposition. The State Department frowned on Trujillo's move. However, his rise to power came at a time—the Great Depression—when Washington sought to leave behind the costly practice of intervening to halt rebellions, supervise elections and put "good men" in power.[51]

The dictator's awareness of the geopolitical conditions and changes occurring in the world allowed him to play up to US expectations. Though at first he flirted with the Axis powers, he conveniently declared war on the side of the United States. Between the end of World War II and the beginning of the Cold War, Trujillo pursued the semblance of democracy and the establishment of diplomatic relations with the Soviet Union. Amidst the Dominican people's rising expectations and the State Department's democratic advocacy, Trujillo inspired the formation of labour unions and the formation of several political parties, though they remained under his control.[52] Once this 'superpower's honeymoon' was over, Trujillo used the Cold War as an opportunity to reinforce the army, to crack down on the opposition, and to suppress the few liberties he had granted.

In power, Trujillo earnestly pursued veneration for himself and his family. He was no longer to be known as a simple mortal, but as "Benefactor of the Fatherland", the "Generalissimo", or "El Jefe." Men in public positions had to pretend a zeal for the Generalissimo that they did not feel. History was rewritten to evince the virtuousness of the Benefactor. In these circumstances, no one could afford to remain neutral; any pause in the glorification of Trujillo could only be interpreted as a sign of antagonism against him.

Enjoying absolute political power over the nation, Trujillo set out to take a firm grip on the country's riches. By 1938, an assessment of the Trujillo fam-

sed in Marvin Goldwert, *The Constabulary in the Dominican Republic and Nicaragua: Progeny and Legacy of United States intervention*, (Gainesville: University of Florida Press, 1962).

50. Jesús de Galíndez, *The era of Trujillo: Dominican Dictator*, (Santo Domingo: La Trinitaria, 1973), p. 9.

51. G. Pope Atkins and Lamar C. Wilson, *The United States and the Trujillo Regime*, (New Brunswick, New Jersey: Rutgers University Press, 1972), p. 39. This period is examined with more detail by Eric Paul Roorda, *The dictator next door: The Good Neighbor Policy and the Trujillo Regime in the Dominican Republic, 1930–1945*, (Durnham and London: Duke University Press, 1998).

52. The Trujillo regime's accumulation of power during the era of the Good Neighbour Policy is also in William Krehm, "La era de un buen vecino." In *Democracias y Tiranias en el Caribe*, (Santa Fe de Bogota: Planeta, (1998) [1984c]), pp. 325–365. See also Eric Paul Roorda, *The Dictator Next Door: The Good Neighbor Policy and the Trujillo Regime in the Dominican Republic, 1930–1945*, (Durnham and London: Duke University Press, 1998).

ily's wealth placed it at forty per cent of the country's resources, exclusive of the sugar industry.[53] Close to the end of his rule, Trujillo employed about eighty per cent of working Dominicans, forty five per cent of whom worked for his private businesses and the remaining thirty five per cent for the state that he tightly controlled.[54] The dictator's graft knew no limits. Often Trujillo forced successful businesses to give him shares or sent unofficial agents to visit owners offering protection in exchange for profits.[55]

The tyrant's absolute power was maintained by a severely brutal state and security apparatus that left no margin for independent activity. Trujillo also targeted every organised social group, placing his men in charge specially if these organisations were likely to undertake a public role.[56] Trujillo's security and espionage apparatus included a network of spies, spreading throughout the United States and Latin America, who informed him of every potentially damaging development. Most of the time, the only political party allowed to exist was the Partido Dominicano (PD), the Jefe's tool for enforcing political compliance and the primary organisational instrument for disseminating and preserving Trujillismo. The press and the radio, even if independently owned, became propaganda organs.

Notwithstanding the utter lack of civil and political liberties, Trujillo camouflaged his iron-fist rule with constitutional liturgies. The Americans had so often conditioned maintaining good relations to the observance of periodic elections and to constitutional procedures that the Generalissimo fitted them suitably into his regime. The PD, for example, received one-hundred percent of the votes cast in every election from 1936 to 1957, with the exception of the 1947 election, where the party received only ninety-three percent as a result of the post World War II's 'political opening.'[57] There were constitutional provisions for the separation of power providing a bicameral legislature, an executive and a judiciary. Elections and "democratic" institutions were simply accessories of a political system that depended chiefly on brute force and intimidation.[58]

Order and change in the Caribbean Basin

Trujillo came and maintained himself as absolute ruler because he managed to turn potentially challenging events in his favour and preserve the weakness of

---

53. Robert D. Crassweller, *Trujillo: The Life and Times of a Caribbean Dictator*, (New York: The Macmillan Company, 1966), pp. 128.

54. Juan Bosch, *Trujillo: Causas de una tiranía sin ejemplo*, (Caracas: Librería Las Novedades, 1959), p. 147; drawing on previously untapped Dominican archives, the author expanded on Trujillo's business deals and wealth later in Juan Bosch, *La fortuna de Trujillo*, (Santo Domingo: Alfa y Omega, 1985).

55. Galíndez, *The era of Trujillo*, p. 178.

56. Bosch, *Trujillo: Causas de una tiranía sin ejemplo*, p. 116.

57. Dieter Nohlen (ed.), *Enciclopedia Electoral Latinoamericana y del Caribe*, (San José: Instituto Interamericano de Derechos Humanos, 1993), p. 553.

58. Charles D McIntosh, "Life with the generalissimo," *American Heritage*, (Nov 1997), pp. 32–37.

Dominican society. During his era he did not face any serious organised nor mass-based affront to his regime from within, since it occupied half an island over whose borders he had complete control (provided Haiti was carefully patrolled). With time, dissatisfaction increased, but this did not translate itself into actions that could have constituted a threat to his rule. He was also aided by the fact that most of the time it enjoyed an auspicious regional environment. But Trujillo's rule faced external influences that he could not control. He had come to and stayed in power thanks to external forces; thus he made every effort to make sure that his most important international environment—the United States, his Latin Caribbean neighbours—remained supportive, or at least neutral toward him. When he felt threatened, Trujillo attempted to carry weight in the international arena, and he did this better when he was not alone as a bulkwark for dictatorships in the Caribbean Basin.

The end of World War II shook the ground of authoritarian rulers in the region. During the war, the rallying cry of freedom targeted against Hitler and Mussolini raised expectations among the populations living under dictatorial regimes. Though the region's strongmen had supported the Allies, they seemed to be unable to escape from the pressures for change even before victory was reached over the Axis powers. On top of these, the United States undertook an effort to democratise its neighbours to the south.[59] In this context, Latin Caribbean dissidents who had dreamed of a dictator-free region coalesced to make sure the thrust for change did not die before they attained their aims. Political activities of exiles of different nationalities revived during the armed conflict. During the war's later years, images of the series of landings leading to the Allied victory served as a model for their planning.[60] And they could have faith in the success of their movement, since every move away from dictatorship reinforced their strength and anticipation of triumph.

But the onset of the Cold War truncated this anti-dictatorial wave.[61] Throughout Latin America, the end of World War II had cleared the way for reforms and political openings. However, the advent of the Soviet-American rivalry stirred Washington to place more emphasis on stability and order, fearing that Communist forces might take advantage from the political effervescence. The cause of democracy again lost ground. Except for Costa Rica, whose revolution in 1948 found the Communist Party on the losing side, and Bolivia, whose revolution in 1952 was led by leaders who were prompt in

---

59. Appointed in September 1945 as Assistant Secretary of State for Interamerican Affairs, Spruille Braden put all his efforts into promoting the democratisation of Latin America— as he did as Ambassador to Argentina against what he considered to be the fascist-prone Juan Domingo Perón barely a few months before being designated to Washington. Braden drove the United States to break diplomatic relations with the Somoza regime in 1947 and targeted the dictatorships of Paraguay and Bolivia.

60. Charles D. Ameringer, *The Caribbean Legion: Patriots, Politicians, Soldiers of Fortune, 1946–1950*, (University Park, Pennsylvania: The Pennsylvania State University Press, 1996), p. 9.

61. This issue is examined by Leslie Bethel and Ian Roxborough (eds.), *Latin America between the Second World War and the Cold War, 1944–1948*, (Cambridge : Cambridge University Press, 1992).

denouncing Communism, in the period between 1948 and 1954 the regional balance of power shifted toward authoritarian rule.[62]

In the mid-fifties, however, international pressures mounted one more time against dictatorships. Despite the intensity of the Cold War, a mix of domestic and international circumstances revived the trend toward democracy in Latin America. The industrialisation and urbanisation spurred by World War II and by government policies thereafter brought new actors into the political arena. Urban labour, middle-class professionals, student movements and peasant organisations rallied to put forward economic and political demands that authoritarian regimes proved unable to meet. In the international realm, east-west tensions had abated for a number of reasons. The tight east-west division of the post-World War II order began to crumble. Stalin had died in March 1953 and his successors in the Kremlin began to seek a loosening of tensions with Washington, bowing down to concentrate on domestic political problems. It was also the time when the Third World began to challenge world powers, giving rise to the Non-Aligned Movement and the re-emergence of the non-intervention cause, and the era of anti-colonialism. Beginning with India's independence in 1947, independence movements throughout Africa and Asia brushed the European powers aside. In addition, the US had no reason to feel threatened by the regime changes. Domestically, the nation-wide anti-Communist campaign led by Senator Joseph McCarthy significantly abated as the American public and the authorities turned their backs on him. As the United States prided itself on defending the cause of independence, many of the new statesmen were looking to the US for aid and guidance. Thus many domestic voices were raised in favour of developing an understanding relationship with the emerging states of the world.

For all of these reasons, this time the winds of change in the Latin Caribbean flowed stronger. One after another, a succession of strongmen/dictators fell. As more transitions succeeded, those struggling for change in countries still under iron-fist rule strengthened their certitude that time was on their side. In 1954, twelve out of twenty Latin American republics were ruled by dictatorships; by 1961, only Stroessner in Paraguay and Trujillo in the Dominican Republic remained.[63]

The turning point

Trujillo did not remain aloof of the trend going on around him and, to avert it, used all the means at his disposal. In 1954 he contributed to the overthrow of the Arbenz government in Guatemala, but a more notorious action was the kidnapping and disappearance in march 1956 of Basque Scholar at Columbia

---

62. Recurring to perceptual factors, the different attitudes of the Eisenhower administration vis-à-vis the Guatemalan and Bolivian revolutions is explained by Martha L. Cottam, *Images & Intervention: U.S. policies in Latin America*, (Pittsburg and London: University of Pittsburg Press, 1994), pp. 51–52.

63. In 1956, both Haiti's Jean Francoise Duvalier and Nicaragua's Luis Somoza, son of the fallen autocrat, had assumed power, but by 1960 they were not pinpointed as dictators since they had assumed—and not yet overturned—constitutional forms.

University Jesús de Galíndez, who had presented his dissertation on the Trujillo regime. Galindez had relied partly on confidential Dominican sources. Maybe the Generalissimo presumed that by eliminating Galíndez he could impede the publication and dissemination of a critique against his regime, but he was soon to be undeceived. Before vanishing, Galíndez had submitted a Spanish copy of his dissertation to a Chilean publisher. By July 1956, seven printings had been made of the doctoral-dissertation-turned best-seller. The episode was further muddled by the disappearance on Dominican territory of Gerald L. Murphy, an American co-pilot in a Trujillo-owned airline. Presumably, Murphy had participated in Galíndez' abduction and became too loquacious, for which he paid with his life.[64]

The Galíndez-Murphy episode turned into a cause célebre, channelling international public opinion against the dictator. Soon after Galíndez' disappearance, the American Press and Latin American public-opinion circles deplored the lack of a solution to the mystery and pointed their fingers at Trujillo, lobbying the Eisenhower administration and Congress against the Generalissimo. Domestic pressures drove the US Congress to order an investigation into the case. Though the Eisenhower administration was not too keen on straining its relations with the Dominican dictator, American public-opinion pressure, heightened by the disappearance of an American citizen, compelled the administration to cool its relations with the Dominican tyrant.

Along with the Galíndez-Murphy episode, various domestic and international circumstances contributed to tense the political situation. Domestically, on the economic side, export revenues dropped as tourism and commodity prices fell. On the political side, there was the increasing middle class, whose rise to the top of their professions had been blocked by associates of El Jefe from earlier generations whom they perceived as unfit to govern.[65] In the United States, a series of political shifts affected US-Dominican relations. In 1955, Democrats regained control of the Senate. Leading Senate figures such as J.W. Fullbright, Frank Church, John F. Kennedy, Wayne Morse and Hubert Humphrey criticised Eisenhower's regional policy and intermittently attacked Trujillo for doing little about Galíndez' disappearance. They reproached the White House for what they perceived to be a decline in US prestige in Latin America and the Third World. In response to the new Congressional realignment, in September 1956 the Eisenhower administration substituted Henry Holland, Assistant Secretary of State for Interamerican Affairs and Trujillo's friend, and appointed a liberal, Richard Rubottom.

The Dwight Eisenhower administration had no reason to be concerned about the Dominican tyrant, but it was driven to take matters in its own hands. Events in Cuba had put pressure on Washington to lower the profile of US sup-

---

64. Piero Gleijeses, *The Dominican crisis: the 1965 Constitutionalist revolt and American intervention,* (Baltimore: Johns Hopkins University Press, c1978), p. 25.

65. US.NA.RG59.Decimal file 739.00/12-1058. "Indications of political tensions," Foreign Service Despatch No. 225 from Ambassador Joseph Farland, American Embassy in Ciudad Trujillo, dated 10 November 1958.

port for dictator Fulgencio Batista in Cuba; the administration became adamant about being regarded as backing dictatorships. Thus in 1958 it issued an arms embargo against the Cuban dictator and later it extended this to the Trujillo regime. The State Department faced a dilemma: how to show it cared while the states in the region proscribed Trujillo and set the Dominican Republic apart? It was a hard choice. "Experience has shown—the State Department argued—that any attempt [to promote democracy] which has involved external pressure has been consistently ineffective and has resulted only in the widespread animosity and a weakening of the fabric of hemispheric cooperation."[66] "We are under directives to seek to avoid giving any impressions that US favours dictatorships in Latin America," said Ambassador Farland; "A part of the picture is that anti-Trujillo attitude in Latin America is considerably high."[67]

Trujillo reacted to the cooling off of US-Dominican relations by looking for ways to win the United States to his side. A pro-Trujillo propaganda campaign carried out throughout 1957 and 1958 in the United States failed to woo American public opinion. Then the Generalissimo reduced military co-operation between the two countries. Trujillo had reasons to believe he was being successful. Until the end of 1958, he had at least got the United States to remain neutral toward him. But in January 1959, Batista fled to the Dominican Republic and, in Cuba, Castro's revolution succeeded; a month later Romulo Betancourt (and Trujillo's nemesis) was sworn in as President of Venezuela, and in April 1959 Secretary of State John Foster Dulles, one of the staunchest supporters of Trujillo within the administration, resigned for health reasons.

Of the range of external circumstances encircling the Trujillo regime, no other had so much impact as Fidel Castro's access to power in Cuba on 1 January 1959. If ahead of this time there was—arguably—a mixture of domestic and international circumstances that might have allowed the Trujillo regime to survive, the arrival of the Cuban revolution made it utterly implausible. This event completely recast the region's political scene. Subsequently, US-Latin American relations would no longer be the same. Neither would Dominican politics; for the years to come, the unfolding of events in revolutionary Cuba would significantly alter the setting for political developments in the country.

The Cuban revolution turned the regional balance of power definitely against Trujillo. With the regime change in Cuba, Trujillo not only lost an important ally, but gained a mighty enemy. Soon after taking power, Fidel Castro, who as a student had participated in operations to topple the Dominican tyrant, joined and supported the region's efforts against Trujillo. But Castro was a menace not so much for what he said or did, but for what he represented. Pressure against Trujillo intensified, as the march of democracy in Latin America seemed irresistible and the overthrow of the Trujillo regime appeared to be only a matter of time to the anti-Trujillo elements within the country.

---

66. US.NA.RG59.Decimal files 739.00/8-1457. Letter by John S. Hoghland II, acting Assistant Secretary of State for Congressional Relations to Senator Mike Mulroney, 20 August 1957.

67. US.NA.RG59.Decimal files 739.00/3-1359. Informal Letter by Ambassador Joseph S. Farland in Ciudad Trujillo, addressed to 'Dear Joe,' dated 13 March 1959.

Batista was a dictator and after his downfall a radical regime took over. Trujillo was a dictator. Therefore, what kind of regime could emerge if the absence of democracy continued? How else could a dictatorship be replaced? Dominicans could look forward to effect a change by following one of the two options that appeared before them: a revolution similar to Castro's, or a peaceful transition modelled after Venezuela's Betancourt. In the end, either to replicate Castro's success or to avoid it, the example of the courageous Cuban revolution, not the quiet Venezuelan transition, enlivened Dominicans to take action against the Generalissimo.

Only seven men had sailed from Mexico and landed in Cuba, and fought a guerrilla war that led to Castro's forces seizing power two years later. How far could a bunch of Dominicans go with Castro's material aid, in addition to Betancourt and other regional political figures' moral backing? Among the many expeditions aiming to emulate Castro's achievement launched against other rulers in the region, two invasions by Dominican exiles landed at Constanza in June 1959. The missions were poorly armed and trained; thus they failed to inflict any harm on Trujillo's forces. However, they had shattering repercussions on the Trujillo regime, for Trujillo did not spare the lives of those who took part in the June landings. The attacking force included many close blood relatives of the Dominican élite. As a result, an astonishingly large number of influential Dominican families became antagonistic toward Trujillo. The Church followed, ending its complicity with El Jefe. A new Nuncio was appointed on June 1959 by John XXIII, Pope since 1958, to replace Salvatore Sino, who had endorsed the Benefactor. However, in January 1960 the Church issued a cathartic, pastoral letter read in all parishes, censuring the regime for the wave of arrests involving Catholics.[68]

Trujillo's regional foes used the situation created by the June invasions to bid for a concerted regional action against the dictator. Convoked by Venezuela to "analyse the recent tensions in the Caribbean," the hemisphere's foreign ministers met in the Chilean capital city of Santiago in August. Venezuela, Chile and Cuba wanted to modify the non-intervention principle to get rid of, or at least to isolate, Trujillo. However, the final Declaration, signed by all member states but Cuba and the Dominican Republic, stuck to the non-intervention clause, merely exhorting all governments to guarantee individual liberties. Newly appointed Secretary of State Christian Herter expressed his opposition to intervention, arguing that "history has shown that efforts to impose democracy in a country, by force and from outside, can easily result in the mere substitution of one form of tyranny for another."[69] Assistant Secretary Rubottom scolded the Venezuelans, arguing that democracy and human rights are not incompatible with the principle of non-intervention. "One only had to consider Venezuela's experience

---

68. US.NA.RG59.Decimal files 739.00/3-760. Confidential telegram from the American Embassy in Ciudad Trujillo to the Department of State, dated 7 March 1960.

69. Bernardo Vega, *Eisenhower y Trujillo*, (Santo Domingo: Fundacion Cultural Dominicana, 1991), p.6; Jose Manuel Sanchez (1972), "U.S. Intervention in the Caribbean, 1954–1965: Decision-making and the information input," Ph.D. Thesis, Columbia University, 1972, pp. 168–169.

during the past year, when the people of that nation had themselves overthrown Perez Jimenez, without outside assistance or intervention. The strict observance of non-intervention is perhaps the best way to promote democracy."[70]

Anti-Trujillo regional leaders had the opportunity to bid once more against the Dominican dictator in the situation created by January 1960's massive wave of arrests that had followed the uncovering of a plot against the Generalissimo. Venezuela denounced the Trujillo regime before the OAS, arguing that the Dominican Republic's human right violations "aggravated international tensions in the Caribbean." A week later, "without expressing an opinion on the internal situation in any member state," the Council Resolution, which the State Department supported, pointed out that the Meeting of Foreign Ministers (MFM) of August 1959 authorised the Inter-American Peace Committee (IAPC) to take cognisance of the relationship between human rights and political tensions affecting hemispheric peace. The Resolution was a precedent-shattering development. Though it did not go as far as condemning the Trujillo regime, it was the first time in OAS history that the denunciation of the political situation within a member state was discussed within the organisation.

At this time, it would apparently have been expedient for Trujillo, in the interest of self-survival, to wait for calmer waters. But the Generalissimo became involved in activities aimed at getting rid of his detractors. The most notorious was Trujillo's conspiracy to overthrow President Betancourt. As evidence linking the Generalissimo to the plot became public, Venezuela called for another MFM to impose the harshest of measures against the Trujillo regime. The tyrant had outreached himself. His neighbours could not forget his repeated interventions supporting anti-democratic revolutions and his master-minding international assassinations. Trujillo had gone beyond the point other governments could tolerate.

In the 1930s, the principle of non-intervention became the cornerstone of US-Latin American relations after the inception of the Good Neighbour Policy. But Washington had unilaterally, breached the principle twice: the first, justifying it as a way to promote democracy during Braden's interregnum after World War II, and the second, on the exclusion of Communist influence in the hemisphere in the overthrow of the Arbenz government in Guatemala in 1954. This principle was born after the observation that, to get co-operation going, states had to commit themselves not to intervene in the domestic affairs of one another. Washington had needed that co-operation when it suffered the Great Depression and when it deemed essential that Latin America backed—or stayed neutral toward—the US war effort against the Axis powers. But now Latin American states wanted to overturn the principle, aiming at promoting a change of regime in the Dominican Republic. This time, most Latin American states wanted intervention in the Dominican Republic before they engaged in co-operation with the United States on Cuba.

---

70. US.NA.RG59.Decimal files 739.00/7-259. "Venezuela's position on possible COAS action on the Dominican Republic's complaint regarding Foreign Intervention." Confidential memoranda of conversation, Department of State, dated 2 July 1959.

The false analogy with the Cuban question haunted US reasoning since the June 1959 landings at Constanza. Since the fall of Batista, Washington began to see Trujillo more as a liability than as an asset. Ambassador Farland had been pleased with Trujillo, for he had done "a lot for his people. He has made this country into a stable and, up to a year and a half ago, a relatively prosperous nation." But barely a month after the first of the Constanza invasions, Farland was unequivocally sure that after Trujillo died or fell, "the Dominican Communists in exile will come rushing back and will attempt to take over the reins of government during the confused period of reorganization."[71] As the Cuban Revolution leaned toward the Soviet Block, US perceptions of threat from the Dominican Republic increased dramatically. By April 1960, Washington reasoned that, in the absence of an alternative, pro-US leadership that could take over after Trujillo left, died or fell, the only alternative was a pro-Castro take-over.

As time passed and no change in the Dominican situation occurred, Washington became even more alarmed about the possibility of facing "another Cuba." Based on Cuban, not Dominican developments, the US perceived "a very real danger" of a Communist take-over in the Dominican Republic, but also of a "violent revolution" that would not stop until "that country is in ashes," probably setting off further revolutions in "Haiti, Nicaragua, Panama, Guatemala, and other Central and Latin American countries."[72] The State Department had little confidence in the institutional strength of Latin Caribbean regimes. The Dominican Republic was no exception. It had a very small number of Communists, nor did it experience a revolt in which a group of them took part, threatening to alter the country's allegiance to the United States. But that hardly mattered because, by this time, "US officials made any Latin American Communist into a superman capable of routing whole armies of 'democrats.'"[73]

The United States could not strike against Castro without engaging first in the regional effort against the most despised regime in Latin America. Castro's recent drift toward the Soviet Union simply did not worry Latin Americans as much as the United States. The memories of the heroic feat by Castro were just too recent; instead, they warned the United States not to engage in any activity that might be interpreted as another "Guatemalazo."[74] Censuring the Trujillo regime could establish the precedent for subsequent action against Castro, for it would breach the norm that had thus far impeded Washington from taking on

71. US.NA.RG59.Decimal files 739.00/7-1459. Secret Informal Letter from Ambassador Joseph Farland to R.R. Rubottom, Jr., Assistant Secretary of State for Inter-American Affairs, dated 14 July 1959.

72. US.NA.RG59.Decimal files 739.00/6-3060. "Views on the political problems in the Dominican Republic and suggestions for possible courses of action by our Government in its future negotiations with the Government of Dominican Republic," Secret Memorandum from Harry M. Lofton, Second Secretary-Consul to Mr. Thomas C. Mann, dated 30 June 1960.

73. According to former Undersecretary of State Thomas Mann, interviewed by Gleijeses. See Gleijeses, *The Dominican crisis*, p. 43.

74. US.NA.RG59.Decimal files 739.00/5-2060. "Transmitting Memorandum of Conversation with President Betancourt," Confidential Foreign Service Despatch from the American Embassy in Caracas to the Department of State, dated 20 May 1960.

measures to topple the Cuban revolutionary. At the OAS meeting held in San Jose in August 1960, all but the Trujillo regime voted to condemn the Dominican acts of aggression and intervention against Venezuela and, for the first time, the OAS agreed to impose sanctions against a member state. Pointing to the danger the Trujillo regime posed to hemispheric peace, the OAS also decided to break diplomatic ties and partially interrupt economic relations.

To influence the San Jose MFM about the imposition of sanctions, Trujillo turned to the 'liberalisation' of his regime. He had his brother Hector resign from the Presidency in favour of Vice-president Joaquin Balaguer, an intellectual who was not related by blood to the Generalissimo. In addition, Trujillo had himself appointed Ambassador to the United Nations, as if to show that his authority was diminishing, since he was expected to leave the country (he never did). The farce was taken to its limits; for the press, Trujillo would take the time to "visit" Balaguer in his office and order the Presidential Guard to render honours to the new President. However, there was no real change in the power structure: Trujillo would enter and exit the Presidential Palace as usual, but through the back door.[75]

Engaging the United States

Seeking a rapprochement with the United States, Trujillo tried every conceivable way to play on US fears about Communism. Trujillo authorised the return of Communist exiles. He then devised a complicated plot to deceive the Americans into thinking that, on Premier Krushchev's request, he was considering abandoning power to Castro.[76] In July, Trujillo set up a radio station, *La Voz Dominicana*, whose editorial line was in defence of socialism. On 1 September, right before the closing of the American Embassy, a Dominican government spokesman announced the selection of the first Dominican Ambassador to Moscow, though the Soviets had not agreed to establish diplomatic relations.[77]

Though these efforts failed to attract the favour of the White House, Trujillo's friends on Capitol Hill let him obtain a temporary victory. In July 1960 the United States deprived Cuba of its sugar quota and distributed it among its Latin Caribbean neighbours. Despite Eisenhower's urgent recommendations to the contrary, Trujillo's friends in Congress provided that one of the countries from which replacement sugar was to be purchased was the Dominican Republic. Possibly bribed by Trujillo, Senator Allen J Ellender, Agricultural Committee President, used his influence in Trujillo's aid.[78] In reaction, following the spirit of

---

75. UK.PRO.FO371/147948. "Interpretation of recent political changes," Confidential correspondence from Mr. Mc Vittie, United Kingdom Embassy in Ciudad Trujillo, dated 8 August 1960.

76. US.NA.RG59.Decimal files 739.00/6-1360. "Possible Abandonment of Power by Trujillo in the Dominican Republic," Secret memorandum of Conversation between Virgilio Diaz Ordoñez, Dominican Republic's Ambassador to the OAS Council, and ARA-Amb. Dreier and RPA-Mr. Redington, dated 13 June 1960.

77. Vega, *Eisenhower y Trujillo*, pp. 99, 119, 122.

78. According to a "realiable dissident" quoted in a telegram from the American Embassy in

the sanctions mandated by the August 1960 MFM, the Eisenhower administration imposed a special fee on Dominican sugar. In reality, however, Trujillo was afforded a psychological victory. Congress did not provide the President with the legal authority to purchase non-quota sugar, thus sugar from the Dominican Republic was going to be purchased anyway, though at world-market prices.[79]

As time passed, many Dominicans resented the US because they interpreted Washington's apparent inaction as support for the dictatorship. The arguments of non-intervention and self-help failed to convince most Dominicans. Thus, State Department analysts thought, Castro could be ready to fill the vacuum and transform Trujillo's demise into a victory for Communism. Not that large segments of the Dominican people were ready to risk their lives, because many thought that any effort to topple the Benefactor without outside assistance was doomed to failure. Many urged the United States to undertake strong measures, including intervention, to help them get rid of Trujillo.[80] Dissidents reasoned they had to take into account possible US reactions. Under what conditions would it provide technical and financial assistance? What if a military garrison or two outside Ciudad Trujillo defected and began military operations against the Trujillo regime? Would the US intervene in these circumstances? Would the US provide the tools for liquidating the old man? The more the United States publicly turned its back on the Generalissimo, the more the dissidents felt at ease talking to US Embassy officers about their prospects for toppling the Benefactor.

Regarding the dissidents, Washington faced a complex predicament: it would not provide material aid until it made sure that the successor regime was not to follow Castro, but at the same time it did not want to discourage Dominicans from engaging in activities aimed at provoking the fall of the Trujillo regime. Could it do so by giving them just some token support? Dominican dissidents looked to the United States, not to themselves, to dislodge Trujillo, and made sure they did what was needed to draw in the US. Accordingly, some dissidents tried to manipulate these fears for their benefit: if they did not receive US aid and guidance, they would go Communist.[81] This attitude posed a different dilemma for Washington.

Ciudad Trujillo, Dominican government agents corresponded at this time on the "amount of money which would be necessary to carry out the program for securing the aid of representative Cooley and Senator Ellender on the sugar program." US.NA.RG59.Decimal files 739.00/8-2560. Confidential telegram from the American Embassy in Ciudad Trujillo to the Department of State, dated 25 August 1960.

79. US.NA.RG59.Decimal files 739.00/10-1860. Confidential Foreign Service Despatch from the American Embassy in Ciudad Trujillo to the Department of State, dated 18 October 1960.

80. US.NA.RG59.Decimal files 739.00/7-1359. "Political Situation in the Dominican Republic," Confidential Memorandum of Conversation between Mr. Alvin E. Gilbert and Mr. Ernest B Gutierrez, Officer in Charge of Dominican Affairs, dated 13 July 1959.

81. US.NA.RG59.Decimal files 739.00/3-2260. Top Secret Informal Letter from Ambassador Joseph Farland to the Assistant Secretary of State for Inter-American Affairs, R.R. Rubottom, Jr., dated 22 March 1960; John Bartlow Martin, *Overtaken by Events: The Dominican Crisis from the Fall of Trujillo to the Civil War*, (Garden City, New York: Doubleday & Company, Inc., 1966), p. 66.

If Trujillo fell and the US had not supported the internal effort against the dictator, how could it exercise influence over any post-Trujillo government?

To avoid estranging the Dominican dissidents, Washington might be forced to deviate from its official non-intervention policy. The only other option was to bolster the Trujillo regime but, with virtually all Latin America against it, it would have been disastrous for US interests abroad precisely at this delicate juncture of the region's history. "The US can gain no credit from their protégé—the British Ambassador observed—since he personifies the final degradation of the American capitalist system ending in extinction of all morality."[82] Washington agreed on what US aims were—keeping Castro out and promoting democracy—and it would strive to work in both directions, though allocating priority to the first. One thing seemed clear to the United States: Trujillo was the major obstacle for realizing both aims.

Thus the Eisenhower administration took the decision to interfere in the Dominican course of events, but it was confused about the best way to achieve both objectives. US policy-makers considered encouraging the formation of a political leadership that, in the event of Trujillo disappearing from the scene, would take over the government. To avoid being singled out by Latin America as unilaterally imposing its will on the Dominican Republic, President Eisenhower instructed the State Department to have the OAS "participate to the maximum extent in any unfolding situation," provided it went along with US interests.[83] The Eisenhower administration also endeavoured, through alleged unofficial channels, to persuade Trujillo to resign.[84] The Generalissimo would take asylum in Portugal or Morocco and a Junta would take over, but Trujillo rejected this proposal outright.[85] In the event that the Generalissimo would not voluntarily leave power, Washington expected to create a civil-military group who would overthrow Trujillo and request the US to send troops to prevent "another Cuba." However, conditions in the Dominican Republic were not conducive for US intelligence operations toward this end. The US mission had little information about the Dominican military, because, since the US had turned its back on Trujillo, members of the Dominican armed forces were not allowed to meet with US Embassy officers without his permission—and, when they did, their language was closely watched.

Since late 1960, Trujillo's cause seemed lost for most observers though not for Trujillo. According to British diplomats, the Generalissimo's henchmen hoped that the US Presidential election, scheduled for November of that year,

---

82. UK.PRO.FO371/147947. "Summary Report on political troubles". Confidential Correspondence from Mr. Mc Vittie at the United Kingdom's Embassy in Ciudad Trujillo, dated 16 February 1960.

83. US.NA.RG59.Decimal files 739.00/4-2560. Secret eyes-only Memorandum for the files, signed by Assistant Secretary of State for Interamerican affairs, R.R. Rubottom, Jr., dated 25 April 1960.

84. US.NA.RG59.Decimal files 739.00/3-2860, XR 739.11. Secret letter from General Norman Clark to Colonel King, dated 28 March 1960.

85. Vega, *Eisenhower y Trujillo*, pp. 65–66.

would lead to a Democratic President with whose more corrupt disciples he could attempt to gain a leverage in the new administration.[86] He expected to slide gradually into the democratic fold. In this regard, Trujillo set to organise early in 1961 a wide-scale political campaign in the United States in preparation for his country's Presidential Election, scheduled for next year, to persuade Americans that his regime would observe democratic principles.[87]

As Trujillo maintained his will to remain in power, the only option left for the United States was to wait for—or encourage—Trujillo's annihilation. If the Generalissimo were left free after his downfall, he could dedicate the rest of his life to overthrowing democracies, fostering dictatorships in the Caribbean or assassinating his enemies. Soon after he abandoned the Dominican Republic in May 1960, Ambassador Farland passed on to the State Department dissidents' requests for rifles and related material. In January 1961, Dominican dissidents were sent arms and supplies. On 10 April 1961 the CIA approved the delivery of four machine guns, but shortly afterwards, following the failed invasion of Cuba, Washington stopped the delivery of the weapons;[88] Castro was still in power and it might be dangerous to create a power vacuum in the Dominican Republic. However, dissidents had already been sufficiently assured: so encouraged were they that on 30 May 1961 they carried out the assassination of Trujillo, despite the United States' last-minute attempts at not precipitating the tyrant's death following the Bay of Pigs fiasco.[89]

The beginning of the end

The dictator's death on 30 May 1961 finished 31 years of the Generalissimo's absolute rule, but his era had not yet ended. The inability of conspirators to attract the loyalty of the Armed Forces allowed Trujillo's family and henchmen to stay in power. Thus the plot ended, as well as the opportunity to initiate a regime transition quickly after Trujillo's death. Though American ships approached the island, Ramfis conducted tortures, murders and mass arrests to avenge his father. Washington deplored Ramfis' "reign of terror," but it was puzzled about how to influence Dominican events.[90]

---

86. UK.PRO:FO371/147948. "Generalissimo Trujillo's awaited speech," Confidential Correspondence from Mr. Mc Vittie at the United Kingdom's Embassy in Ciudad Trujillo, dated 29 September 1960.

87. UK.PRO.FO371/155986. "Wide scale political campaign in USA in preparation for the Presidential election," Confidential correspondence from Mr. Mc Vittie, United Kingdom's Embassy in Ciudad Trujillo, 5 May 1961.

88. United States Senate, 94 Congress, 1st. session, *Alleged Assasination Plots Involving Foreign Leaders: An Interim Report of the Select Committee to Study Governmental Operations with Respect to Intelligence Activities, An Interim Report,* (Washington, DC: U.S. Government Printing Office, 1975), part D.

89. Dissidents told US Consul Dearborn that they would not adjust their plan to US whims. By 30 April 1961, it was common knowledge in Washington's higher echelons that an attempt at Trujillo's life was going to be committed any time. See US Senate, *op. cit.,* loc. cit.

90. UK.PRO.FO371/155987. "Conversation between Mr. Achilles and Head of Chancery: State Department concerned at reports received from the [US] Consul General," Confidential Cor-

Once the Generalissimo had disappeared from the scene, Dominicans faced a whole new situation. For the political opposition, the pillar that sustained the dictatorship was forever gone. But to become politically active against Trujillo's heirs they would have to wait until the Dominican government changed the rules of the game. The impact of the dictator's death was stronger in Trujillo's followers, because the absence of the Benefactor forced them to reassess their strategies in their effort to retain power. Notably, their calculations were not to take place in a vacuum, but under a degree of international pressures unparalleled in the region's history.

Since the United States was the most powerful of its regional antagonists, the Dominican regime set out to find ways to appease Washington. Weeks after the assassination of his father, Ramfis Trujillo, visible head of the regime, sent conciliatory messages to the American Consul. Ramfis expressed his government's willingness to do "anything reasonable" that the US requested, and his desire that the US "take the leadership in specifying what should be done."[91] If the United States wanted them to become democrats, they would comply. The State Department pondered whether the Ramfis-Balaguer duo, if given US support, were likely to maintain political stability over the short run and to evolve "along lines similar to the Somoza's relatively moderate rule in Nicaragua." However, bolstering the Trujillos could weaken the "drawing power" of the Dominican opposition, turning them unable to counter either the Trujillistas or the Left. In addition, the State Department felt, US support or tolerance of a continuation of the Trujillo dynasty was likely to be poorly received in the hemisphere.[92]

Within these limited range of options, the United States undertook to guide the Ramfis-Balaguer dyad into 'democratisation.' The US hoped there could be "a smooth and orderly transition from the previously repressive regime to a more liberal and enlightened regime." This did not mean, the State Department underlined, the departure of Balaguer. In fact, the US stated that he could remain and "lead the Government toward such liberalisation, hopefully with the support of Ramfis and other members of the Trujillo family."[93] Though the fallen tyrant's son was depicted as leading a 'reign of terror,' he was assured that the US "would not be swayed by the difficulties and frictions of the past." He could preserve Trujillo's "accomplishments" and begin to establish his own reputation by "fully observing human rights." The US had an exclusionary vision of the future political system. For example, next steps had to be the adoption of measures to establish a "political climate and system which would allow free elections" and

respondence from Mr. Rennie at the United Kingdom's Embassy in Ciudad Trujillo, dated 3 June 1961.

91. US.NA.RG59.Decimal files 739.00/6-1261. Confidential Telegram from the American Embassy in Ciudad Trujillo, dated 12 June 1961.

92. US.NA.RG59.Decimal files 739.00/7-361. "Dominican Republic," Secret Memorandum from RA Stevenson to Mr. Coeer, Department of State, dated 3 July 1961.

93. US.NA.RG59.Decimal files 739.00/6-2461. Secret Memorandum from U. Alexis Johnson to the Secretary of State, dated 24 June 1961.

the participation of "all non-Castro, non-communist elements who adhere to the Dominican Constitution."[94]

In its communications with the Dominican regime, the US encouraged Ramfis to effect basic political changes. However, in private it believed that, to bring about a real democratisation, the Trujillo family—still in powerful positions in the military and security apparatus—would have to go. President Kennedy had launched the Alliance for Progress, which was to herald a new era in interamerican relations, and Castro was being criticised as a dictator who violated human rights. Thus for the State Department the transition required more than holding elections. Ramfis could stay, at least as long as he were needed to keep the Armed Forces together. Balaguer had little power of his own. Thus, the State Department recommended that the US should not press for things he could not do and probably build up Balaguer's image in Dominican and outside opinion.

Washington's determination to curtail the Trujillos' repressive power and to press Balaguer for reforms tilted the Dominican balance of power in favour of civilian dissidents. But if this process was to reach a point of no return in the direction of democratisation, President Balaguer also needed to show the Generalissimo's heirs that he would get the United States to resume normal diplomatic relations and the OAS to lift its sanctions. Balaguer argued that this was "a matter of life and death" for his regime.[95] Balaguer did his best at making his country a convincing case of liberalisation. He as well as Ramfis invited denunciations or arbitrary or unlawful acts by Government or Armed Forces officials and announced that exiles could participate in the 1962 elections.[96]

Balaguer insisted that the US had to assume responsibility to help maintain stability while the reforms were being enacted, but the US was constrained by the fact that the OAS had been clear about how and when were they to consider lifting sanctions against the Dominican government. An OAS delegation to the Dominican Republic—invited by Ramfis and Balaguer—took note of the regime's "intention of bringing about a democratic transformation." However, politely it responded that it was "too early" to determine the degree of change.[97] The link between the regime's domestic policies and its international conduct had been set by the OAS Resolutions. Because of pressures from Venezuela, the only evidence the OAS was to consider as proof of the Dominican government's 'change of heart' was its acquisition of credible democratic credentials.[98]

94. US.NA.RG59.Decimal files 739.00/6-2661. Confidential Memorandum from the American Consulate in Ciudad Trujillo, dated 26 June 1961.

95. US.NA.RG59.Decimal files 739.00/6-1361. Secret Telegram from the American Consulate in Ciudad Trujillo, dated June 13 1961.

96. UK.PRO.FO371/155988. "Show of liberalisation by the Balaguer Government," Confidential Correspondence from Mr. Mc Vittie, United Kingdom's Embassy in Ciudad Trujillo, dated 15 June 1961.

97. US.NA.RG59.Decimal files 739.00/7-1861. Unclassified Airgram from the Department of State to all ARA diplomatic posts and US/UN, dated July 18 1961.

98. US.NA.RG59.Decimal files 739.00/6-2061. "Venezuela: Caribbean Problems," Confidential Memorandum of Conversation between Jose Antonio Mayobre, Ambassador of Venezuela, Dr. Rafael Caldera, President of Venezuela's Chamber of Deputies, and the Undersecretary,

The road toward a "more enlightened regime," as Washington expected, was full of complications. Balaguer and Ramfis were not accomplishing much. The personality cult of the Generalissimo persisted as the regime's official policy, and the PD continued its activities without breaking stride.[99] By August, young military officers were restless about Balaguer's inability to show progress and considered installing a military junta to replace Balaguer, leaving Ramfis as "mediator and counsellor." Some State Department officials supported the idea, but it was rejected on the grounds that a military government could hardly govern without diplomatic recognition and substantial economic aid, both of which were not to be granted by most Latin American states until all of the Trujillos left.[100] Only when the US threatened to tighten rather than relax sanctions was the conspiracy aborted.[101] Ramfis and Balaguer required some token support from the US to deter the oft-mounting criticisms within the regime. However, whatever action they took would have been counterproductive with the opposition, who at this time accused the United States of forcing a "Nicaraguan solution" upon the Dominican Republic.[102] In this context, raising the status of Consulates to Consulate Generals was as far as the US and the Venezuelan governments went.

The uncertainties of the transition, at a time when the Kennedy administration was ostensibly championing the cause of democracy in the Americas, prompted most dissidents to expect—and ask—the US to come in their aid. In the interest of promoting democracy in the Dominican Republic, Washington had to deal with the Ramfis-Balaguer duo, and believed it could not openly take sides, lest support for one result in the lack of co-operation of the other. As a result of Balaguer-Ramfis' liberalisation, the political opposition had barely begun to emerge, and were looking for ways to engage Washington. A spokesman for a group of dissidents told the US Consul that US armed intervention was the "only thing which could be counted on." To make sure that the non-intervention issue did not represent an obstacle, this group considered sabotaging American property and investments, since this would leave the United States no option but armed intervention to safeguard American lives and property and, in the process, rid the country of the Trujillos.[103] President Balaguer also asked whether the US would intervene should his position be threatened by the military, but Hill cautioned Balaguer and the dissidents to expect it exclusively in the event of a

dated June 20 1961.

99. US.NA.RG59.Decimal files 739.00/7-1661. Confidential Foreign Service Despatch from the American Consulate in Ciudad Trujillo, dated 16 July 1961.

100. US.NA.RG59.Decimal files 739.00/8-2261. Confidential Telegram from the American Consulate in Ciudad Trujillo, dated 22 August 1961.

101. US.NA.RG59.Decimal files 739.00/8-1161. Secret Telegram from Ciudad Trujillo, dated 11 August 1961.

102. US.NA.RG59.Decimal files 739.00/8-1161. Secret Telegram No. 307 from the American Consulate in Ciudad Trujillo, dated 11 August 1961. The 'Nicaraguan solution' was a way to describe the course of events in Nicaragua after the death of dictator Somoza, where, despite the fact that the tyrant died, his family kept control of the country.

103. US.NA.RG59.Decimal files 739.00/6-1761. Secret telegram from the American Embassy in Ciudad Trujillo, dated 17 June 1961.

Castro-led invasion and not to expect it in advance.[104]

Ramfis and Balaguer imagined that the United States would support their half-baked liberalisation effort, but Washington had conflicting interests in mind. Kennedy instructed US officials to express, in dealings with the Dominican regime, his government's interest in the implementation of measures designed to exclude "Communists and Castroists" from the country.[105] Yet Communist subversion could be prevented by strengthening the Balaguer regime, at the expense of democracy, or by providing the Dominicans with the opportunity to engage in democratic politics, at the cost of political stability. Provided the course of events did not go out of control, Washington's decisions would also be influenced by Balaguer's effectiveness in accomplishing both objectives, and on the Dominican people's willingness to bear the pace and the extent of the regime's reforms.

Two major political forces emerged during the effervescence of the transition. At this moment, the most important seemed to be the Unión Civica Nacional (UCN), which was created as a loosely organised alliance between the discontented business and professional classes and the landed élite, who united to bring the downfall of Trujillato and get hold of the government, with no plan to interfere with the country's social structure.[106] Its most visible leader, and later, its presidential candidate, was Viriato Fiallo, a medical doctor with scarcely any political experience before he was propelled into the UCN's leadership. Fiallo was virtually unknown outside the Dominican Republic.

The other, but oldest and better organised was the Dominican Revolutionary Party (PRD), founded in 1939 in Cuba by Juan Bosch and other Dominican exiles seeking the overthrow of Trujillo's dictatorship. Bosch, its most important leader, and later its presidential candidate, was a writer, well known among the region's literary and political circles. His activities within the so-called 'Caribbean Legion' in the late 1940s and in support of the democratic revolutions of Guatemala (1944–1954), Venezuela (1947–48 and 1958) and Costa Rica (1948), where he taught at a political training institute, made him a well known figure in the Latin Caribbean's democratic left.

But the opposition remained wary about Balaguer, no matter what he said or did. The Dominican President promised that no member of the Trujillo family would be a candidate in the 1962 elections and that he would withdraw from politics unless it were found "necessary" for the good of the nation and the furtherance of democratisation.[107] However, no opposition party would participate

---

104. UK.PRO.FO371/155989. "President Balaguer had consultation with US Consul-General about members of Trujillo family who are likely to oppose him", Confidential Correspondence from Mr. Harding, United Kingdom's Embassy in Ciudad Trujillo, dated 15 July 1961.

105. Delesseps S. Morrison, *Latin American Mission: An adventure in Hemisphere Diplomacy*, (New York: Simon and Schuster, 1965), pp. 124–125.

106. Thomas Jay D'Agostino, "The evolution of an emerging political party system: a study of party politics in the Dominican Republic, 1961–1990," Ph.D. Thesis, Syracuse University, 1992, pp. 113–114.

107. UK.PRO.FO371/155989. "Points made in a statement by President Balaguer published in La Nacion," Restricted correspondence from Mr. Harding, United Kingdom's Embassy in Ciudad Trujillo, dated 12 August 1961.

until the PD was dissolved and key Trujillos remained in control of the military and security apparatus.[108] Balaguer was willing to negotiate the departure of all the military members of the Trujillo family, but not of Ramfis, whom he regarded as indispensable to maintain stability.[109]

Washington's most practical course of action was to induce military and civilian support for the Balaguer government. It encouraged the "non-communist opposition" to use "moderate" methods and the Trujillo family to depart gradually and to give up enough property to dissolve their power-hold. All actors were also warned that they should take forceful actions against "Castro-Communists." Time had to be allowed for the military and the opposition to "achieve a constructive relationship."[110] Equally important was the decision to enunciate US policy with "greater clarity" because, when the US remained silent, the Balaguer regime interpreted the silence as lack of support for its programmes, and the opposition interpreted it as indifference to the government's repression.[111]

Beginning of the Dominican transition

The Trujillo era ended when, unexpectedly, Ramfis Trujillo resigned as Chief of the Armed Forces and announced his departure from the island. Conditions were propitious for staying in power and seeking to 'liberalise' the dictatorship and present a 'new face' of Trujillismo, as the Americans, momentarily, seemed to be ready to accept. However, Ramfis chose to leave and have his uncles Hector and Arismendi return to Dominican soil. The Generalissimo's eldest son explained that his decision derived purely from personal reasons and said that his uncle Hector would remain in the country but outside the armed forces, "as a symbol of continuity of the Trujillo name."[112]

Whatever the reasons for Ramfis to relinquish his post as head of the Armed Forces, once he announced his decision all forces vying for power made an effort to turn unsettled matters in their favour. Adopting a passive role, Balaguer threatened to resign if the Trujillo brothers did not leave. The opposition took the streets and demanded that all the Trujillos part. The United States began to contemplate the execution of its contingency military plans for the Dominican Republic. Cuban radio stations issued broadcasts calling the Dominican youth and workers to rebel against the government. The military was divided about where to stand.

---

108. US.NA.RG59.Decimal files 739.00/9-2161. Secret telegram from the Department of State to the American Consulate in Ciudad Trujillo, dated 21 September 1961.

109. UK.PRO.FO371/155991. "Public correction appeared in 'El Caribe' of a statement made by President Balaguer about exiling army officers," Restricted correspondence from Mr. Harding, United Kingdom's Embassy in Ciudad Trujillo, dated 13 October 1961.

110. US.NA.RG59.Decimal files 739.00/9-161. Secret Telegram from the Department of State to the American Consul in Ciudad Trujillo, dated 1 September 1961.

111. US.NA.RG59.Decimal files 739.00/10-361. "Program for the Dominican Republic," Secret Memorandum of Conversation between Dr. Joaquin Balaguer, President of the Dominican Republic; the Honorable George Ball, Undersecretary of State, and Mr. John Calvin Hill, Consul General in Ciudad Trujillo, dated 3 October 1961.

112. US.NA.RG59.Decimal files 739.00/11-1661. Secret Telegram from the American Consulate in Ciudad Trujillo, dated 16 November 1961.

Of all the actors involved in the Dominican crisis, only the United States had the influence to oppose the new political arrangement desired by the uncles. Balaguer was virtually alone: the opposition disavowed him and Ramfis, his sole nexus with the military, had just left his post. The opposition had no ties with the Armed Forces and the United States was its sole interlocutor in the crisis. The only ones in which the Trujillo uncles could trust were their henchmen in the military, but at this moment, with all the international and domestic pressures against it, most of them could not anticipate the successful reimposition of the dictatorship. The United States had a large ascendancy over Balaguer and the opposition, both of which expected Washington to come in, and perhaps might have some over the Armed Forces, if it used its power to sway most of them against the 'wicked uncles.'

Thus the United States took command of the Dominican crisis. In Washington, Secretary Rusk publicly expressed his country's firm determination against the reimposition of dictatorship.[113] The State Department reassured Balaguer of US support, and sent US naval units to approach Dominican waters and to position themselves below the horizon, to provide a "calming effect" and "an element of security" for Balaguer.[114] For his part, US Consul Hill demanded Hector and Arismendi to leave, threatening military intervention to assure that the Dominican Republic does not "fall into Castro-Communist hands."[115]

The impressive display of force by the United States altered the internal balance among the groups seeking power. Soon after Ramfis departed on 17 November, Dominican Air Force officers led by General Pedro Rafael Rodriguez Echavarria succeeded in concentrating in Santiago all aircraft and pilots. Echavarria declared his loyalty to Balaguer, his opposition to the Trujillo family, and bombed the air force base near the capital.[116] Co-ordinating some of his groups' actions with an American Navy Officer serving at the US Consulate, Rodriguez Echavarria was instrumental in enabling Balaguer to hold his own and oust the Trujillo brothers.[117]

Yet the opposition was emboldened and would not stop there. To force the resignation of Balaguer and form a provisional government, the UCN, the most active political force during the course of these events, called a general strike in late November. But the Armed Forces sided with the President. Their chiefs were suspicious about the UCN and disagreed with the opposition's effort to

---

113. UK.PRO.FO371/155991. "Mr. Rusk's statements about the return to the Dominican Republic of Hector and Arismendi Trujillo," Confidential Correspondence from Sir Ormsby-Gore, United Kingdom's Embassy in Washington, dated 19 November 1961.

114. US.NA.RG59.Decimal files 739.00/11-1861. Secret Telegram from the Department of State to the American Consulate in Ciudad Trujillo, dated 18 November 1961.

115. US.NA.RG59.Decimal files 739.00/11-1961. Secret Telegram from the American Consul in Ciudad Trujillo, dated 19 November 1961, 2 p.m.

116. UK.PRO.FO371/155991. "Echavarria declared his loyalty to Balaguer," Restricted correspondence from Mr. Mc Vittie, United Kingdom's Embassy in Ciudad Trujillo, dated 20 November 1961.

117. US.NA.RG59.Decimal files 739.00/11-1961. Secret Telegram from American Consul in Ciudad Trujillo, dated 19 November 1961, 1: 39 p.m.

force their way into power. Negotiations between Balaguer and the UCN started and continued as the strike went on, mediated by US Consul Hill and Undersecretary of State Morales Carrion (who moved into the US Embassy). The Americans virtually took over the negotiations, rejecting the beginning of a mediation effort by OAS Secretary General Mora. The military made an effort to condition their support for the agreement, but they refrained from going ahead after the State Department publicly disavowed it.[118] The United States was not happy about the UCN's intransigence either. Forcing Balaguer out was essentially a coup—the State Department understood—and the United States would not participate in it.[119]

But the UCN refused to be led. Their cause was aided by an OAS Subcommittee's unanimous decision to leave the sanctions in place as long as the country's situation "remained unstable and the possibility of reinstitution of the military dictatorship is real."[120] Balaguer had no other choice but to yield. Congress would be dissolved and both the executive and the legislative branches of government would be fused into a Council of State. Balaguer became a member of the Council, over which he presided while the sanctions were removed. By the end of the year, the PD had dissolved itself and transferred its property and financial assets to the state.

The Council of State

Early in January 1962, the seven members of the Council of State were sworn in and the OAS Council voted to rescind its sanctions to the Dominican Republic and to re-establish diplomatic relations. The Council included pro-American elements of the UCN and the only survivors of the plot against the Generalissimo, Antonio Imbert and Luis Amiama Tio; the US insisted on their inclusion believing that their 'hero' status would attract the population's respect for the new regime. The Council brought in a momentary political détente but did not solve the old antagonism between the Dominican military and the UCN. Once the Council began to operate, the military demanded, with Balaguer's acquiescence, that the former President remain in charge. Otherwise, they would resort to the installation of a seven-man military junta headed by General Rodriguez Echavarria. Worried about this turn of events, the State Department offered to mediate, but privately informed UCN leaders that they could count on US support. The US also kept its naval units visible.[121] Reassured by the US, the UCN refused to yield, but on 16 January General Rodriguez Echavarria took over anyway. In response, Dominicans turned in large numbers to the streets, engaging in general

---

118. US.NA.RG59.Decimal files 739.00/12-1261. Secret telegram from the State Department to the American Consul in Santo Domingo, dated 12 December 1961

119. US.NA.RG59.Decimal files 739.00/12-3061. Secret telegram from the American Embassy in Santo Domingo to the Department of State, dated 30 November 1961.

120. US.NA.RG59.Decimal files 739.00/12-161. Confidential telegram from the Department of State to the American Consul in Santo Domingo, dated 1 December 1961.

121. US.NA.RG59.Decimal files 739.00/1-1262. Secret telegram from the Department of State to the American Consul in Santo Domingo, dated 12 January 1962.

strikes and walkouts. The US refused to recognise the new Junta and threatened to reimpose sanctions and break diplomatic relations. The Council of State was reinstated when, two days later, Dominican Air Force officers arrested Echavarria and the members of his Junta, while Balaguer fled to the Nunciatura.

With the countercoup, seven months of political turmoil ended. However, the transition had yet to confront a greater challenge: For thirty-one years, Dominicans had had no experience in democratic institutions and practices. Dominicans had to create them, and experience them, with all the allurements and tensions brought forward by the latest turn in the Cold War, provoked by the radicalisation of the Cuban revolution. The United States had played, and would continue to play, a decisive role, but first in Washington's agenda for the region was fighting Castro. "Now that the Dominican Republic is moving from a dictatorship of the right, we are hopeful that the voice of the hemisphere will speak against dictatorships of the left which are sustained and supported from outside the hemisphere," stated President Kennedy.[122]

The United States was critical in the creation of the Council of State and it remained so for its survival. The United States had organisational, material, human and analytical resources dedicated to accomplish clear objectives, while Dominicans were far from it. In addition, the US was widely believed to have played the key role in ending the Trujillo dictatorship and in forcing Balaguer and the military to give in to the opposition's pressures. Consequently, not only the Council was over-friendly to the US but in fact heavily dependent on it. Bonelly, President of the Council of State, and US Ambassador John Bartlow Martin saw or called each other at least once a week, and in times of trouble, several times a day.[123] Sometimes, cabinet or Council members requested meetings with high-ranking US officials in an effort to gain leverage over their peers. To avert coups, the Council resorted to identifying closely with Washington by having high US officers pay public visits to them, by appearing with Ambassador Martin at public meetings or by having Martin express US support for the Council.[124] To attract Washington's attention they often claimed "Castro/Communist subversion" as the root of their problems or pointed out the possibility of revolution.[125] If they did not get the backing of the US Embassy in Santo Domingo, they tried to influence Washington directly.[126]

The US acted to give some variant of democracy a chance in a country where democrats were scarce. The US strove to take advantage of this situation by teach-

---

122. John F. Kennedy, "The President's News Conference of January 15, 1962," *Public Papers of the Presidents of the United States: John F. Kennedy*, (Washington, DC: USGPO, 1963), m. 8, p. 19.

123. Martin, *Overtaken by events*, p. 87.

124. At one time, Martin gave a speech on US support for the Council just before the latter purged the military unopposed. Martin, *Overtaken by events*, pp. 92—93, 111.

125. Martin, *Overtaken by events*, p. 7.

126. UK.PRO.FO371/173871. "In 1962 the Council of State used Francisco Aguirre to influence a pro-Dominican lobby in the US for a fee of $150,000 dollars a year," Confidential Correspondence, from Mr. Lockhart, United Kingdom's Embassy in Santo Domingo, dated 2 January 1964.

ing the Dominican political élite to behave 'democratically,' going beyond electoral practices and procedures. Ambassador Martin encouraged all parties to proceed with ordinary political activities to clarify issues, and to permit candidates to emerge. The Council considered postponing the general elections for two years, but Martin urged—and got—the Council to firmly commit to holding them on December 1962, as previously scheduled.[127] This task proved to be more difficult than Washington had imagined. Amiama and Imbert, whose status as national heroes was supposed to help the Council lead the country toward democracy, frequently plotted to overthrow the government. There were many in the Council, in the military and in the political parties who distrusted democracy. Therefore US officials, both in its Embassy in Santo Domingo and in Washington, felt the need to repeatedly express their support for democracy in the Dominican Republic.[128]

The Cuban Missile Crisis in October offered the US the opportunity to show how serious it was. A month and a half before the holding of presidential and congressional elections in the Dominican Republic, the US discovered the arrangements between the Soviet Union and the Castro regime to install a Missile base on Cuban territory, alarming Washington and its allies throughout the world. Imbert and Amiama seized the opportunity to show they were great friends of the US and great enemies of Communism and to gather support for a "benevolent dictatorship" led by themselves. The Council proceeded to order arrests with vigour. Bosch threatened to leave the country and abandon the electoral race. A handful of party leaders visited Martin to inquire whether US policy was still the same, pleading a 'strongman' to control the Dominican people and the "Castro-Communist" threat.[129] The US Ambassador restated Washington's policy of support for the elections, altering people's impressions that he was behind a coup. Washington had committed its prestige by announcing its intention to make the Dominican Republic a show-case of the Alliance for Progress. At this critical point in time, in the context of the Cold War, the US could not afford to be indifferent to the success of the elections.

Throughout the Council's tenure, the UCN and the PRD secured the allegiance of the majority of the population. Minor groups around Amiama and Imbert, on the one hand, and around Balaguer, who was unauthorised to run by the Electoral Board, on the other, did not gather significant support. Amiama and Imbert sought the Ambassador's acquiescence with their candidacy, but Martin refused on the grounds that "the US would have nothing to do with influencing the outcome" of the election.[130] Balaguer sought to vindicate himself, but most of the Dominican élite identified him with all the discredit of Trujillismo.

---

127. US.NA.RG59.Decimal files 739.00/5-862. Secret telegram from the American Embassy in Santo Domingo, dated 8 May 1962.

128. Martin often underlined the official US policy line that it would find it "extremely difficult to recognize and almost impossible to assist any regime that took power by force or threats of force." Martin, *Overtaken by events*, pp. 121–122.

129. US.NA.RG59.Decimal files 739.00/10-3062. Secret telegram from the US Embassy in Santo Domingo, dated 30 October 1962.

130. Martin, *Overtaken by events*, p. 248.

Throughout the electoral campaign, the US strove to make sure that the most important political actors followed its script. It sent its attachés to talk to the Chiefs of the Armed Forces to assess whether they would accept the results of the elections. When in private conversations UCN members suggested a wish to deny Bosch the electoral victory, US Embassy officers reiterated that the United States would support the winner, whoever this might be. When Bosch threatened to withdraw from the race unless the Electoral Board provided different colours for the ballots, alleging discrimination against illiterates, Martin sent him word that "if he pulled out now he had no future with [the US]."[131] Concerned about the potential rifts between the major political forces and about a plot by Imbert and Amiama Tio to take power, the State Department arranged a pact between Fiallo and Bosch. The agreement imposed obligations on the winner to permit the loser's party to survive, to offer them Cabinet seats, and to consult the losing party in matters affecting the supreme national interest, including foreign policy.[132] To avoid charges of interventionism, the State Department invited the Betancourt government to participate.[133] Both candidates signed the agreement, though Fiallo had accepted only at the urging of Martin.[134]

By the time the elections approached and it became evident that the UCN was losing ground to the PRD, the electoral campaign received a heavy blow from within. Although officially neutral, the Catholic Church turned against Bosch. Nuns at Catholic Schools and priests before their pulpits threatened to excommunicate Bosch's supporters. Catholic radio stations broadcast messages likening Bosch to Hitler and Mussolini and inviting voting against Bosch.[135] Then, a few days before the election, the Spanish Jesuit Láutico García published an article expanding on the charge that Bosch's ideas were Marxist-Leninist. Bosch seized the opportunity and challenged the Jesuit Father to a TV debate on the allegations. The debate, which lasted several prime-time hours served to increase Bosch's standing before the electorate.

The blows did not prevent Bosch from winning but did put considerable tension into a fragile political process. On 21 December, Bosch won nearly two-to-one over Fiallo. The PRD won an overwhelming majority in both houses of Congress, which would act as a Constituent Assembly to write a new Constitution before undertaking their legislative duties. Resentful, Fiallo waited several weeks, until the results were official, to congratulate Bosch for his victory. The Armed Forces were "proud" and "satisfied."[136] The course toward democracy seemed to be on the right track.

---

131. Martin, *Overtaken by events*, p. 292.

132. The text of the agreement is in Martin, *Overtaken by events*, pp. 227–228.

133. Juan Bosch, *The Unfinished Experiment: Democracy in the Dominican Republic*, (London: The Pall Mall Press, 1966), pp. 102, 104–105.

134. US.NA.RG59.Decimal files 739.00/12-1362. Secret telegram from the US Embassy in Santo Domingo, dated 13 December 1962.

135. Gleijeses, *The Dominican Crisis*, p. 84.

136. US.NA.RG59.Decimal files 739.00/12-2262. Confidential telegram from the Navy Attaché in Santo Domingo, dated 22 December 1962.

Giving democracy a chance

On March 1963, Juan Bosch took office as the first freely-elected President in the Dominican Republic in more than thirty years. The tasks ahead seemed insurmountable. Upon taking office, the Bosch administration found itself without a single study of any of the country's problems; the government budget, running in its third month, faced a serious deficit; the currency situation was in crisis. In addition, the new administration had to rely on inexperienced personnel.[137] It would also have to provide meaningful economic improvements; combat corruption, which remained high during the Council of State's administration; and undertake the deepening of democratic institutions and practices.

Auspiciously for Dominican democracy, its most important regional environment was, for the time being, firmly sympathetic. President Bosch enjoyed the good will of most Latin American statesmen and had many ties with a handful of them—in particular, with the respected Venezuelan President Rómulo Betancourt.[138] The United States, the most powerful actor in the region, fully supported Bosch.

Yet the greatest challenge to the transition toward democracy was not external but domestic. Dominicans had little experience with the basic rules of democracy, and the most powerful elements of the Dominican power structure were not eager to abide by them. He was viewed with deep suspicion by important segments of the military and the Church. Simply, Bosch's opponents were not disposed to endure four years of a PRD government in the hopes of winning the next election. The US had effectively "taken over:" Most actors could deal with the US, but not with whomever the electorate had chosen. Thus, only Washington's will to support Bosch kept his government afloat. Before and after the new President was sworn in, people from various affiliations asked the US Embassy its opinion about a coup to depose Bosch, but they constantly met with the US Embassy's disapproval.

Dominican democracy faced some of its most serious challenges in the domestic handling of external threats. In early April, acts of terrorism were directed against the Duvalier regime. A member of Duvalier's armed forces was granted asylum in the Dominican embassy but Haitian police forces then broke into the the diplomatic office. Bosch, believing US support for his regime would be extended for this purpose, began to formulate a plan of action that included the mobilisation of troops to the border near Port-au-Prince, in such a way as to give the unmistakable impression of a military advance on Haiti.[139] Bosch expected that a victory over the Haitian dictatorship would strengthen his own government so that he could move ahead with internal social reforms.[140]

---

137. Bosch, *The Unfinished Experiment*, p. 157, 160.

138. Martin, *Overtaken by events*, p. 343.

139. US.NA.RG59.POL DOM REP-HAI. Limited Official Use Telegram from the American Embassy in Santo Domingo to the Department of State, dated 30 April 1963.

140. US.NA.RG59.POL DOM REP-HAI. Top Secret Telegram from the American Embassy in Santo Domingo to the Department of State, dated 2 May 1963.

But neither the military nor the United States followed. The State Department warned Bosch against taking unilateral military actions in the absence of OAS sanctions and pushed him into the OAS fold. The Venezuelan President advised Bosch against invading Haiti and not to expect OAS or Venezuelan assistance in an armed conflict unless the Dominican Republic were attacked.[141] The OAS did not follow him either. As a result, the military grew disenchanted with Bosch; they felt the new President had asked them to prepare for an invasion they were incapable of performing successfully, and that he had mobilised the armed forces not for the defence of his country but for his own political ends.[142]

With so many domestic challenges, the success of the Dominican transition to democracy depended on Bosch and Washington's ability to maintain the appearance of a unified front against the return of dictatorship. As his predecessors, Bosch sought to be identified with the United States. Bosch often sought advice from Martin before undertaking actions and requested the American Ambassador to tell his military attachés to "spread the word" that the US was behind his government.[143] Time after time, either Ambassador Martin himself or Bosch made efforts to establish bridges between the new government and powerful actors such as Dominican and foreign newspaper editors, businessmen, 'enlightened' members of the oligarchy, bankers, respected professionals, sugar industrialists, and the UCN[144] Ambassador Martin would often lecture them on the virtues of democratic government and on the US official policy line against the overthrow of freely-elected Heads of State.

Despite these efforts, the sense of unease persisted. Throughout Bosch's tenure, the perception of an existing Communist threat endured among the many actors participating in the Dominican political process. Ambassador Martin, for example, was nearly hysterical about the presence of a handful of Communists on Dominican soil, to whom he and most other political observers attributed an enormous capacity to turn the Dominican government, overnight, into a Communist regime. The United States, and most of the Dominican power echelon, wanted them expatriated or expected the Bosch government to crash down on them; but the new Constitution banned the government from expelling Dominican citizens and Bosch, who had spent his political and literary career in exile, refused to circumvent it.[145] The handling of the issue was made peremptory by

---

141. US.NA.RG59.POL DOM REP-HAI. Secret Telegram from the American Embassy in Caracas to the Department of State, dated 10 May 1963.

142. US.NA.RG59.POL DOM REP-HAI. Secret Telegram from the American Embassy in Santo Domingo to the Department of State, dated 5 May 1963.

143. In one instance, he set up a cruise with Ambassador Martin, inviting the Chiefs of the Dominican Armed Forces, in order to "overwhelm the military" and to show them how "close" he was to the US diplomat. Martin, *Overtaken by events*, pp. 360, 408.

144. US.NA.RG59.POL 2 DOM REP. Confidential telegram from the American Embassy in Santo Domingo to the Department of State, dated 23 August 1963.

145. By mid-1963, some 150 alleged Communists who had been deported by the Council of State were allowed to return, upon the promulgation of the new Constitution, and were allegedly active in student groups, civic organisations and labour unions. Martin, *Overtaken by*

unfavourable criticism of the US Press and Congress, who accused Bosch of being "soft on Communism."[146]

The handling of Communists or alleged Communists poisoned the Dominican Republic's domestic environment, badly hurting both Bosch and Dominican democracy. Perception of threat from Communists or alleged Communists in the United States had significantly increased, particularly after the
Cuban Missile Crisis and events in Vietnam. This environment spread to the
Dominican Republic rapidly, particularly within the Right, who was prone
to identify measures that threatened their vested interests as ways in which
the Dominican Republic could end up in the Soviet camp. At such an early stage in the transition toward democracy, the new Dominican regime had
few bulkwarks to withstand the rightist attacks. Like Mexico's post-revolution
Constitution, the new Dominican Statute asserted labour's right to participate
in business profits and permitted the state's expropriation of private property
with indemnification. To make matters worse, Bosch sent a Confiscation Law
to Congress making that Legislative entity the supreme tribunal in cases alleging that property had been acquired illegally; though the law was aimed at
Trujillo's estate, the Right exploited it as if this act were 'proof' that Bosch was
going the Castro route.[147]

In this environment, Americans began to view Bosch with suspicion. In
Washington, at a time when Bosch was being publicly praised as a reform-mind-
ed democrat, mid-level Agency for International Development (AID) officials
were cooling off on Bosch. As time went on, reserve and doubt replaced the United States' initial enthusiasm toward the new democratic experiment.

Under such conditions, what the actors believed was perhaps more important than what the official US policy line was or the reality of the Communist
threat.[148] Talk on Bosch's failure to address this danger tended to undermine
confidence in him and ran counter to US basic policy. During the Trujillo years,
Dominicans had learned to distinguish between what American Embassy officials did and what the government in Washington said. They had seen times
when the US Ambassador was personally friendly with Trujillo while Washington frowned on at him. Bosch himself came to believe that anti-government
activities were part of a vast plot involving US military attachés at the US
Embassy, the Pentagon and the CIA, who evaded the White House's control.
Though he had doubts about Bosch, Martin appealed to important members
of the Dominican élite to support constitutionality, but the latter blamed the

---

events, p. 455.

146. Some American reporters, friendly to Castro early in his career, were playing it safe on
Bosch. US.NA.RG59.POL 2 DOM REP. "The Dominican Situation", Secret Airgram from
the American Embassy in Santo Domingo to the Department of State, dated 11 June 1963.

147. Martin, *Overtaken by events*, p. 495.

148. Bosch put it more bluntly, "if a Captain in the US mission had said that the government
should be overthrown, this would have been done withing an hour, because a US Captain
had greater authority over the Dominican military high command than the people, the
Constitution, and the President." Bosch, *The unfinished experiment*, p. 217.

US Ambassador for Washington's failure to realize the "need" to get rid of the Dominican President.[149]

Bosch had a different view of his own situation and of the issues involved in handling the Communist Left. Bosch was obsessed with avoiding giving the impression that he was a puppet of the Americans.[150] In addition, Bosch felt he faced a more direct threat from the Right, whom he saw as actively engaged in conspiracies to topple his administration. Bosch sought to be in a stronger position before confronting Communists, because engaging the military would enhance its prestige. On the other hand, he also wished to avoid an open break with the extreme Left to avert the likely sabotage and terrorism such as that faced by his friend Betancourt in Venezuela after taking that course of action.[151]

In such an unpropitious domestic environment, not acting on the Communist issue proved more detrimental to the Dominican transition than the danger posed by the unconstitutional laws and procedures against alleged Communists that were demanded from the President. On 20 September, businesses went on strike to repudiate the "growing communist infiltration in the country." Though the government declared it illegal, almost all urban businesses closed down.[152] Finally, Bosch began drafting a special message to Congress asking for constitutional reforms to prohibit travel to Cuba and the Communist bloc.[153] Meanwhile, on 24 September the Chiefs of Staff met Bosch to demand immediate measures against Communism. Led by Air Force General Elias Wessin y Wessin, the officers sought actions to demonstrate that the Dominican government was not aiding the Communist cause. But Bosch was adamantly against his authority being questioned by the military and insisted on Wessin's removal. Otherwise, faced with such an open disobedience, he would go before Congress next day and resign. Bosch felt sure of himself; that night he had attended a gathering at the Officer's Club of the Armed Forces in honour of US Vice-admiral William Ferrall, who had arrived for an official visit. Bosch and his closest allies thought that the presence of such a high American military officer lessened the chances for a coup.[154] But the military decided they could not afford Bosch to go before Congress. Consequently, the military took over, justifying the coup on the armed forces' 'sacred role' of safeguarding the country from Communism.

---

149. Martin, *Overtaken by events*, p. 489, 498, 501–502.

150. Miguel Guerrero, *El Golpe de Estado: Historia del Derrocamiento de Juan Bosch*, (Santo Domingo: Editora Corripio, 1993), pp. 111–112.

151. US.NA.RG59.POL 15-1 DOM REP. "President Juan Bosch of the Dominican Republic." Secret Memorandum from the Executive Secretary, William H. Brubek, to Mr. McGeorge Bundy, the White House, dated 4 June 1963.

152. Guerrero, *El Golpe de Estado*, pp. 163–164.

153. US.NA.RG59.POL 2-1 DOM REP. Confidential Airgram from the American Embassy in Santo Domingo to the Department of State, dated 1 October 1963.

154. US.NA.RG59.POL 2-1 DOM REP. Confidential Airgram from the American Embassy in Santo Domingo to the Department of State, dated 1 October; Guerrero, *El Golpe de Estado*, pp. 163–164.

Back to authoritarian rule

Once in power, the military annulled Bosch's Constitution, dissolved Congress, and invited Bosch's political opposition to join a provisional government, all confirming Bosch's views that the real danger laid in the Right. The politicians and the military officers behind the coup had convinced themselves that their anti-Communist virtues made it inevitable that the US would promptly recognise their regime.[155] A large segment of the political élite believed that the coup had had active assistance or at least the blessing of the Pentagon, who "knew better" the Communist danger than did the State Department.[156] But early confidence that diplomatic recognition would come almost automatically faded away in the following weeks. Ambassador Martin refused to endorse the coup or even receive the Triumvirate that succeeded Bosch or its envoys into the Embassy. Secretary of State Dean Rusk announced his intention to withdraw military and AID personnel and, in line with the philosophy of the Alliance for Progress, President Kennedy issued a strong statement condemning the coup.[157]

But neither Bosch nor those who had pledged to uphold constitutionality acted effectively against the coup. No general strike was called. The deposed President was exiled to Puerto Rico. Aiming at reversing the coup, Congress secretly elected Senate President Juan Cassanovas as Bosch's constitutional successor but gathered few supporters in the Dominican Republic and in Washington, who lost this opportunity to influence Dominican events to restore some variant of democracy because it feared, without grounds, the possible implication of "Castro-communist elements" in this manoeuvre.[158]

Washington could not afford to adopt a passive role. The coup involved the whole US foreign policy toward the hemisphere. Among other considerations, the State Department feared the dominant role of the military in the coup, for they were seen in the United States as "arbitrary perpetrators of endless series of coups against elected civilian governments."[159] The United States decided it would not use force because its commitment to democracy was contingent upon another set of priorities. First on its foreign policy agenda was the "adherence of the Dominican Republic to the free world and the prevention of a Castro/Communist take-over." The commitment of the government of the Dominican Republic to the Alliance for Progress was second. Third, was the maintenance of

155. US.NA.RG59.POL DOM REP-US. Confidential memorandum from Assistant Secretary Edwin Martin to the American Ambassador to Rio de Janeiro, dated 4 November 1963.

156. US.NA.RG59.POL 15 DOM REP. Confidential telegram from the American Embassy in Santo Domingo to the Department of State, dated 1 October 1963.

157. US.NA.RG59.POL 2-1 DOM REP. Confidential Airgram from the American Embassy in Santo Domingo to the Department of State, dated 8 October 1963; John F. Kennedy, "The President's News Conference of October 31, 1963," *Public Papers of the Presidents of the United States: John F. Kennedy, 1963*, (Washington, DC: USGPO, 1964), m. 448.

158. US.NA.RG59.POL 15 DOM REP. Secret Telegram from the Department of State to the American Embassy in Santo Domingo, dated 13 October 1963.

159. US.NA.RG59.POL 15 DOM REP. Confidential Telegram from the Department of State to the American Embassy in Santo Domingo, dated 17 October 1963.

democratic government and last, the continuation of the constitutional order.[160] Bosch's return was not contemplated.

In the background was the fact that by 1963 authoritarian forces had gained strength throughout Latin America. The Argentinean military deposed President Arturo Frondizi in March 1962; in July, the Peruvian military refused to allow President-elect Haya de la Torre to take office. The Kennedy administration severed diplomatic relations and cut off economic aid, to reinstate them later when both military regimes promised to hold elections. In March in Guatemala, the Ydigoras government fell. In July, it was Ecuador's turn. Then, a few days after the overthrow of Bosch, his Honduran counterpart followed. Washington was concerned about a possible chain reaction. Its response could affect the course of events in other Latin American countries where the situation seemed to be unstable, such as Venezuela—whose elections were scheduled for December—Ecuador, El Salvador and Brazil.[161]

The State Department felt it could afford pressing for the maintenance or continuation of the democratic government. In exchange for recognition, some semblance of constitutionality and plurality had to be reached; the government would have to adopt reforms in accordance with the Alliance for Progress and hold Presidential elections within a year.[162] The State Department waited for the Junta to back down, expecting influential sectors would have to seek a formula that could satisfy the Americans.

The lessons of Argentina and Peru did not escape the Triumvirate, who countered by following the tactic of denouncing Communism. A powerful factor in shaping attitudes in the Dominican Republic was the fact that the US recognised the new regime in South Vietnam, which was led by men who had assassinated its Chief of State and his relatives, in the context of a war involving the Communist regime of North Vietnam. Security considerations shadowed the Kennedy administration's commitment to democracy in South Vietnam;[163] most likely, Dominican actors expected, the US would have to follow the same approach in their country. "The eagerness with which the US has acted, in announcing the rapid recognition of the Military Junta in Vietnam, is a denial of the so-called 'political rigidity' of the Department of State in cases of coups," editorialised the local press.[164] Time was on the Triumvirate's side; the United States, sooner or later, would have to resume diplomatic relations. For as long as they did not, the Triumvirate reckoned, they could survive without US aid owing

---

160. US.NA.RG59.POL 1-1 DOM REP. "Contingency Plan," Secret Airgram from the American Embassy in Santo Domingo to the Department of State, dated 22 September 1963.

161. UK.PRO.FO371/167994. "State Department's attitude toward recent military coups," Confidential correspondence from Sir D. Ormsby-Gore at the United Kingdom's Embassy in Washington, DC, dated 12 October 1963.

162. Martin, *Overtaken by events*, p. 600.

163. This case is carefully studied by Mark Peceny, *Democracy at the Point of Bayonets*, (University Park: Pennsylvania University Press, 1999), p. 92.

164. US.NA.RG59.POL 2-1 DOM REP. Confidential Airgram from the American Embassy in Santo Domingo to the Department of State, dated 5 November 1963.

to the high price of sugar in international markets.[165]

The more Washington delayed recognising the new government, the more isolated the US became. Many US citizens living on Dominican soil, including members of the Embassy, had thought all along that the Kennedy administration had been wrong in supporting Bosch. To US embarrassment, neither of its allies held for long enough their support for Washington's policy of non-recognition. By late October, Spain, Nationalist China, Portugal, and all of the European powers recognised the Triumvirate.[166] Likewise, US agribusiness interests, who expected to buy the entire 1963–1964 sugar crop, pressed for a policy change.[167] Congressmen and editorialists in the United States recommended recognizing the Dominican government. When these issues were being discussed, President Kennedy was assassinated and Vice-President Lyndon B. Johnson, a conservative Texan, took office. By mid December 1963, the Venezuelan elections had taken place and Washington was ready to recognise the new Honduran regime—after the latter made arrangements with the opposition to set up an election schedule. But also guerrilla fights had started in the Dominican countryside—a fact that the Triumvirate skilfully exploited.[168] Finding no other option, on 14 December the United States recognised the Triumvirate unconditionally.

Soon after Washington recognised the new Dominican government, the Foreign Minister, Donald Reid Cabral, became the visible head of the Triumvirate. Though Reid was backed by the armed forces and by influential men in the Dominican Republic, the United States, and particularly, the US Embassy, became his most important source of support. In February 1964 the Johnson administration appointed career diplomat William Tapley Bennet, Jr., as Ambassador to the Dominican Republic; Bennet had served in the Dominican Republic in the Trujillo years and had friends among the wealthiest families. Throughout his stay in Santo Domingo, economic, military and other missions built up to their former strength. During Reid's administration, Washington provided more aid in direct and guaranteed loans than it had made available to Bosch or to any other previous Dominican government.[169]

Reid Cabral, as had his predecessors, sought not only Washington's backing but also to be closely identified with the United States. He lost no opportunity in expressing his support for the Alliance for Progress.[170] Despite US backing,

---

165. UK.PRO.FO371/167995. "Dominican government has been recognised by certain European governments," Restricted correspondence from Mr. Lockhart, United Kingdom's Embassy in Santo Domingo, dated 1 November 1963.

166. UK.PRO.FO371/167995. "Possible return to constitutional legality because of American threats to withdraw aid," Confidential correspondence from Mr. Lockhart, United Kingdom's Embassy in Santo Domingo, dated 18 October 1963.

167. US.NA.RG59.XR POL DOM REP-US. Confidential letter from the Deputy Undersecretary of Agriculture, James L. Sundquist, to the Deputy Assistant Secretary for Economic Affairs, Jerome Jacobson, dated 1 November 1963.

168. Martin *Overtaken by events*, p. 606.

169. Theodore Draper, *The Dominican Revolt*, (New York: Commentary, 1968), pp. 15–17

170. Abraham Lowenthal, *The Dominican intervention*, (Cambridge, Mass : Harvard University Press, 1972), p. 46.

or perhaps because of it, the Reid regime became one of the most unpopular governments in the history of the Republic. Sensing Bennet and Washington's endorsement, Reid had less incentive to cultivate the support of his countrymen. Reid purged the original coalition cabinet and frequently ordered the suppression of public meetings, disregarded judicial procedures, exiled political undesirables and occasionally closed down the press. Congressional and Presidential elections were to be held on 1 September 1965, but political demonstrations were forbidden until nearer the time.

In this context, the support, admiration and efforts for the return of former Presidents Bosch and Balaguer multiplied. Had Bosch stayed in power, maybe his failures would have damaged his reputation so that he would have had few chances in a future election. But by striking him down and with Reid's unpopularity in the background, the military made a myth of the former President. In the meantime, Bosch and PRD leaders succeeded in organising groups of upper- and middle-class professionals and intellectuals in support of the constitution. Further improving Bosch's standing was the publication in December 1964 of his persuasive account of his rise to power and overthrow.[171] In Latin America, hundreds of copies of the book were sold within a day, becoming a best seller; in the Dominican Republic, the book circulated widely but privately. Equally, Balaguer conducted skilful campaigns through the press and radio against the Triumvirate. Though exiled in New York City since early 1962, Balaguer reacquired a number of avid followers in Dominican political and military circles. By January 1965, Bosch and Balaguer's followers began to find common ground against Reid: leaders from the PRD and Balaguer's Social Christian Party (PRSC) signed the Rio Piedras Pact, agreeing "to build a common front to reestablish constitutional order and to act together if faced with any event that might bring a democratic solution to the problems of the country."[172] Satisfied with Reid, the State Department chose to refrain from pressuring him into holding elections, arguing the way the Dominican Republic went back to democracy was a "strictly internal problem" in which the United States should not be involved."[173] The United States was no longer interested in what the Dominicans wanted.

Reid drove his enemies together, in particular since he expressed his wish to remain in power. Dominicans were unconvinced that Washington would put pressure on Reid to assure free elections, in particular since the US Embassy did not issue pronouncements favouring the electoral contest. Balaguer wished to return to power but, trying to vindicate himself, he would do so only through

---

171. The book was first published in Mexico in 1964 under the title *Crisis de la Democracia de América en la República Dominicana*. The english translation, by Frederick Praeger, was published in 1966 under the title *The Unfinished Experiment: Democracy in the Dominican Republic*, (New York: The Pall Mall Press).

172. José A. Moreno, *Barrios in Arms: Revolution in Santo Domingo*, (Pittsburg: University of Pittsburg Press, 1970), p. 24.

173. US.NA.RG59.POL 1 DOM REP "Dominican political situation." Confidential memorandum of conversation between expresident of the Dominican Republic, Joaquin Balaguer, and Kennedy Crocket, Director of the Office of Caribbean Affairs, and Henry W. Shlaudeman, Chief of Dominican Affairs, dated 21 August 1964.

free elections. Considering that elections were unlikely to be held as scheduled, Balaguer's sympathisers pressed for a coup against the Triumvirate. Though the plot was thwarted in mid-April 1965, the impetus for a coup did not abate. In the military, a pro-Bosch cadre had been preparing to bring back the former President, but camouflaged their movement by hiding their plans and aligning themselves with several other groups trying to overthrow Reid.[174]

The countercoup and the United States military intervention

Unexpectedly for the United States, the countercoup against Reid was launched on 24 April. Fighting to take over the government started and, as it became clear that discussions were taking place to form a military junta among senior military officers, a group of junior Army officers led by Lieutenant Colonel Francisco Camaño entered the Presidential Palace, arrested Reid Cabral, and expressed their intention to restore what had been taken from the people on 25 September 1963. Pending Bosch's return, the only high-ranking member of the Bosch administration on Dominican soil, Chamber of Deputies President José Rafael Molina Ureña, was sworn in as provisional Chief. The rebel officers seized Santo Domingo that night and, aiming at defending the city against what they felt was a military superior enemy, distributed arms to civilians.

As a result, what began as an élitist coup of one faction of the military against another turned into an uprising of the populace against the oligarchy.[175] Balaguer's supporters in the Armed Forces were surprised at finding that the rebels were determined to bring Bosch back. Impressed by the clamouring of the crowds around the Presidential Palace, they were convinced that public opinion favoured Bosch's return and chose not to oppose them.[176] The Air Force, led by General Elias Wessin y Wessin, tried to put down the rebellion and impede Bosch's return, but he was soon abandoned by the Navy, who, on the face of events, went to the side of the newly formed government.[177]

The rebel leadership ascertained that the United States' attitude toward the countercoup would prove to be a determinant in the course of events. Reid was known to be cherished by the US Embassy; most likely, the US would be displeased at the countercoup. But the rebels had assumed that Washington would not intervene. After all, the era of US armed intervention in the area seemed to be over. Only a few years had passed since the United States had championed the anti-Trujillo cause and had fully supported Bosch's constitutional government. Coup leaders had no reason to think that Bosch's return threatened vital US interests; thus, they did not consider whether the US Embassy would at least incite loyal Dominican officers to resist the revolt. In any case their triumph, rebel lead-

---

174. Lowenthal, *The Dominican intervention*, p. 53–54.

175. According to an estimate by Moreno, *Barrios in Arms*, pp. 65–67, about 90 percent of the rebel rank and file were not active in party politics and about 60 percent were unemployed immediately before the countercoup.

176. Lowenthal, *The Dominican intervention*, pp. 74–76.

177. US.NA.RG59.POL 23-9 DOM REP. Confidential telegram from the American Embassy in Santo Domingo to the Department of State, dated 26 April 1965, 7:59 a.m.

ers pondered, would be so rapid that the United States would have to face a fait accompli before it had the opportunity to act.[178] This certitude was reinforced by the US Embassy's inaction during the first 24 hours of the revolt, which the rebels happily but wrongfully interpreted as a sign of US neutrality.

The US Embassy's initial aloofness toward the countercoup was due to the fact it did not expect it. The US Embassy was near empty and the situation in Washington was not much different.[179] Had it been more attentive to the course of developments, however, the ensuing events might not have been too different. The Johnson administration was no longer interested in promoting the return of constitutional rule and, in the context of its involvement in Vietnam, would not let things go uncontrolled. But it contributed to its gross miscalculation. Throughout the Triumvirate's hold on power, the US Embassy had developed no ties either with the PRD or with the disenchanted military officers who undertook the coup.[180] As a result, not only did the US Embassy fail to discover the strength of the plot against Reid, but also during its first 24 hours it greatly misjudged the rebel's aims and both the government and the rebel's strength.[181] The US Embassy watched the collapse of the Triumvirate unmoved, convinced that the rebels would endorse the creation of a military junta and that the loyalist military could control the situation without US interference. Bosch's return to power by means of a military revolt carried out by a Constitutionalist faction of the military, the PRD and the support of the masses was simply not an option the US Embassy ever contemplated. Disregarding Dominican wishes, and oblivious to its previous role in supporting Dominican democracy, the US equated Bosch and the uprising it did not control with Communism; hence, Washington worked to prevent Bosch's return.

The unpopular Reid was no longer an option around which a government could be formed, since he no longer commanded the loyalty of the armed forces or of any significant segment of the population. US strategists in the Embassy and in Washington thought that the anti-Bosch cause required an entity to which the anti-Bosch military could rally and to which rebel defectors could surrender. Seeking to avoid further commitments, the Embassy encouraged the formation of a military junta.[182] Sensing the opportunity, Imbert volunteered; however, his proposal was hastily—but momentarily—shelved when Wessin's forces at the San Isidro Air Force base announced the formation of a Junta headed by Colonel Benoit.[183]

---

178. Gleijeses, *The Dominican crisis*, p. 154, 186.

179. Lowenthal, *The Dominican intervention*, pp. 63–64; Gleijeses, *The Dominican crisis*, pp. 177, 382, n. 8.

180. Three days after the beginning of the countercoup, the US embassy reported that they had no information from rebel military sources yet. US.NA.RG59.POL 23-9 DOM REP Confidential telegram from the American Embassy in Santo Domingo to the Department of State, dated 27 April 1965, 2:43 p.m.

181. Gleijeses, *The Dominican crisis*, pp. 177–178.

182. US.NA.RG59.POL 23-9 DOM REP. Confidential Telegram from the American Embassy in Santo Domingo to the Department of State, dated 26 April 1965, 3:39 a.m.

183. Lowenthal, *The Dominican Intervention*, p. 99.

Despite its desire not to taint US prestige against Bosch's return, the US Embassy soon adopted an active role against the rebels. US Service attachés encouraged the loyalist military leaders to do "everything possible" to prevent a "communist takeover."[184] The Embassy simply chose sides believing that no direct US participation needed to be forthcoming.[185] Sometimes Ambassador Bennet disobeyed the Department's instructions or misreported Dominican events.[186] Though the US official policy line was to seek an unconditional cease-fire, decisions taken by US Embassy officials were instrumental in preventing any arrangement between rebels and loyalists. Ambassador Bennet himself reassured Wessin that the US would not let the Dominican Republic fall to Communists. On 27 April, negotiations aborted as Wessin—with the US Service Attaché's approval and guidance—strafed the National Palace, where the talks were taking place.[187] In so doing, the US boycotted the opportunity for a peaceful and 'national' return to democratic rule.

Once it committed itself to halt Bosch's return to power, the United States was drawn in further into the Dominican Republic by elements that shared this aim. Conditioned to work with the US Embassy to settle domestic political matters, Dominicans readily asked for US intervention to further their own purposes. They knew how to entice Washington to their side. Benoit, for instance, asked for US military intervention, in writing. But to make his appeal more dramatic— possibly following US Embassy officers' advice—he added that "American lives are in danger and conditions are of such disorder that it is impossible to provide adequate protection."[188] Others called the US Embassy, already concerned about alleged Communist participation in the revolt, to warn that Communists would claim and exert strong influence should Bosch return to the Presidency.[189]

Cuba's spectre haunted the reasoning of US officials throughout the Dominican crisis, causing them to magnify even the slightest possibility of a victory by

---

184. US.NA.RG59.POL 23-9 DOM REP. Confidential telegram from the American Embassy in Santo Domingo to the Department of State, dated 25 April 1965, 5:00 p.m.

185. Lowenthal, *The Dominican intervention*, p. 80.

186. Ambassador Bennet, for example, despite overwhelming evidence to the contrary, reported to the State Department that "at no time did both sides sat down seriously to seek an amicable solution. It should be noted that insurgents, on several initiatives taken by Embassy officers, were even more unbending than loyal armed forces elements." US.NA.RG59.POL 23-9 DOM REP. Confidential telegram from the American Embassy in Santo Domingo to the Department of State, dated 28 April 1965, 12:59 p.m.

187. British diplomats in Santo Domingo received copies of two of seven tapes proving a substantial record of signal traffic between Wessin's headquarters, the Air Force, the Navy and the US Service Attaché, Colonel Heywood. Heywood was reported to have agreed that fire should be opened after the negotiations had begun. UK.PRO.FO371/179342. "Reports on tape recordings which have been obtained by monitoring radio frequencies used by San Isidro and Wessin-controlled out station during fighting between 25-29 April," Secret Correspondence from Mr. Campbell, United Kingdom's Embassy in Santo Domingo, dated 17 August 1965.

188. US.NA.RG59.POL 23-9 DOM REP. Confidential telegram from the American Embassy in Santo Domingo, dated 29 April 1965, 1:16 a.m.

189. Lowenthal, *The Dominican Intervention*, p. 79.

Communists. Washington did not understand how Cuba went over to the Soviet Bloc and would not let Dominican events to go on uncontrolled. Since February 1965, the United States had been escalating its involvement in Vietnam; a disaster in its backyard might bring opposition to this most recent adventure. Given the power differentials, what mattered was Washington's vision of Dominican events, regardless of what Dominicans constructed among themselves. No evidence existed to support the claim that the revolutionary movement had been taken over by Communist conspirators, but the State Department instructed the American Embassy to produce the material to support it.[190] US Embassy officers, encouraged by State Department officials who feared "another Cuba' in their hands, reported cases of Communist involvement even when sources were known to be unreliable.[191] Stories of alleged atrocities committed by the rebels and with no foundation in facts were readily believed and transmitted. For example, the US Embassy reported that there were 12,000 Communists in the city, glossing over the large number of non-Communists who were fighting for democracy.[192] President Johnson echoed these exaggerations by publicly claiming that "some 1500 innocent people were murdered and shot, and their heads cut off... [plus the fact that] they were firing on Americans and the American Embassy."[193] Washington had not much information about rebel military leader Camaño. However, sufficiently incriminatory was the observation that, like Castro in Cuba, Camaño was intelligent and was leading an uprising from below.[194]

But the rebels were winning anyway, despite the bombings and US Embassy encouragement to the Junta group to go on. In the aftermath of Wessin's strafing of the Palace, little was known in the US Embassy about what was going on in the city, nor about the real strength of the rebels, but the worst was assumed anyway.[195] One thing was certain: the Dominican Armed Forces had virtually disintegrated. According to the State Department, Bosch could be put in power by Communists who would leave him there for appearance's sake but would quickly

---

190. UK.PRO.FO371/179331. "The State Department has requested any additional material available on the President's statement that the revolutionary movement has been taken over by a band of Communist conspirators," Confidential correspondence from Sir P. Dean, United Kingdom's Embassy in Washington, DC, dated 3 May 1965.

191. This anxiety may be explained in part in that a whole generation of China specialists had been wiped out after Mao's victory and Cuban specialists found their careers aborted after Castro's victory in Cuba. Therefore, before the 1965 crisis in the Dominican Republic, there was an overwhelming predisposition to err on the 'safe' side. Jerome Slater, *Intervention and negotiation: the United States and the Dominican revolution* , (New York : Harper & Row, 1970), p. 308.

192. UK.PRO.FO371/179332. "Camaño has been proclaimed President of the rebel provisional government," Confidential correspondence from Mr. Campbell, United Kingdom's Embassy in Santo Domingo, dated 4 May 1965.

193. "The President's News Conference of June 17, 1965," *Public Papers of the President of the United States: Lyndon B. Johnson, 1965*, vol. II, (Washington, D.C.: USGPO, 1966), m. 319, pp. 678.

194. Martin, *Overtaken by events*, p. 668.

195. UK.PRO.FO371/179330. "Complete breakdown of law and order," Confidential correspondence from Mr. Campbell, United Kingdom's Embassy in Santo Domingo, dated 29 April 1965.

dominate and probably discard him.[196] Whether their anxiety led them to seriously believe this or it was a way to justify further US involvement is uncertain. In any case, nothing short of major US intervention could prevent the victory of the Constitutionalists.

In this context, President Johnson ordered the intervention of the Dominican Republic. On 29 April, 400 marines landed in Santo Domingo; on 1 May, these were increased to 14,000. In outlining the objectives of the intervention, Johnson said it was to "save the lives of US citizens" and to "help prevent [the emergence of] another Communist state in the hemisphere." No prior consultation with the OAS, the UN or its allies were made. Privately, it aimed at interposing itself between the insurgents and Benoit's forces and to enforce an effective cease-fire, thus rescuing the Junta from collapsing altogether.[197] The sending of Marines was supposed to be part of a low-key intervention that would serve to encourage the loyalists and discourage the rebels, while also serving to provide secret logistical support for Wessin's forces.[198] Washington wanted to avoid "another" Cuba and serving as the springboard for another dictatorship, but also wished to avoid provoking "another Hungary" by fully occupying the country.[199]

The intervention of the United States precluded a Constitutionalist victory, thwarting rebel efforts at gaining control of the country. It halted the disintegration of loyalist troops and boosted the morale of Wessin's forces. Despite the claim that the intervention had humanitarian purposes and that the US was neutral to both factions, on Dominican soil American troops were told that their mission was to prevent another Cuba, and that a victory of the rebels would produce that outcome.[200] But loyalists had no incentive to fight, since they believed the US had come to do the job for them. As a result, the US was led to conduct the effort against the rebels and guide the Benoit Junta, aiming at preserving it as an alternative to Camaño's forces. American attachés became in-field advisers, developed operational plans and provided the intelligence and communication capabilities for the Benoit Junta to carry out operations.[201] Though officially the State Department endorsed the cease-fire, in practice the US military on Dominican soil turned a blind eye to this, if not actually encouraging it, when it was violated by Wessin's forces.[202]

196. US.NA.RG59.POL 23-9. Secret EXDIS Telecon between Deputy Assistant Secretary Mann, Ambassador Bunker and Assistant Secretary Vaughn to the American Embassy in Santo Domingo, dated 29 April 1965.

197. US.NA.RG59.POL 23-9. Secret telegram from the Department of State to the American Embassy in Santo Domingo, dated 29 April 1965, 11:11 p.m.

198. US.NA.RG59.POL 23-9. Confidential telegram from the American Embassy in Santo Domingo, to the Department of State, dated 29 April 1965, 3:54 a.m.

199. The term referred to the Soviet occupation of Hungary in 1956, when a neutral government in Budapest was deposed by Soviet troops, fighting local forces.

200. Bruce Palmer, Jr., *Intervention in the Caribbean: The Dominican Crisis of 1965*, (The University Press of Kentucky, 1989), pp. 5–6.

201. US.NA.RG59.POL 23-9. Secret Telegram from the American Embassy in Santo Domingo to the Department of State, dated 29 April 1965, 5:13 p.m.

202. UK.PRO.FO371/179336. "Although Wessin has broken the cease-fire he seems to have incurred US sympathy," Confidential Correspondence from Mr. Campbell, United Kingdom's

Propping up a political alternative to Bosch required that the US reach other political sectors beyond those few to which Bennet had confined itself. But Bennet refused to negotiate with the rebels, believing that this strategy left Washington free to do things without consulting with the rebel leadership.[203] Washington doubted Ambassador Bennet was up to the task and sent former Ambassador Martin to the Dominican Republic. As the former Ambassador who aided Dominican democracy, Bosch and Camaño had confidence in him. But Martin was understanding what was required from him in Washington, and was now more interested in buttressing Wessin. Martin attempted to get Bosch's support for the intervention, but neither Bosch nor Camaño were disposed toward accepting US tutelage. Martin promised that Washington could recognize the Molina Ureña government, provided Bosch publicly accepted the danger of a Communist takeover and accepted the presence of US forces to maintain order. Bosch, however, went on to denounce US intervention, while Camaño insisted that any negotiated solution had to list "constitutionality" as an essential precondition.[204]

Despite the bolstering of Wessin's group by the United States, Camaño's forces resisted and maintained the upper hand. Swept by events, Camaño became impassioned about the cause for which he was fighting, capturing the imagination of the people around him. After PRD leaders subtracted themselves from leading the movement, Camaño took control of the Constitutionalist cause. The Constitutionalist leader refused to negotiate with the loyalist Generals, arguing he could do so directly with the United States. The Constitutionalists at first welcomed and encouraged OAS mediation, to counterbalance the US, but soon lost faith in the interamerican organisation as it accused them of tolerating Communist infiltration in their movement. Thus Camaño formed a government and sought diplomatic recognition from other Latin American and European states. However, arguing "security considerations," the State Department discouraged other OAS Member states to accord recognition to Camaño.[205] To develop an alternative to Bosch, the loyalist Generals formed, on Martin and Bennet's encouragement, the Council of National Reconstruction (CNR). Because of Martin's pressures, Imbert, the assassin of Trujillo, was put in charge.[206] Martin expected to get the support of the main political currents for the junta, but gathered none outside the loyalist generals, who had to be pressured nonetheless for the inclusion of Imbert.[207]

Embassy in Santo Domingo, dated 13 May 1965.

203. US.NA.RG59.POL 23-9. Secret telegram from the American Embassy in Santo Domingo to the Department of State, dated 4 May 1965, 3:30 a.m.

204. US.NA.RG59.POL 23-9. Secret telegram from the American Embassy in Santo Domingo to the Department of State, dated 12 May 1965, 8:39 a.m.

205. US.NA.RG59.POL 23-9. Confidential Telegram from the Department of State to the American Embassy in Santo Domingo, dated 4 May 1965, 4:46 p.m.

206. US troops provided Imbert's security, while Washington provided the government's payroll. US.NA.RG59.POL 23-9. Secret telegram from the American Embassy in Santo Domingo to the Department of State, dated 7 May 1965, 8:48 p.m.

207. US.NA.RG59.POL 23-9. Secret telegram from the American Embassy in Santo Domingo

The intervention was full of complications, and the formation of another Junta did not contribute to solve the political stalemate. The CNR did not gather any significant support from the population. Washington's unqualified affirmation that the American nations would not permit the establishment of another Communist government had yet to be affirmed by the American nations themselves assembled in the OAS. It also could be interpreted as meaning that, even if Dominicans were to choose Communism in a free election, the US would deny them that choice, thus countering the non-intervention policy that had served the US and its allies well. On the other hand, no evidence of Communist involvement in the Dominican crisis was forthcoming. In the international arena, the intervention was being harshly criticised by allies and non-allies alike; they blamed Washington for blurting out its own image in the world. France and Uruguay differed from the United States when the situation was brought to the Security Council, which to Washington's displeasure, sent a fact-finding mission to the Dominican Republic. In Latin America, leaders lamented in private their disappointment at US unilateralism and Washington's apparent insensitivity to Latin American opinions.[208] French President Charles De Gaulle criticised the intervention and promised the recognition of Camaño's as the legitimate government of the Dominican Republic. Key political leaders in Congress and in the mass media challenged Washington's version of events and criticised what they perceived as a policy leading to propping up a military dictatorship.[209]

In this context, Washington shifted to seeking a formula that would satisfy the Constitutionalists but would not lead Bosch back to power. The prospect that the United States would soon have to be engaged directly to quench the rebels—so Bennet and US military representatives on the Dominican Republic recommended—pushed President Johnson to seek a political solution to the stalemate. Johnson instructed Secretary of State Rusk to involve the OAS quickly and to end its isolation from its Latin American allies.[210] This was also meant to peter out debate at the UN Security Council, where the United States had few friends on the Dominican issue. Washington send emissaries to speak to selected, influential Latin American leaders to seek their advice and understanding, and their support for the creation of an Inter-American Peace-Keeping Force (IAPF) that would cooperate with the OAS in the restoration of normal conditions in the Dominican Republic.[211] Washington also disavowed Bennet and Martin, and sent another team, headed by White House advisor McGeorge

---

to the Department of State, dated 5 May 1965, 11:02 p.m.

208. US.NA.RG59.POL 23-9. "Situation in the Dominican Republic," Confidential memorandum of conversation between Former President Betancourt and President Lyndon Johnson, dated 3 May 1965.

209. Slater, *Intervention and negotiation*, pp. 85–86. \

210. Martin, *Overtaken by events*, p. 661.

211. Hugo Panasco Alvim, A Brazilian General, was nominally in charge of the IAPF while an American General, Bruce Palmer, was put in as deputy commander. Alvim, contrary to the Brazilian government's policy, proved to be as anticommunist as the loyalist Generals and the US marines, and tended to side with Imbert.

Bundy. On Bundy's recommendations, Washington swung to a Constitution-alism-without-Bosch formula. After speaking to rebel leaders, Bundy came up with a plan: Former Bosch's Agriculture Minister, Antonio Guzman, would serve the remainder of the term, the 1963 Constitution would be restored and the government would be purged of communist influence.

Washington decided that both Wessin and Imbert would have to go, but this task was not going to be an easy one. Time was on Imbert's side: if a compromise formula was not reached and implemented, it meant that he had a chance to consolidate his position. Imbert, constantly in the company of US attaché, Colonel Heywood, may have hoped that what he thought were his ties with the Pentagon would allow him to hold on long enough until the United States swung back to its original idea of a Communist menace. If Trujillos' ties to the US marines served the late Generalissimo, why wouldn't these ties work for him?

The 'Guzman solution' gained momentum but was soon defeated by anti-Bosch forces that arrayed against the return of this variant of democracy. Bundy's solution had not been reached without dissension: Bennet, Martin and Under-secretary Mann, who was also a member of Bundy's team, insisted that Imbert could still be supported. Powerful anticommunist quarters in the United States would raise an alarm if it became known that Washington had started to deal with Camaño, whom they considered a Communist, despite the fact that they had nothing to prove it.[212] But for Bundy it was clear that Imbert had no popular support and that Camaño was "a figure of importance" with ascendancy over the rebels.[213] Bosch and Camaño agreed to Bundy's plan; Bosch would drop his demand that US troops be immediately withdrawn and Guzman's cabinet would include a majority of PRD members and some conservatives acceptable to Imbert's military. Control of the armed forces would be given to a Chief not associated with either side and leaders from both sides would leave the country for six months. The sticking point was, again, the disposition of the 'Communists.' Washington sought, and Bosch finally agreed, to have them expelled or interned, but Guzman did not agree, because it violated the 1963 Constitution over which he was supposed to preside.[214] As soon as this deal was made public, conservatives in the Dominican Republic and in Washington, Martin and Bennet in particular, torpedoed the agreement, aided by Guzman's refusal to go along with the control measures and ask the rebel leaders to go.[215] OAS Secretary General Mora

---

212. UK.PRO.FO371/179335. "Conversation with Mr. Schlaudeman of the State Department: affirms that Wessin's removal was ordered from Washington," Confidential correspondence from Mr. Campbell, United Kingdom's Embassy in Santo Domingo, dated 11 May 1965.

213. UK.PRO.FO371/179338. "Mr. Bundy's views on the Dominican situation," Confidential correspondence from Mr. Campbell, United Kingdom's Embassy in Santo Domingo, dated 27 May 1965.

214. US.NA.RG59.POL 23-9. Secret telegram from the American Embassy in Santo Domingo to the Department of State, dated 24 May 1965, 3:00 p.m.

215. US.NA.RG59.POL 23-9. Secret telegram from the American Embassy in Santo Domingo to the Department of State, dated 25 May 1965.

also rejected the Guzman formula, because it "favoured rebels too much."[216]

As the Guzman solution failed, Washington sought the OAS cover and sent another envoy, the US representative to the OAS, Ellsworth Bunker, who also headed the OAS mission to the Dominican Republic. Though the OAS group also included Bunker's Brazilian and Salvadoran counterparts, in practice Bunker commanded what was nominally an OAS mission.[217] Bunker swung back to the "third' force formula, only stipulating that this time it would not be headed by the military. The formula required, above all, an "OAS flavour."[218] Mediation was not possible, for neither side would make any meaningful concession to the other, and a solution through the force of arms was unacceptable, Bunker underlined.[219] To extricate itself from the Dominican Republic, the United States decided to hold elections supervised by the OAS and install a provisional government operating under an 'institutional act.'

But Imbert did not want to step down. Latin American diplomats and US correspondents who were fond of him encouraged him to stand fast against any concessions. Extreme right politicians counselled Imbert on alleged divisions in Washington. Occasional fire between the contending forces, sometimes with the connivance of US troops, increased the CNR's ability to claim control of the country and bred Imbert's intransigence. Neither could the US force him out. The US could not decline to acknowledge Imbert's "services." If the US did not arrange a graceful exit for Imbert, others would not be inclined to step forth on the United States' behalf in the future. In the end, Imbert accepted the turning of power to a provisional government, but only at the last minute and after being reassured by the US military commander and Ambassador Bennet that he was confronting a unified American position on the subject.

Facing the military superiority of the US and confronting weariness and divisions within its ranks, the Constitutionalists accepted the establishment of an interim government with a 'neutral' as its President. Elections would be scheduled between six and nine months after its inauguration. Constitutionalists would 'demilitarise' their areas as the new regime effected a restructuring of the Armed Forces' staff. Negotiations focused on the selection of the person to preside over the provisional government. The rebels put forward lists of candidates, but Bunker had no confidence in Dominican choices and thus had only one candidate to offer: Hector Garcia Godoy. A respected Dominican, Godoy had been an Ambassador to Great Britain under Trujillo, Foreign Affairs Minister in the last weeks of the Bosch administration, and Vicepresident of Balaguer's party in

---

216. US.NA.RG59.POL 23-9. Secret telegram from the American Embassy in Santo Domingo to the Department of State, dated 24 May 1965, 12:26 p.m.

217. Audrey Bracey, *Resolution of the Dominican Crisis, 1965: A Study in Mediation*, (Washington, DC: Institute for the Study of Diplomacy, School of Foreign service, Georgetown University, 1980), pp. 1–3.

218. US.NA.RG59.POL 23-9. Confidential telegram from the American Embassy in Santo Domingo to the Department of State, dated 10 June 1965.

219. US.NA.RG59.POL 14 DOMREP, XR POL 15 DOM REP. Secret telegram from the American Embassy in Santo Domingo to the Department of State, dated 14 June 1965.

1964. The rebels accepted him anyway, after delivering a note of protest to the OAS denouncing Bunker's imposition.[220] The war ended on 3 September when Garcia Godoy was sworn in as Provisional President, after Camaño signed the Institutional and Reconciliation Act on behalf of the Constitutionalists.

The Provisional Government and the elections of 1966

Garcia Godoy had in mind a 'truly independent' regime with 'normal' powers, freedom of action and the "necessary authority."[221] But the US, and many others on Dominican soil, were on a different track. Influential Dominicans expected to be guided by the United States, and they acted accordingly. Civic leaders in Santiago and the Capital assembled a package of proposals to be carried out by the interim government, but first they delivered it to the US Embassy assuming that the programme and the names of those who would carry them out had to be cleared at the highest levels of the US government.[222] Before Garcia Godoy took over, Washington made sure he would follow the script. He was pressured into agreeing, in writing, to associate himself with Washington in opposing Communism; to choose appointments at the National Department of Investigations after "appropriate consultations" with the OAS and Washington; and to prohibit the organisation of parties whose principles were against representative democracy.[223] Washington insisted that all members of Garcia Godoy's cabinet had to be men with anti-Communist credentials, but it went along with the new President's cabinet, which included rebel and PRD sympathisers, only after he threatened to quit the assignment.[224]

The United States believed that a strong Dominican army was needed as a bulkwar against Communism and made sure that it be kept intact under Garcia Godoy. Garcia Godoy dismissed Reid's Minister of Defense Rivera Caminero, but Bunker stubbornly insisted that he be kept on. Washington officially supported the interim Prsident, but US military attachés continued to work with Imbert, who was now outside the government, and Wessin, who had yet to be removed, in opposing the new President's measures.[225] With such powerful backers, the Chiefs of Staff remained in a state of insubordination and resisted their

---

220. US.NA.RG59.POL 15. Secret telegram from the American Embassy in Santo Domingo to the Department of State, dated 4 July 1965.

221. US.NA.RG59.POL 14 DOM REP, XR POL 15 DOM REP. Confidential telegram from the American Embassy in Santo Domingo to the Department of State, dated 26 June 1965.

222. US.NA.RG59.POL 15 DOM REP. Confidential airgram from the American Embassy in Santo Domingo to the Department of State, dated 15 July 1965.

223. US.NA.RG59.POL 23-7. Secret telegram from the American Embassy in Santo Domingo to the Department of State, dated 2 August 1965.

224. Some of Garcia Godoy's appointments were allegedly made with the aim of "sugaring the pill" for the Americans. UK.PRO:FO371/179345. "Details of meeting with Provisional President," Secret Correspondence from Mr. Bell, United Kingdom's Embassy in Santo Domingo, dated 4 November 1965.

225. UK.PRO.FO371/179342. "Comments on Mr. Slater's letter of 2 August in connection with Mr. Killick's visit to the Dominican Republic," Secret Correspondence from Mr. Killick at the United Kingdom's Embassy in Washington to Mr. Slater, dated 19 August 1965.

removal, even after some of them were implicated in plotting the assassination of the new President.[226] Garcia Godoy became a powerless Executive: under his eroded authority, paramilitary groups apparently supported by right-wing military forces and IAPF Commander Alvin spread everywhere, killing PRD labour and local leaders.[227] The armed forces remained in a virtual state of rebellion: on December 1965, they launched an attack on the Constitutionalists, killing many of them. Garcia Godoy created an avowedly impartial "investigating commission" to delve into this event, but the US and the military warned that they would not accept the blaming of the Armed Forces.[228]

So reassured was the Right of US complicity that they twice attempted a coup against Garcia Godoy. The first attempt took place in September, but the US stopped it outright. The second was effected in late November. Imbert and Fiallo among them, the plotters believed that the United States would not intervene.[229] US actions on Dominican soil seemed to foreign observers that the United States was looking for a more reliable leader.[230] However, due to the lack of a better alternative, the US and the IAPF intervened on Garcia Godoy's behalf, thus preventing the coup.

The electoral campaign took place under these ambivalences and understandings. The leading contenders were former Presidents Bosch and Balaguer. Despite their continuous meddling against the Constitutionalists, Bunker and the new Ambassador, John Crimmins, regularly met Dominican political leaders to persuade them of the sincerity of US policy of 'neutrality' regarding the elections. Understandably, most sceptical was Bosch. The US worried about the prospects of his dropping his candidacy, thus undermining the legitimacy of the process. Therefore, the US Embassy urged Garcia Godoy to arrest terrorism and expressed to Imbert, and other Rightist Dominicans suspected of being behind destabilizing actions, of "Washington's 'disapproval.'"[231] But the Right surmised that, in the final analysis, it was hard to believe that Washington wanted Bosch in power more than they did. This time, the military gave Bosch no chance of winning. On 1 June 1966, the elections produced the expected result: Balaguer was elected with 57 percent of the votes to Bosch's 39 percent. It had been perhaps the most watched election in history: journalists from all over the world, missions from the United Nations and the OAS and

---

226. Slater, *Intervention and negotiation*, p. 153.

227. UK.PRO.FO371/179345. "Situation in October 1965," Confidential correspondence from Mr. Bell, United Kingdom's Embassy in Santo Domingo, dated 26 October 1965.

228. UK.PRO.FO371/179347. "An opinion is that Constitutionalists started the recent fighting in Santo Domingo," Confidential Correspondence from Sir P. Dean, United Kingdom's Embassy in Washington, dated 23 December 1965.

229. UK.PRO.FO371/179346. "Details of recent coup d'etat at Santo Domingo," Secret Correspondence from Mr. Bell, United Kingdom's Embassy in Santo Domingo, dated 25 November 1965.

230. UK.PRO.FO371/179345. "Comments on the growing American disenchantment with Garcia Godoy," Confidential Correspondence from Sir P. Dean, United Kingdom's Embassy in Washington, dated 27 October 1965.

231. Slater, *Intervention and negotiation*, pp. 165–167.

some 70 American liberals observed and agreed that the elections had been 'free and fair.'[232]

Reappraising the Dominican experience

The struggle for democracy acquired different meanings throughout the Dominican regime trajectory. The continuation of autocracy in the Dominican Republic was no longer viable once Trujillo died. The armed forces lost cohesion as the last Trujillo left. Aspiring democrats sought a pluralist political system, reform-oriented, open to the participation of political parties, based on free elections. Yet, throughout the transition the United States dictated the terms for the country's security policy and the most powerful actors, the armed forces and the dominant business elite, did not feel confident with the new rules of the game, contributing to preserve the authoritarian option if the new President did not deliver. Evidently, the emerging institutions remained severely limited. After the United States thwarted the Constitutionalist uprising, the armed forces' reppressive role was strengthened, resulting in the inauguration of an authoritarian presidential system presided by former Trujillo's protege, Joaquín Balaguer, where political and civil rights remained restricted for more than a decade.

The study of the evolution of the Dominican political system has to incorporate the role of the United States and the way domestic actors handled US influences. The fact that the country is located on a small island, so close and so valuable to the United States, meant that US policy-makers and politicians paid great attention to the course of events in the Dominican Republic. Within the Dominican domestic environment, this fact afforded those engaging in power struggles with opportunities for gaining leverage over their rivals. As long as these actors associated themselves fully with what they regarded as US "real" interests, they usually had a better chance at gaining or maintaining power than their counterparts who did not. Throughout the period under study, the establishment of the political institutions of democracy was not the top priority in the foreign policy agenda of the United States. Thus most powerful actors adapted their political interactions, producing outcomes that reflected real or perceived US preferences. Local actors allured the US to their side, most often to their personal advantage and to the detriment of democracy.

The course of the Dominican regime transition was also conditioned by the sequence of events in neighboring countries. Venezuela's recent experience out of authoritarian rule buttressed Dominican democrats, while the Cuban revolution emboldened those seeking social and political change. The Cold War impregnated the political interactions between the United States and the Latin Caribbean, undermining the efforts toward regime change effected by the few and inexperi-

232. A recent account about the Johnson administration's alleged orchestrating of events surrounding this election, ostensibly aimed at insuring an outcome favourable to US interests is in Eric Thomas Chester, *Rag-Tags, Scum, Riff-raff, and commies: The US Intervention in the Dominican Republic, 1965–1966.* New York: Monthly Review Press, 2001; similar arguments were previously laid out in Edward S. Herman and Frank Brodhead, *Demonstration elections: US-staged elections in the Dominican Republic, Vietnam, and El Salvador,* (Boston: South End Press, 1984).

enced local democrats. Conditions prevailing in this sub-region also influenced the formulation of policy in Washington regarding the Dominican Republic. The regime trajectory is a result of the interaction of domestic and international circumstances and events that often influenced each other.

NICARAGUA

Dictatorship, Revolution and Democracy

The Nicaraguan political trajectory was similarly shaped by the interaction between domestic and external influences and events. Two consecutive processes preceded the inauguration of democratic rule in this Central American country. The first was the struggle against the Somoza family's dynastic dictatorship (1936–1979) that paved the way for the establishment of a revolutionary regime led by the Sandinista Front for National Liberation (FSLN) in 1979. The second was the revolutionary regime's effort—carefully scrutinised and questioned by Washington—to institutionalise itself, leading to the victory of the political opposition in February 1990.

Though the roots of both the Dominican Republic and Nicaragua's dictatorships lie in their respective American military occupations, Nicaragua did not undergo, in the term under study, a direct military intervention by the United States. Yet, it did go through substantial, and equally traumatic, US involvement. The road toward democracy in Nicaragua was full of domestic and international complications. Shifts in the international arena, and particularly in US policy, as interpreted and handled by local actors, afforded much weight on the sequence of choices that led from one regime to the next.

The rise of the Somoza's dynastic dictatorship

Like Trujillo's dictatorship in the Dominican Republic, the regime of General Anastasio Somoza García (1936–1956) in Nicaragua was an unwitting consequence of US policy in the Caribbean Basin in the first three decades of the twentieth-century. From the end of the Spanish-American War to the end of World War I, aiming at securing Nicaragua as an alternative site for the interoceanic waterway, Washington exercised its influence to mediate historically rooted political disputes between the two major contending political forces in Nicaragua, the Liberal and the Conservative Parties. Fearing these quarrels would lead to foreign encroachments, the United States intervened in 1927 to restore order and to create conditions for future political stability.[233] Unlike its occupation of the Dominican Republic, in Nicaragua US Marines were confronted by

---

233. This period was first narrated by Henry L. Stimson, *American Policy in Nicaragua*, (New York: Charles Scribner's Sons, 1927); and Harold Norman Denny, *Dollars for Bullets: American rule in Nicaragua*, (New York: L. MacKeagh, The Dial Press, 1929).

domestic forces commanded by Augusto Cesar Sandino. In 1933, after supervising elections and creating an avowedly apolitical constabulary charged with maintaining order, the United States withdrew its Marines from Nicaragua.[234] Somoza García took advantage of the new circumstances left by the departure of the marines to concentrate power in his own hands.

The new head of the National Guard was in a position to gain the most with the US military occupation and subsequent withdrawal of Nicaragua. The recently created constabulary replaced the previously existing but highly ineffective forces and, to avoid the customary political mingling of incumbent Presidents, it was set up as an autonomous entity.[235] After consulting with the US Legation, President Sacasa appointed the husband of his niece and the American Legation's interpreter, Somoza García, as *Jefe Director* (Chief Director) of the National Guard.[236] In 1934, he ordered the assassination of rebel leader Augusto César Sandino. In 1936 he deposed Sacasa and arranged his own election, following Trujillo's step in the Dominican Republic a few years earlier. Many in Nicaragua urged Washington to stop Somoza, but the State Department—once the Good Neighbour Policy had begun to be implemented—was uninterested in arbitrating Nicaragua's domestic affairs. In any case, Somoza's constant tête-à-tête with the American Legation Minister created the impression that the Americans were sanctioning his acts; "denials from the Legation were rather mild or written in such a form that the Nicaraguan public did not take them seriously."[237] Somoza García thus benefited from this change in US policy and, aided by his control of the Guard, established a dynastic dictatorship that outlived the Trujillo regime for almost two decades.[238]

Throughout the era of the Somozas, Nicaragua enjoyed a greater democratic potential than the Dominican Republic under Trujillo. The Somoza's main instruments for retaining power were the National Guard, which became intertwined with the dictator's family, and the Liberal Party (PL), through which it controlled the running of the government and Congress. Other political parties existed and participated in periodical electoral processes—particularly the Conservative Party, which had a strong following prior to the arrival of the Somozas to power—that nonetheless were always "won" by the Somozas. The Nicaraguan Constitution prohibited re-election, but most times the Somozas circumvented it. These, among other independent political practices, coexisted

---

234. This period is explained with more detail by Thomas Dodd, *Managing democracy in Central America: United States election supervision in Nicaragua, 1927–1933*, (Miami: The University of Miami/North-South Center, 1992).

235. Marvin Goldwert, *The Constabulary in the Dominican Republic and Nicaragua: Progeny and Legacy of United States intervention*, (Gainesville: University of Florida Press, 1962.), p. 17.

236. Mark Everingham, *Revolution and the multiclass coalition in Nicaragua*, (Pittsburg: University of Pittsburg Press, 1996), p.44.

237. Ternot MacRenato, "Somoza Seizure of Power, 1926–1939," Ph.D. Dissertation, University of California, San Diego, 1991.

238. How Nicaragua fitted into the Cold War is explained by Michael D. Gambone, *Eisenhower, Somoza, and the Cold War in Nicaragua, 1953–1961* (Wesport, CN: Praeger Publishers, 1997).

with a regime that remained relatively "liberal" compared to several Latin Caribbean dictatorships.

The dictator's awareness of the political changes occurring in the world and of Washington's political complexities allowed him to weather US pressures against the continuation of his rule. At the end of World War II, inspired by the triumph over the Axis powers, the State Department advocated democracy in Latin America. Then, Somoza's attempt to re-elect himself as President, prohibited by the Nicaraguan constitution, countered Washington's aims. The United States pressured Somoza not to run for office. The dictator complied, only after he had found a man who would "serve patriotically and loyally to the interests of Nicaragua and of the United States." Somoza's candidate, Liberal Leonardo Arguello, "won" the February 1947 elections, while he retained control of Congress and remained as *Jefe Director* of the National Guard. Yet, Somoza García deposed the new President only a few weeks after taking office. Seeking US recognition for his government, he promised to produce a new Constitution in line with US concerns about regional security and military strength, with provisions to outlaw Communist propaganda and to allow US military bases on national soil.[239] Washington maintained the policy of non-recognition but the dictator stood still. As Trujillo did with the Marines, Somoza García cultivated the Head of the US military mission in Managua, who departed for Washington but left his family behind in a house provided by the Nicaraguan government, and arranged for the visit of Conservative US Congressmen.[240] During this interregnum, the State and War Departments differed about how to handle Somoza. Once the United States became more involved in the Cold War, security concerns eclipsed the interest in promoting democracy. In line with this, months later Washington recognised the Somoza García regime. Thereafter, Washington used Somoza's services to keep an eye on Latin Caribbean political developments that might threaten US interests. Along Trujillo, Somoza became one of the pillars of the Cold War order in the Latin Caribbean.

The dictatorship outlived the assassination of Anastasio Somoza García in 1956 by twenty-three years. His sons Luis and Anastasio, Jr., were in positions of power at the time of their father's death and worked together to retain control of the regime. Somoza's eldest son Luis was President of the Nicaraguan Congress and in that capacity he inherited, according to the Constitution, his father's office. Luis served the remainder of his father's term and had himself elected in 1958, after promising not to seek re-election. His brother Anastasio, who graduated from West Point Military Academy in 1947, headed the Presidential Military Staff of the National Guard and, upon the death of his father, Luis appointed him Commander of the National Guard.

Unlike his father, Luis favoured a more enlightened dictatorship. Echoing the winds of change flowing in the region since the mid-fifties, once in power

---

239. Walter Knut, *The regime of Anastasio Somoza, 1936–1956*, (Chapel Hill and London: The University of North Carolina Press, 1993), pp. 145–147, 155, 166–167.

240. Paul Coe Clark, Jr., *The United States and Somoza, 1933–1956: A Revisionist Look*, (Westport, Connecticut, and London: Praeger, 1992), pp. 167–168.

Luis co-opted some of the political leaders who had opposed Somoza García. He also conferred autonomy on the University of Nicaragua—which served as a springboard for independent political organising—and granted social security to workers from private enterprises. In 1960, thirty-seven percent of the national budget was apportioned to public works and health.[241] Thus the political opposition had a hard time in gathering mass support and, once Nicaraguans sought to emulate Castro's feat in Cuba, the regime remained solidly in power. Between Castro's rise to power in January 1959 and 1961, Nicaragua experienced twenty-three different uprisings, yet none came close to succeeding; the regime adopted a lenient attitude which contributed to keepinig stebility.[242] Unlike Trujillo, who did not undertake social reforms and massacred those who had risen against his regime, the Nicaraguan dictatorship survived the region-wide pressures for change that came after the triumph and subsequent radicalisation of the Cuban revolution.

At the height of President Kennedy's (1961–1963) Alliance for Progress' stated aim of promoting democracy and social reforms in Latin America, Luis Somoza relaxed political restrictions and announced he would not seek his re-election. Instead, he nominated the older Somoza's former private secretary, René Schick, as the Liberal candidate. Schick "won" the February 1963 electoral contest after the Conservative Party's nominee, Fernando Aguero, withdrew from the race. In office, Schick enjoyed considerable autonomy, although Anastasio Somoza Debayle retained control of the National Guard. Luis, the most accommodating of the Somoza family, died from natural causes in 1967.

After suppressing the political opposition, Anastasio, Jr. had himself elected to the Presidency in 1967, while retaining his post as *Jefe Director* of the National Guard. Anastasio, Jr., was the hard-liner of the family, but in any case he did not confront the pressures for change that had induced his brother Luis to adopt an 'enlightened' approach. The election of Richard Nixon in 1968 brought to the White House a man who sympathised with the Nicaraguan dictator. Nixon sent an Ambassador to Managua, Turner Shelton, who went out of his way to help Somoza in times of trouble. The US Ambassador was not crucial for Somoza to stay in power, but it did contribute to the impression that he was an American protégé. As his term in office was about to expire, at the end of 1971 Somoza conspired to remain in power. With substantial help from Shelton, Somoza reached an agreement with former presidential candidate and opposition leader Fernando Aguero. Both agreed to set up a three-man junta that included two members from the Liberal Party; the junta would be presided over by Aguero while Somoza retained his position as Chief of the National Guard.

---

241. Luis Herrera Zúñiga, *Relaciones internacionales y poder político en Nicaragua*, (Mexico City: El Colegio de México, 1991), pp. 1112–113, 116.

242. Under instructions from Luis Somoza, the National Guard thwarted the insurrections but later freed most of those who had taken up arms, the majority of which were sons of the Conservative Party's élite. See Institute for the Comparative Study of Electoral Systems (1966), *Nicaragua Election Factbook: February 5, 1967*, (Washington, DC: Institute for the Comparative Study of Electoral Systems), p. 24.

The turning point

The late sixties and early seventies offered an auspicious international environment for the consolidation of regimes such as Somoza's. Dictators ruled most of Latin America, and most of the few democracies there were broke down, giving way to authoritarian regimes. Washington, occupied with Vietnam and other conflicts of the Cold War, was uninterested in exerting any effort to uphold or promote democracy in the Third World. Somoza, in particular, shared President Nixon's view about the Communist threat in the hemisphere. No domestic group posed any significant threat to Somoza's rule. Yet, an unforeseen natural distaster in Nicaragua definitely recast the whole political scene.

The earthquake of December 1972 almost completely shattered Managua's downtown. Between eight and ten thousand Nicaraguans were killed, and more than fifty thousand homes and over eighty percent of the city's commercial establishments were destroyed. The National Guard practically vanished, as most officers either abandoned their posts to take care of their families and belongings or engaged in massive looting.[243] Somoza himself siphoned off funds from USAID projects and ransacked state institutions like the National Lottery and the Social Security.[244] With Ambassador Shelton's encouragement, Somoza imposed a state of siege, reducing the Triumvirate to a symbolic entity. The state of siege was used by Somoza to shut off criticism from the principal opposition leader and editor of La Prensa, Pedro Joaquin Chamorro, who also led the anti-Somoza political coalition, the Democratic Liberation Union (*Unión Democrática de Liberación*, UDEL).

Somoza's actions to take advantage of the natural disaster alienated most sectors of Nicaraguan society and, in time, weakened his regime. The United States and international financial institutions provided generous resources towards reconstruction and development. But corruption and mismanagement ensued. Somoza insisted that relief aid be distributed through the Liberal Party's precincts and not through the Church whose hierarchy, since 1970, had openly criticised his government. Merchants lost everything and were required to pay custom duties on all goods previously ordered that were now entering the country. Unable to pay, they saw their merchandise being sold at bargain prices by wives of National Guard officers.[245]

The political and economic crisis that followed the earthquake activated a process of mass mobilisation unprecedented in Nicaraguan history. Political conditions changed dramatically: popular unrest increased, while the lower and middle classes lost faith in the political system. The guerrilla group Sandinista Front for National Liberation (FSLN), active since the 1960's, became more active and visible. The widespread corruption further damaged Somoza's domestic and international standing. Yet, among widespread apathy, and after the Con-

243. Richard Millet, *Guardians of the Dynasty: A History of the US created Guardia Nacional and the Somoza Family*, (United States: Orbis Books, 1977), pp. 236–238.

244. Everingham, *Revolution and the multiclass coalition in Nicaragua*, p. 110.

245. Bernard Diederich, *Somoza and the legacy of US involvement in Central America*, (London: Junction Books, 1982), pp. 97–101.

stituent Assembly promulgated a new constitution extending the term in office to seven years, in 1974 Somoza ran for the presidency and "won" the elections. With these actions, Somoza polarised Nicaraguan society and exposed the character of the dictatorship.

The mid-seventies also saw a qualitative change in US foreign policy toward the Somoza regime. The dictatorship customarily sought advice and assistance from Washington, usually in an effort to be identified with the United States and use the pretended support as an advantage against its opponents. Ambassador Shelton, designated by Nixon, had frequently and publicly showed his appreciation for Somoza and his contempt for the dictator's opposition. But after Nixon's resignation in 1974 and despite Somoza's protest, the Ford administration appointed James Theberge as new Ambassador to Managua. Theberge arrived with instructions to keep a distance between himself and the dictator and to establish contacts with the Conservative Party and its leader, Pedro Joaquín Chamorro.[246] This step attested the State Department's new attitude toward Somoza. Coming as it did from Nicaragua's most significant external environment, this policy shift drastically altered the Nicaraguan élite's expectation vis-à-vis Washington, encouraging the opposition to be more outspoken.

Equally consequential for Nicaraguan politics was the fact that, since the mid-seventies, respect for human rights climbed in Washington's foreign policy agenda.[247] Because the Nixon and Ford administrations seemed to be giving low priority to human rights, starting in 1973–74 Congress took measures to take these into account for a variety of military and economic aid programmes. Congress banned military and development aid to those countries that were notorious human rights violators. To monitor human right violations in countries that were recipient of US aid, Congress later established a Co-ordinator for Human Rights and Humanitarian Affairs who would submit an annual report to Congress. One of the most thunderous reports was heard on 8–9 June 1976, when the subcommittee on international organisations of the House Foreign Relations Committee proceeded to hear a report on Nicaragua, Guatemala, and El Salvador. The hearings included testimonies of the abuses committed by the National Guard, thus raising awareness on among US Congressmen and the media.[248]

Somoza believed he would endure these pressures as comfortably as his father and brother had done. This was not the first time in which chilly winds had blown in from the United States. He could hold still and wait for the human rights euphoria to pass. After all, his ties to influential Congressmen in Washington, the history of his and his family's collaboration with the United States, and his experience with the intricacies of Washington's politics constituted important assets

---

246. Clark, *The United States and Somoza, 1933–1956*, p. 204.

247. This is seen as a starting point for what has been termed the "democratisation of the [US] foreign policy process," which made it increasingly difficult for incumbent Presidents to circumvent republican institutions in their foreign policy toward Latin America. See Jonathan Hartlyn, Lars Schoultz and Augusto Varas (eds.), *The United States and Latin America in the 1990s*, (Chapel Hill: University of North Carolina Press, 1992), pp. 6–9.

248. Millet, *Guardians of the Dynasty*, pp. 10–11.

in helping him to hold up until a more congenial administration took office. In the wake of Watergate and Vietnam, and due to his proximity to Nixon, Somoza thought he was just being singled out and that, in due course, US-Nicaraguan relations would return to normal.[249] The 1976 US election campaign thus became a pressing issue for the Somoza family, in particular since the Democratic platform stressed it would restore moral values to US foreign policy. Subsequently, James Carter's victory shocked the dictator and delighted his opponents.

Somoza reacted by making an effort to accommodate the new administration's wishes. If Carter wanted him to observe human rights, he would comply. In any case, neither the political opposition nor the FSLN represented a real threat to his regime, though their activities had significantly increased. Six months after Carter took office—and only after the new administration showed it was serious about the issue—Somoza lifted martial law, ended censorship and restrained the National Guard. At once the independent daily La Prensa began to publish harsh criticisms of the Somoza regime. Somoza had done his part, but whether the US would release aid now that he had was a complex issue for the Carter administration.

The Carter administration sought to induce Somoza to liberalise his regime but at this point it had no reason to adopt a stronger role for this purpose. The Nicaraguan dictatorship seemed to be stronger than ever, and the new administration in Washington, wary of involvements that might lead to further commitments and oblivious to the legacy of US intervention, hoped that Nicaraguans would effect a change by themselves. Washington had withheld aid as an instrument to induce Somoza to liberalise his regime. However, releasing it would have been interpreted, in this context, as the United States being ready to live with Somoza, thus demoralising the opposition. If the US granted aid again, policy makers argued, Somoza would have no incentive to enact reforms. So the Carter administration opted not to be seen as buttressing the dictator and continued to withhold aid. Only up to May 1978 did it approve two human-need loans to Nicaragua, after taking pains to explain to domestic and Nicaraguan opinion that this should not be interpreted as an expression of political support for the Somoza regime.[250] Somoza was amenable to suggestions by the United States so he proceeded with further concessions. In June 1978, he announced that he would allow the return of exiles and that he would permit the visit of the Inter-American Human Rights Commission (IAHRC) into Nicaragua, two actions that President Carter rapidly commended.[251] Somoza felt reassured, and interpreted this as proof that he was finally making progress in the United States.[252]

Unexpectedly, the ensuing political opening in Nicaragua was followed not only by increased political opposition activities but also by a new FSLN offen-

---

249. Diederich, *Somoza and the Legacy of US involvement in Central America*, p. 123.

250. Robert Pastor, *Condemned to repetition: The United States and Nicaragua*, (Pittsburgh: The University of Pittsburgh Press, 1987), p. 56.

251. NSA 1991, Document No. 00132. Letter from President James Carter to the President of the Republic of Nicaragua, General Anastasio Somoza Debayle, dated 30 June 1978.

252. Pastor, *Condemned to repetition*, p. 66.

sive against the Somoza regime. But Somoza could not go back. The State Department warned him that if he reacted to those events in a repressive way, the political crisis and the human rights situation could worsen, and 'advised' him to maintain his declared intention to effect political reforms and respect for human rights.[253] Somoza had no wish to alienate Washington, thus he did not unleash a wave of repression against his opponents. Yet he did not enact any significant political reform nor engage in a dialogue with the political opposition.

Dwindling choices

Though important local political actors declared their wish to open up the political system and effect a peaceful transition, not all shared this aim. Somoza's opponents included the Conservatives, the Catholic Church, an association of 500 businessmen known as the Nicaraguan Development Institute (INDE) and other leaders of distinct political orientations grouped under the umbrella of UDEL, but also the more organised and armed FSLN. Since 1974, the Sandinistas had gained notoriety, credibility and recruits thanks to a series of feats such as the capture of the home of wealthy businessman and Somoza associate Jose María Castillo. Though beset by internal divisions throughout the seventies, and after a severe blow by the National Guard in 1976, a faction known as *Terceristas* gained ascendancy within the FSLN. Encouraged by their backers in Panama—who sought to teach them the importance of attracting international sympathy to their cause—and Cuba—who did not believe the US would allow another revolution in the Caribbean—Terceristas made sure of avoiding leftist rethoric and presenting potential collaborators an option for the elimination of the Somoza regime. The FSLN revitalised itself domestically and internationally by developing a series of strategic alliances with Somoza's non-Marxist opponents in Nicaragua and abroad. The strategy soon paid off. A coalition of businessmen, clergy and intellectuals known as Group of Twelve (G-12) formed and demanded the participation of the FSLN in the political process.[254] The FSLN, however, was more interested in undertaking a social revolution than establishing a political democracy.

By 1977 both the political opposition and the FSLN intersected; the history of the opposition's failed attempts to dismantle the Somoza regime contributed a great deal to link all sectors of the political spectrum in the effort to unseat the dictatorship. Concerned about the FSLN's success in mobilising workers, students and the general public for demonstrations against the regime, at times, some of the members of the political opposition and the private sector sought to establish a dialogue with Somoza, fearing they were losing their ability to influence future events.[255] Yet, as Somoza refused to effect concessions and the Carter

---

253. NSA 1991, Document No. 00182. "Human rights demarche," Confidential cable No. 218953 from the Secretary of State, Warren Christopher, to the American Embassy in Managua, dated 29 August 1978.

254. The G-12 was a front for the FSLN but then it made an effort to appear as an independent grouping.

255. NSA 1991, Document No. 00100. "Opposition attitudes toward dialogue," Confidential

administration refused to exercise US influence to remove him, more of them trusted in the insurrectionist line as the only way to accomplish this objective.[256]

The assassination in January 1978 of the most outstanding opposition leader and director of La Prensa, Pedro Joaquin Chamorro, catalysed the trend toward a closer collaboration between the political opposition and the FSLN.[257] Chamorro's death left the political opposition without a leader, but it also ignited the highly explosive political environment. Businessmen organised a work stoppage and the FSLN escalated its attacks on the National Guard. Enthusiasm for confrontation subsided rapidly among the business élite as they could not endure the heavy toll of the economic standtill they generated. However, a process of radicalisation ensued. From this moment on, facing insurrections in Managua's neighbourhoods and in other cities, the National Guard targeted civilians indiscriminately.

As long as the situation seemed under control, the Carter administration refrained from undertaking a stronger role in the Nicaraguan crisis. It departed from its policy of non-interference only when events indicated that violence could continue to increase without an agreement being reached on the future of the Somoza regime. For instance, whereas prior to Chamorro's slaying the State Department merely provided opinions about how to approach the crisis, now it told Somoza what to do. He was told to exercise restraint in dealing with the general strike and lockouts, continue to seek conversations with "responsible" opposition leaders, avoid vengeance or reprisals against individuals or firms that had participated in the general strike, and appoint a national investigatory commission on Chamorro's slaying.[258] Washington told Somoza it was reevaluating its aid relationship to Nicaragua, and Somoza was promised that, if he acted in this direction, the United States would exercise its ascendancy over both the political opposition and Nicaragua's neighbours, some of which were active in promoting or acquiescing the armed cause against the dictatorship.[259] Somoza, instead, adopted a hard-line attitude. The opposition, emboldened by the Carter administration's disassociation from Somoza, asked Somoza to resign, but he argued that his departure before 1981 was unconstitutional and did not follow Washington's lead.

cable No. 02058 from the American Embassy in Managua to the Department of State, dated 4 May 1978; NSA 1991, Document No. 0099. "Embassy-Opposition Dialogue," Confidential Cable No. 02057 from the US Embassy in Managua to the Department of State, dated 4 May 1978.

256. Everingham, *Revolution and the multiclass coalition in Nicaragua*, p. 230.

257. Apparently not under Somoza's instructions, his son and an associate killed Chamorro for making public before the US Congress and the General Accounting Office the illegal export of blood by a Somoza-owned company. Everingham, *Revolution and the multiclass coalition in Nicaragua*, p. 230.

258. NSA 1991, Document No. 00050. "Proposed initiatives with Somoza and the opposition," Confidential cable No. 030739 from the Secretary of State to the American Embassy in Managua, dated 5 February 1978.

259. NSA 1991, Document No. 00055. "Demarche to President Somoza," Secret cable No. 000621 from the American Embassy in Managua to the Secretary of State, dated 8 February 1978.

To intervene or not to intervene

Somoza did not follow Washington's advice in part because US policy remained ambivalent. US policy was, "without interfereing in Nicaraguan affairs" (sic), to encourage "orderly movement" towards honest and open national elections, and discouraging Somoza to effect policies and actions that might be conducive to heightened military and political tensions. The State Department publicly repudiated Chamorro's assassination and the ensuing violence, but the situation in Nicaragua still seemed to be under control and did not undertake additional actions to push Somoza in the intended direction. Rather, the US Embassy in Managua was instructed to avoid direct involvement in the internal political manoeuvring and not to go beyond counselling both sides to avoid violence and reprisals against each other. The US would play no role in the crisis; the US Embassy was instructed not to offer Nicaraguans any specific suggestions on how to resolve their differences.[260] Neither would the United States ask Somoza to step down. The absence of a clear statement either in favour of or against the Somoza regime, or on the parameters of the proposed dialogue between the dictator and the opposition, bewildered Nicaraguans of all persuasions and contributed to Somoza's perception that the US could still live with him.[261]

How would not interfering in Nicaragua's domestic affairs would help the United States achieve its objectives? The State Department chose not to interfere because it assumed that both Somoza and the political opposition, in time and free from external pressures, would eventually find a "made in Nicaragua" solution that would put Nicaragua on the road to democracy. Given the history, and Nicaraguans' perception of US-Nicaraguan relations, this conjecture may have been utterly implausible. Despite US policy of neutrality, Nicaraguans never stopped considering the United States as an essential actor in the crisis.[262] In this context, despite all attempts to maintain a low profile, US officials had to be extremely careful, because every word or action they expressed was subject to varying interpretations, depending on the political viewpoint of the local analyst.[263]

This ambivalence allowed Somoza to use the unclearness of US policy to his advantage. He exploited any news that he could use to impress the Nicaraguan public, such as the announcing of new loans from USAID and international financial institutions. Lacking any clear public or private statement against his regime from Washington, Somoza understood and explained the crisis to his subordinates as a byproduct of actions by a handful of State Department officials

---

260. NSA 1991, Document No. 00064. "Role of US Embassy in Nicaragua," Secret cable No. 041757 from the Secretary of State to the American Embassy in Managua," dated 16 February 1978.

261. NSA 1991, Document No. 000325. "Perceived needs of Nicaraguans for US involvement," Secret cable No. 04609 from the American Embassy in Managua to the Secretary of State and the American Embassy in Panama City, dated 24 September 1978.

262. NSA 1991, Document No. 00093. "Opposition plotting," Confidential cable No. 04609 from the American Embassy in Managua to the Secretary of State, dated 26 April 1978.

263. NSA 1991, Document No. 000121. "Political update," Confidential cable No. 02671 from the American Embassy in Managua to the Secretary of State, dated 12 June 1978.

who misreported Nicaraguan events. Nicaraguan troubles stemmed, according to Somoza, from American Embassy and State Department activities giving the impression that he was not being backed by the United States.[264] Somoza blamed the Carter administration for the increase in political activities against his regime. Consequently, he did not perceive a need to enter into a meaningful dialogue with the political opposition, since all that it was needed was to convince the Americans that unless they changed their policy, "another Cuba" would follow. But the Carter administration attributed the political instability to Somoza's policies and did not buy Somoza's arguments.

Washington's non-interference also allowed Somoza to believe he could extract concessions from the United States. Somoza asked for guidance: "What reforms do you want me to implement in exchange for continuing to provide aid?," he asked. Somoza had a long list of grievances, including a decision not to sell weapons to Nicaragua in 1977, the suspension in military supplies, refusal to sign new aid agreements, votes against Nicaraguan loans at the Inter-american Development Bank and the World Bank, and similar actions at the United Nations. But on the other hand, he noted, the Constitution had been negotiated by none other than Ambassador Shelton himself.[265] Somoza attempted to make Washington pay him back for his and his family's past support for the United States. Had Washington forgotten that Nicaragua supported the US Bay of Pigs invasion in 1961 and the intervention of the Dominican Republic in 1965?[266] What was at stake was the character of the Cold War's regional order, of which the Somoza regime had been one of its most important pillars, but influential policy-makers in Washington had changed gears and considered that the Nicaraguan dictatorship was no longer useful.

Most Nicaraguan actors understood this change and expected the United States to use its power to turn events in their favour. Throughout the crisis that followed Chamorro's assassination, Ambassador Solaun and nearly all Embassy officers were approached by Nicaraguans and US citizens living on Nicaraguan soil to ask the United States to intervene.[267] Even when other regional leaders were involved, and sometimes to a much greater extent than Carter, such as Presidents Rodrigo Carazo of Costa Rica and Carlos Andrés Pérez of Venezuela and Panama's military Chief General Omar Torrijos, some opposition politicians believed in the indispensability of the White House's approval for their plans to be

264. NSA 1991, Document No. 000191. "Ambassador meets Somoza 30 August," Confidential cable No. 04099 from the American Embassy in Managua to the Secretary of State, dated 31 August 1978.

265. NSA 1991, Document No. 000205. "Conversations with Somoza: 5 September," Confidential cable No. 04176 from the American Embassy in Managua to the Secretary of State, dated 6 September 1978.

266. NSA 1991, Document No. 000211. "Conversations with Somoza: 7 September," Confidential cable No. 04197 from the American Embassy in Managua to the Secretary of State, dated 7 September 1978.

267. NSA 1991, Document No. 00070. "Item for Ambassador Solaun," Confidential cable No. 01005 from the American Embassy in Nicaragua to the Secretary of State, dated 1 March 1978.

carried out successfully.[268] Liberal and Conservative party leaders also sought So-laun's participation as mediator and, in fact, the Conservatives refused to engage in a dialogue with Somoza unless the US played the role of guarantor.[269] No one believed the US would leave them alone to settle matters by themselves, interpret-ing Solaun and Washington officials' repeated concern with the growing strength of what they called the "radical left". As a result, both Somoza and the political opposition expected Washington would eventually change its mind to undertake actions in their favour, aiming at preventing "another Cuba" in Nicaragua.

Regional leaders also understood what was at stake and were already taking part in the Nicaraguan crisis, but the United States was scarcely participating in that exchange. Costa Rica, whose leaders pretended neutrality, served as a stag-ing ground for the FSLN and broke diplomatic relations with Nicaragua. Both Venezuela and Panama declared they would come to aid Costa Rica were the Somoza government to undertake any action against its eastern neighbour. The G-12 members frequently met Mexican, Costa Rican, Panamanian and Venezu-elan leaders to discuss their plans. Panama, in particular, was unusually active in training and arming the Sandinistas. But General Torrijos and President Perez also sought US involvement, and to do so they warned they were ready to take direct actions to remove Somoza.[270] On the other hand, Somoza had also ac-quired new friends at this stage of the crisis, in particular the military regimes of Guatemala, El Salvador, Brazil and Argentina, all of which had been singled out by the Carter administration for their human rights violations. To all extents and purposes, there were so many expectations and pressures about US involvement and external actors eagerly engaged in the Nicaraguan crisis that a totally "made in Nicaragua" solution was illusory.

The heightened international attention on Nicaraguan affairs brought the Carter administration to the fore. At the Organization of American States, Ven-ezuela convoked member nations in early September 1978 to call for a Meeting of Foreign Ministers to consider events in Nicaragua, following the increase of violence in that Central American country. Building upon the experience against Trujillo in the Dominican Republic less than two decades earlier, Venezuela ar-gued that the Nicaraguan crisis constituted a threat to the peace and security of the hemisphere. In that capacity, discussion of Nicaragua's domestic conflict jus-tified breaching the norm of non-intervention. Somoza, like Trujillo before him, made the effort to stop it, arguing that affairs in Nicaragua were purely an inter-nal matter. Somoza well remembered the Dominican precedent, and was wor-ried about repeating Trujillo's steps.[271] The Carter administration was dragged

268. NSA 1991, Document No. 000325. "Perceived need of Nicaraguans for US involvement," Confidential cable No. 04609 from the American Embassy in Nicaragua to the Secretary of State, dated 24 September 1978.

269. NSA 1991, Document No. 00093. "Opposition plotting," Confidential cable No. 01939 from the American Embassy in Nicaragua to the Secretary of State, dated 26 April 1978.

270. NSA 1991, Document No. 000630. "The Caracas Caucus," Confidential cable No. 00305 from the American Embassy in Managua to the Secretary of State, dated 19 January 1979.

271. NSA 1991, Document No. 000205. "Conversation with Somoza: 5th September," Confi-

on. Conceding it was a matter of common concern (but not a security threat) to the hemisphere, it supported the call for the meeting.[272]

The Carter administration was impelled to review its stated policy of strict non-interference in Nicaraguan. The Nicaraguan opposition and Latin Americans would have interpreted not supporting the call as if Washington had taken the side of the Nicaraguan dictator. In addition, the US Embassy observed, Somoza had not expressed his willingness to undertake reforms.[273] Talks had been taking place between Conservative and Liberal Party Deputies, including one on restructuring the National Guard, but they did not seem to be reaching meaningful conclusions. Besides, past US policy was not seen as neutral, but as ambiguous and vacillating.[274] Since 9 September, the FSLN had launched co-ordinated attacks on National Guard detachments in Nicaragua's major cities. Opposition and business leaders organised a strike and demands for Somoza's resignation increased. Somoza, however, became more intransigent and imprisoned between 600 and 800 opposition activists. These considerations motivated Washington to seek a new role regarding the Nicaraguan crisis.

In the post-Vietnam international order, the Carter administration was interested in avoiding unilateral measures that could be used to accuse the US of interventionism. Thus the Carter administration worked with the hemispheric organisation to reach a resolution that would leave an open door for its involvement. The OAS resolution stated that it "hoped that the Somoza government would be willing, in principle, to accept the friendly co-operation and conciliatory efforts that several OAS member states may offer toward establishing the conditions necessary for a peaceful settlement." It followed that the opposition and the government would request mediation and several OAS member states would volunteer, but neither would happen without the United States.[275]

From there on, the United States guided the mediation process and, within the administration, the National Security Council took over the formulation of policy toward Nicaragua. US objectives were to induce Somoza to surrender power, permit the National Guard and Somoza's Liberal party to remain cohesive forces and allow new actors to enter the political system.[276] But Washington's ability to handle the process would be more difficult to reach if these objectives

---

dential cable No. 04176 from the American Embassy in Managua to the Secretary of State, dated 6 September 1978.

272. NSA 1991, Document No. 000202. "Nicaragua-OAS consideration," Confidential cable No. 04147 from the American Embassy in Managua to the Secretary of State, dated 5 September 1978.

273. NSA 1991, Document No. 000166. "GON-opposition dialogue," Secret cable No. 03921 from the American Embassy in Managua to the Secretary of State, dated 23 August 1978.

274. NSA 1991, Document No. 000325. "Perceived need of Nicaraguans for US involvement," Confidential cable No. 04609 from the American Embassy in Nicaragua to the Secretary of State, dated 24 September 1978.

275. Pastor, *Condemned to repetition*, p. 91.

276. NSA 1991, Document No. 000366. "Mediation: a difficult road," Confidential cable No. 04858 from the American Embassy in Managua to the Secretary of State, dated 5 October 1978.

were clear initially.[277] There were other "negotiators," namely from Colombia and the Dominican Republic, but the United States took the leading part. The role of the US would be central to achieve these objectives. US negotiators were instructed to facilitate the "solution" to emerge, to the greatest extent, from the play of positions taken by the two sides. The opposition, however, would have to be helped to articulate its interests. The United States would consider resuming economic and military assistance once they reached an agreement.[278]

But the Nicaraguan dictator refused to step down and, having the threat of major actions by the Sandinistas in the background, finally the Carter administration told Somoza that he had to go.[279] To avoid unilateral appearances, the group of mediators delivered the message. The ultimatum delivered to the Nicaraguan dictator underlined that, in exchange for providing a constitutional transition to a provisional government, Somoza would be granted amnesty and a "reasonable guarantee of protection" for his "essential interests," including those of the Liberal Party and of the National Guard.[280] The US plan included a three-year transitional government led by a Triumvirate and agreement on the non-prosecution of Somoza officials in a future government. The opposition, gathered in the Broad Opposition Front (FAO, the new umbrella organisation created after Chamorro's murder), devised, after being prompted by the United States, a transitional government that would take over after he resigned. The plan included the departure of Somoza's family from both the National Guard and the country, a timetable for elections for a constituent assembly and the reorganisation of the National Guard.[281] Nevertheless, Somoza did not accept the need for his resignation, and neither the opposition nor the FSLN wanted to be associated to a formula that did not mean a complete break with the past.

In any event, none of the most significant actors had been interested in mediation. Somoza had accepted mediation only as a way to gain time to rearm the National Guard. FAO leaders had accepted it believing that by undertaking mediation the Carter administration would remove the dictator and isolate the Sandinistas. The United States expected FAO to be able to take over the government, but FAO leaders waited to be told by the US Embassy what to do next.[282] The FSLN was not interested in mediation either. The FSLN had backed the effort and participated in it through the G-12, but abandoned it upon realising

277. Pastor, *Condemned to repetition*, p. 79.

278. NSA 1991, Document No. 000365. "Nicaragua mediation: negotiating instructions," Confidential cable No. 252512 from the Secretary of State to the American Embassy in Managua, dated 4 october 1978.

279. NSA 1991, Document No. 000443. "Nicaragua mediation No. 81: Demarche to Somoza," Secret cable No. 05430 from the American Embassy in Managua to the Secretary of State, dated 30 October 1978.

280. NSA 1991, Document No. 000436. "Nicaragua mediation No. 58: proposed talking points for use with Somoza," Confidential cable No. 05273 from the American Embassy in Managua to the Secretary of State, dated 24 October 1978.

281. Pastor, *Condemned to repetition*, p. 101.

282. Everingham, *Revolution and the multiclass coalition in Nicaragua*, pp. 132–133.

that the process could lead to the installation of a government that precluded them from real power.[283]

Pressured by the United States to give in to FAO's demands, Somoza offered instead to hold a plebiscite on his future. Before he went on with the idea, Somoza sent an emissary to ask the US envoys whether Washington would, if he won, respect the results of the election and resume normal relations. If he lost, he wondered whether he would receive asylum and count on Washington's legal and economic protection. Somoza was less interested in the concessions he could get from the opposition than those he could get from the government of the United States.[284] In December, only after the Carter administration expressed its support for the plebiscite did the FAO and Somoza government representatives sit down to negotiate the specifics. The FSLN rejected the plebiscite altogether, while the FAO, now pressured to prove its revolutionary credentials, conditioned it to Somoza leaving the country and handing over power to an interim government during the campaign, conditions that would have been difficult for Somoza to accept.[285] But Somoza was not interested in holding a free election and thus changed his mind and instructed his cabinet to reject the plebiscite.[286] On 8 February 1979 the State Department announced that, due to Somoza's unwillingness to accept the most essential elements put forward by the negotiators, it would terminate the military assistance programme and reduce by more than half the number of US Embassy personnel.[287]

The Nicaraguan dictatorship challenged the Carter administration because it had reasons to be optimistic about its future. The National Guard increased its size from 7,500 in September 1978 to 11,000 in March 1979, and was receiving arms shipments from Israel, Guatemala, Brazil, and Argentina.[288] At the OAS, it was unlikely that sanctions be approved against the Somoza regime, for they required at least two thirds of the votes and dictatorships targeted by the Carter administration for their human rights violations ruled most of Latin America.

---

283. Diederich, *Somoza and the Legacy of US involvement in Central America*, p. 208.

284. Somoza expected the US government promise to co-operate so that he and his family would not be forced out of the United States to answer legal charges in Nicaragua on the basis of a bilateral extradition treaty. In another occasion, Somoza sent an emissary to Washington, who insisted to find out what was the Carter administration's "fall back position." NSA 1991, Document No. 000548. "Nicaragua mediation No. 203: Somoza's request to USG," Secret cable No. 06297 from the American Embassy in Managua to the Secretary of State, dated 4 December 1978; NSA 1991, Document No. 000623. "GON wants to make a deal," Secret cable No. 00235 from the American Embassy in Managua to the Secretary of State, dated 15 January 1979.

285. Diederich, *Somoza and the Legacy of US involvement in Central America*, p. 211.

286. NSA 1991, Document No. 000482. "Nicaragua mediation No. 121: Conversation with Somoza." Secret cable No. 05775 from the Secretary of State to the American Embassy in Managua, dated 11 November 1978.

287. Pastor, *Condemned to repetition*, p. 109.

288. In April 1979, Somoza bragged on TV that he had stood up to the Carter administration. Pastor, *Condemned to repetition*, p. 123; Diederich, *Somoza and the Legacy of US involvement in Central America*, p. 215.

Somoza was sure he could control the FSLN and reduce it to manageable proportions in time for the 1981 elections.[289] Backed by his supporters on Capitol Hill, who advised him to stick around and not give in to the "Communists" in Nicaragua and Washington, the Nicaraguan dictator decided to bypass the Carter administration and the political opposition's demands for his departure.[290] There were men in Washington, in Congress and at high levels of the administration to whom Somoza appealed for help. At times, policy makers spoke about possibilities and options, such as sending troops. Though these comments were not directly told to Somoza, he was so well-wired in Washington that usually he found out about the discussions going on inside Washington's inner circles. Even when these options were rapidly discarded by the Carter administration, knowing they were a matter of conversation may have made Somoza think that the US would send troops at the last minute.[291]

The failure of mediation accelerated the process of polarisation in Nicaragua. Both Somoza and the FSLN intensified their resolve to fight to the finish, bringing an increase both in revolutionary violence and repression. To most observers, it seemed as if Somoza would be able to stay until the end of his term. Demoralised, the political opposition demobilised itself, thus ceding the leadership of the anti-Somoza struggle to the FSLN. By late May 1979, CIA analysts concluded that the fighting could get to the level it reached during September 1978's insurrection, but it would not be enough to topple Somoza before 1981.[292]

Finding itself with no further tools to influence Nicaraguan events, and believing that the situation did not merit further involvement, the United States adopted a "correct but not supportive" relationship with the Nicaraguan regime.[293] The State Department realised it could not negotiate or mediate successfully a real solution to the succession issue, especially since Somoza appeared to be relatively strong. This meant a retreat to the previous policy of non-involvement. Even at rumours of coup plots to topple Somoza, the State Department chose not to provide any backing, blessing, acquiescence, or moral support. It was essential that the administration's "absolute non involvement be unequivocally clear to anyone."[294] Some Nicaraguans, however, interpreted Carter's inaction as proof of undercover support for the Nicaraguan dictatorship, insofar as the US was

---

289. NSA 1991, Document No. 000626. "Demarche [excised] January 17," Secret cable No. 00285 from the American Embassy in Managua to Secretary of State, dated 17 January 1979.

290. Diederich, *Somoza and the Legacy of US involvement in Central America*, p. 124.

291. Larence Pezzullo, Association for Diplomatic Studies, Foreign Affairs Oral History Program, Lawinger Library, Georgetown University, 24 February 1989.

292. Since the sharp reduction in US Embassy staff in February 1979, the amount of information the US gathered on the National Guard declined further, thus providing poor intelligence information to the Carter administration. Pastor, *Condemned to repetition*, p. 128.

293. NSA 1991, Document No. 000639. "Nicaragua meeting," Classification Unknown Memorandum from Barbara Bowie to Ms. Patricia derian, dated 24 January 1979.

294. NSA 1991, Document No. 000647. "Coup plotting," Secret cable No. 033931 from the American Embassy in Managua to the Secretary of State, dated 9 February 1979.

not using its power to halt the arms flow from countries such as Israel.[295] Both Somoza and FAO sought to involve the United States on their behalf. However, the Carter administration could not normalise relations with Nicaragua without discouraging and radicalising the political opposition but, at the same time, it was left with few options to deal with the crisis.

In practice, the Carter administration did take sides. It was not for the continuation of the Somoza regime, but did not take actions because it believed that a revolution was not at hand. As in the Dominican Republic between Bosch's fall and the constitutionalist uprising, the US government distrusted the FSLN and avoided contacts with its leadership, even when requested by the Sandinistas themselves.[296] Thus the United States foreclosed the only channel it could have used to exercise its influence in Nicaragua, short of US military intervention, in particular since early March all FSLN factions decided to establish an unified leadership. Having no one else to turn to, and to prove its revolutionary credentials, the political opposition pushed in the forefront of the movement to dismantle the dictatorship. By 4 June, the FAO and the FSLN co-ordinated some of their activities. Later, fighting broke out virtually everywhere, while the FSLN captured and kept towns. By mid-June, both the FSLN and FAO had set up an alternative Government of National Reconstruction (GNR) inside Nicaragua.

Too little, too late

Only then did the Carter administration realise that Somoza's days were numbered and began to devise a plan for a successor regime that would not be under the control of the FSLN. Somoza, recognising he was not in a position to defeat the FSLN, seemed to be prepared to resign, but wanted assurances from the United States that the National Guard would not collapse.[297] The Department of Defense proposed sending in an Inter-American Peace Keeping Force. For this strategy to work, the OAS would have to vote in favour of a military force large enough to pacify the Sandinista-led insurrection. Somoza would also have to resign immediately, so that the successor government would not be perceived as negotiating on his behalf. The new regime's survival would also require the presence of external military forces.

Despite the objection of the State Department, the United States did propose sending in an inter-American force to maintain peace and guarantee the transition process. The Carter administration sought the support of Latin American governments, arguing the situation in Nicaragua had reached grave

---

295. NSA 1991, Document No. 000678. "G-12 continues anti-US statements," Limited Official Use Cable No. 01619 from the American Embassy in Managua to the Secretary of State, dated 2 April 1979.

296. NSA 1991, Document No. 000753. United States Bureau of Human Rights and Humanitarian Affairs Memorandum from Patricia Derian to Brandon Grove, Department of State, dated 12 June 1979.

297. NSA 1991, Document No. 000833. "Somoza-The First Visit," Secret cable No. 02857 from the American Embassy in Managua to the Secretary of State, dated 28 June 1979. In this meeting, Somoza tells the US Ambassador that the United States is paying him poorly for his contributions to the overthrow of Arbenz in Guatemala and the Bay of Pigs Invasion.

proportions. It argued that, due to Cuban aid to the FSLN and the tangible prospects for an internationalisation of the conflict, an inter-American effort to sponsor and supervise Nicaragua's political process and an inter-American presence were urgently required.[298] On June 21, however, the US proposal was defeated at the Organisation of American States, thanks in part to lobbying by Panama and Venezuela. The Carter administration thus joined a resolution stating that Somoza was the fundamental cause of Nicaragua's troubles, called for his replacement, denounced intervention and did not invite the participation of the OAS. The US had attempted to replicate the strategy that paid off when it intervened against the Constitutionalist uprising in the Dominican Republic in 1965, but the character of the region had changed considerably and most governments were wary of this option.

Washington made an effort to prevent what seemed to be the most likely outcome of the current situation, the FSLN's military victory. Yet, by this stage it may have been too late to influence the course of events in Nicaragua, unless it may have been willing to undertake an unilateral military intervention in Nicaragua. For a month before Somoza's departure from Nicaragua on 17 July 1979, the Carter administration had been occupied with other matters it considered more important.[299] Regional powers had already filled the vacuum left by the vacillating policy of the Carter administration and they were not lenient toward leaving the United States to retake that role. Mexico broke diplomatic relations with Nicaragua in late May, and Panama, after the House of Representatives passed the implementing legislation for the Panama Canal Treaties, followed in mid-June. Venezuela and Panama were strongly supporting the FSLN. Costa Rica, though playing neutral, allowed the free transit or goods and arms for the FSLN throughout its territory. Since April, with the new administration of Carlos Herrera Campins, Venezuela had reduced its material support for the FSLN, but Cuba had filled the void. Despite Washington's request to the contrary, Andean Pact countries declared in mid-June that a "State of Belligerency" existed in Nicaragua, a political bolstering for the FSLN. In fact, to deal at this stage with the Nicaraguan crisis, the Carter administration was compelled to consult with Torrijos, Carazo, President Herrera and former President Pérez, who still wielded considerable influence in the region even after leaving office.[300]

---

298. NSA 1991, Document No. 000765. "OAS action Nicaragua," Secret cable No. 153522 from the Secretary of State to All American Republics diplomatic posts," dated 15 June 1979.

299. Former NSC advisor Robert Pastor explains that Carter flew to Vienna for the signing of the Salt II Treaty from June 15 to 18, visited Japan and South Korea from 23 June to 1 July, and around 3 July retreated to Camp David to work on a speech about energy, staying there for about two weeks to reassess the state of the nation and his presidency, at a time when his popularity was at its lowest. Pastor, *Condemned to repetition*, p. 137.

300. Panama's General Torrijos, in particular, wielded considerable influence with the FSLN. The Carter administration used Torrijos as a channel with the Sandinistas. In early July, Torrijos was secretly brought to the White House to discuss the state of Nicaraguan events with President Carter, but this meeting reached Somoza's ears. The fact that Somoza heard about this "secret" meeting is in NSA 1991, Document No. 000866. "Somoza: The Fourth Meeting," Secret cable No. 02990 from the American Embassy in Managua to the Secretary of State, dated 5 July 1979.

The Carter administration's options to attempt to influence Nicaraguan affairs were even more limited now. It could not openly or covertly support Somoza without endangering its relationship with the democratic opposition in Nicaragua and the regional leaders who were seeking Somoza's ousting. It would discredit US human rights policy, would undermine its capacity to work toward other foreign policy goals in the hemisphere and raise questions about the Carter administration's international purposes. Disassociation from the dictator and public support for the opposition was necessary, not only as a way to bolster a non-FSLN alternative to Somoza in Nicaragua but also to encourage the steps away from rigid repression taken in Guatemala, Honduras and El Salvador. Supporting Somoza, or for that matter, an authoritarian alternative, would most likely promote hard-line and repressive responses to the unsettled social and political conditions in Central America.[301] Particularly since the uproar caused by the murder of ABC correspondent William Stewart by a National Guard soldier in June, bolstering Somoza was even less popular in Washington's circles.

In these circumstances, the Carter administration sought to impede the successor regime falling under the FSLN's dominance but understood that it would have to show a large degree of broadness and include the FSLN. To work in this direction, in late June the State Department attempted to reconstitute the National Guard and form an alternative Nicaraguan Executive that could compete for power with the FSLN-led GNR. To make it viable, Somoza would have to depart first, and the new Executive, representing a clean break with the past, would have to take over and request such support for the reconstituted Guard.[302] To have time to achieve both objectives, the State Department agreed with Somoza to delay his departure, until it found the persons willing "to take up the baton."[303] The State Department contacted former National Guard officers not tainted with Somoza's excesses to lead a reconstituted National Guard, as well as respectable Nicaraguan civilians to join the Executive Committee. However, most of the important organisations, disillusioned with Washington's inaction, had already endorsed the Provisional Government. An expanded Executive without Sandinista representation was not a viable aim. The best the US could hope for was for Somoza to turn over power either to a member of Congress or of his cabinet and make the successor call for a cease-fire, co-operation in forming a government of reconciliation and appeal for humanitarian assistance.[304] Somoza told the US press his agreement with the Carter administration, provoking

301. NSA 1991, Document No. 000634. United States Bureau of Human Rights and Humanitarian Affairs, "Options," Secret memorandum from Mark L. Schneider to Ambassador Bowdler, dated 19 January 1979.

302. NSA 1991, Document No. 000835. "Talk with Somoza," Secret cable No. 166874 from the Secretary of State to the American Embassy in Managua, dated 28 June 1979.

303. NSA 1991, Document No. 000846. "Nicaraguan scenario," Confidential cable No. 168715 from the Secretary of State to the American Embassy in Managua, dated 30 June 1979; NSA 1991, Document No. 000848. "Somoza: The third Meeting," Secret cable No. 02911 from the American Embassy in Managua to the Secretary of State, dated 30 June 1979.

304. NSA 1991, Document No. 000836. "The current scene," Secret cable No. 02870 from the American Embassy in Managua to the Secretary of State, dated 28 June 1979.

criticism in the United States and Nicaragua for the continuing bloodshed, and compelling Washington to seek a rapid settlement of the crisis.[305]

The Carter administration made an effort toward establishing a transition scenario that offered political moderates the opportunity to participate and prevent the FSLN from dominating the post-Somoza political scene. The State Department sought to make sure that a new National Guard Commander be in place as soon as Somoza departed, who would announce a total reformation of the Guard and exile the most corrupt and repressive officers.[306] Washington aimed at enlarging the Junta with the support of the Costa Rica, Venezuela, Panama and the Andean nations, who acquiesced to helping the Carter administration for this aim. The United States, however, found many obstacles it was not able to circumvent. Specifically, the "moderate" elements already included in the Provisional Government, Violeta Barrios de Chamorro, widow of the slain leader, and businessman Alfonso Robelo, refused to yield to Carter's request, thus thwarting the possibility of enlarging the Junta.[307] Finally, on the eve of Somoza's departure, the Carter administration was able to set up a transition scenario with the Junta. The Nicaraguan Congress would designate Somoza's successor, the interim President would appoint a new National Guard's Chief of Staff (selected by the United States and approved by Somoza and the FSLN), call for a cease-fire and arrange for a transfer of power to the Junta within seventy-two hours.[308]

Yet Somoza and his associates chose not to follow the script the US laid out for them. Two days before, Ambassador Pezzullo had reviewed with Congress President Urcuyo the steps he was going to take following Somoza's departure. However, Urcuyo defended his position as Constitutional President and declared that he would not surrender power to the Junta nor would he arrange a cease-fire.[309] Urcuyo and Somoza's decision not to abide by the agreed scenario was based on their interpretation that the Carter administration would have no choice other than supporting them because it was going through a period of extreme weakness due to an alleged cabinet crisis.[310] In addition, Somoza had not informed the National Guard about his plans. To forestall panic as he left, he had told his military officers that the US would provide aid. The United States, however, did not provide support to the Guard. As soon as Somoza resigned,

305. NSA 1991, Document No. 000873. "Somoza tells Post reporter he made commitment to USG," Confidential cable No. 03035 from the American Embassy in Managua to the Secretary of State, dated 7 July 1979.

306. NSA 1991, Document No. 000886. "Nicaragua: The National Guard," Secret cable No. 176171 from the Secretary of State to the American Embassy in Managua, dated 7 July 1979.

307. Pastor, *Condemned to repetition*, p. 168.

308. NSA 1991, Document No. 000937. "Transition scenario," Secret cable No. 183735 from the Secretary of State to the American Embassy in Managua, dated 15 July 1979.

309. NSA 1991, Document No. 000961. "GON backs off from agreement," Secret cable No. 03250 from the American Embassy in Managua to the Secretary of State, dated 17 July 1979.

310. NSA 1991, Document No. 000968. "(Excised) explains attitude of Urcuyo," Secret cable No. 05458 from the American Embassy in Panama to the Secretary of State, dated 18 July 1979.

the FSLN advanced toward Managua. As a result, National Guard officials lost confidence in their ability to withstand the war and broke down within two days, and Urcuyo, realising he had no support, abandoned the country. To disassociate itself from Somoza and Urcuyo, the State Department recalled its Ambassador and most of its staff. Unrestrained, on 19 July the FSLN took the Capital and the GNR swore in as the Revolutionary Government of Nicaragua.

The Nicaraguan revolution

After 19 July 1979, Nicaraguans faced a qualitatively different domestic political setting. The revolution effectively destroyed Somoza's dynastic dictatorship and its instruments and installed a new regime enjoying initial substantial national and international legitimacy. As the undisputed leader of the effort that toppled Somoza, the FSLN found itself in an unexpectedly predominant position and with a clear path to exercising nearly unrestrained political power. Seeing itself as the "vanguard" of the insurrection against Somoza, the FSLN moved to take full responsibility for the political direction of the government.

From the start, the FSLN commanded the majority of the votes within the Junta. The five-member Junta of the Government of National Reconstruction included Daniel Ortega, a Sandinista Commander; intellectual Sergio Ramírez, from the Group of Twelve, and Moisés Hassan, from an organisation of professionals, both supporters of the FSLN; Joaquin Chamorro's widow and majority shareholder of *La Prensa*, Violeta Barrios, and a prominent member from the private sector, Alfonso Robelo.

Among the population, enthusiasm for revolutionary change did not abate. The FSLN's revolutionary rethoric was shared by *La Prensa*'s editorials and even by members of the Conservative Party's élite, some of whom called for the construction of socialism and for joining "the revolutionary wave that runs over Central America." Junta member Robelo himself, for example, travelled to Cuba to participate in a political event sponsored by the government of Fidel Castro.[311]

The Sandinistas stepped in this momentum to claim a larger power quota. The Interior Ministry fomented the creation of mass organisations everywhere, purportedly in defence of the revolution, and the new armed force, the Popular Sandinista Army, was formed following the political orientation of the FSLN. Soon it became clear that real power was held by the Sandinistas and that they were uninterested in binding themselves by the formal institutions of democracy which, after all, had been recurrently used and abused by the Somoza dictatorship. Technically, the collegiate Junta led the government and shared legislative powers with a Council of State composed of representatives from 33 organisations. Later, in April 1980, it was expanded to include representatives from labour, middle class, youth, peasant and professional organizations created by the FSLN, leading to Violeta and Robelo's resignations. Despite the fact that the latter two were replaced with two prominent independents, Arturo Cruz and Rafaelo Córdova Rivas, differing viewpoints about how to handle the tasks ahead

---

311. Rafael Córdova Rivas, *Contribución a la Revolución*, (Managua: Centro de Publicaciones de Avanzada, s.a., 1983), pp. 37, 95.

led to the deterioration of the once-open lines of communication between the FSLN and the Superior Council of Private Enterprise (COSEP). The institutional basis for running and partipating in government decision-making and the extent to which revolutionary fervours would extend to other areas were open questions that remained unanswered for many years.

In any case, the tasks ahead seemed unsourmountable. Public administration and security forces had to be rebuilt. Social services were minimal and income distribution patterns were highly skewed. A revolution to correct these ills, more than a political system modelled after industrial democracies, had great appeal in Nicaragua. The framework for transformation, previously agreed by the FSLN and the groups who opposed Somoza, committed the government to upholding a mixed economy, political pluralism and an independent foreign policy. Among the first measures the Junta announced were the confiscation of Somoza-owned properties, an agrarian reform, free unionisation and the nationalisation of natural resources and foreign trade.

Fortunately for the new regime, the Carter administration chose to establish a constructive relationship. As Somoza fell, the analogy with the Cuban revolution had haunted Washington's policy-makers. Based on the earlier experience, the National Security Council concluded that the United States had pushed Castro to the left and to the Soviet Union. To contribute to the Nicaraguan revolution not becoming anti-American, Washington could assist the GNR to fulfil its stated promises of political pluralism, elections and a vigorous private sector. This approach would contribute to deny the Sandinistas a reason for relying on Cuban and Soviet assistance and to make clear that a good relationship with the United States was contingent upon Nicaraguan non-interference in the internal affairs of her neighbours.[312] To achieve these goals, the Carter administration moved rapidly to establish a warm relationship with the new government, providing emergency food and relief supplies. Potentially conflictive issues were dealt with on a bilateral basis, while in public it remained supportive. The GNR exercised its independence and called for Cuban military advisors to rebuild the internal security forces. Yet, rather than presenting Cuba's influence as a large threat vto the United States, the Carter administration continued to provide aid and made sure to point out that it expected the new regime to respect human rights and avoid exporting revolution.[313]

In 1980, events in the United States turned sour what could have developed into a constructive relationship providing a positive environment for the attainment of the revolution's stated goals. In November, Republican candidate Ronald Reagan won the presidential elections, defeating Carter. Public since March, the Republican platorm deplored the "Marxist Sandinista takeover of Nicaragua" and its attempts to destabilise the rest of Central America. It stated that the United States had endured a series of humiliations during the Carter administration (the Soviet invasion of Afghanistan, the Iranian revolution and the kidnapping of US citizens by Iranian revolutionaries, the recognition of Panamanian sover-

---

312. Pastor, *Condemned to repetition*, p. 192.

313. Pezzullo, Oral History Program.

eignty over the Panama Canal, among others), and that Reagan would work to reverse that trend. Going back to the Cold War's rhetoric prevalent in Washington before the seventies, Reagan claimed that the Soviet Union underlay all the unrest in the region. Policies and discourse based on these views, rather than local conditions, shaped US-Nicaraguan relations for the following decade.

Ronald Reagan's victory provided the ground for events in Nicaragua and the region even before he took office. Violeta and Robelo's resignations from the GNR in April 1980, though ostensibly caused by the FSLN's enlargement of the Council of State, took place against the publication and diffusion of the Republican Party's platform. As public opinion polls in the United States showed Reagan was likely to win, expectations about the likely future course of US policy entered into the calculations of all actors. Regionally, those who had supported the Nicaraguan revolution feared the effects Reagan's policies would have in Central America. President Aristides Royo of Panama, for example, convoked a meeting of Central American Heads of Government to discuss how to deal with the new US President.[314] "Realists" in Managua believed that Reagan would have to realise that the revolution was a fact and that he would have to find a modus vivendi with Nicaragua. Others in the FSLN opted to establish contacts with the Soviet Union and those countries threatened in Reagan's speeches.[315] Some of the FSLN's opponents perceived it as an opportunity to take actions furthering theifr own purposes, foreseeing they would be welcomed by the incoming administration. Against the background of Reagan's likely triumph, for example, in October important members of the Nicaraguan business community contacted former officers of Somoza's National Guard exiled in Honduras with the aim of overthrowing the FSLN's national directorate.[316] Right after Reagan's victory, even rightist political parties in Nicaragua such as the Social Christians worried about what they saw was the likely course of events.[317]

Handling Reagan's obsessions

Once in power, the Reagan administration put in practice what it had been preaching about US-Nicaraguan relations. Within two days of President Reagan's inauguration, the United States suspended aid to Nicaragua citing a continued flow of arms to the guerrillas in El Salvador, though by that time it had not gathered evidence of the alleged flow of weapons. Diplomacy was not among Washington's chosen instruments in dealing with the GNR. Based on perceptions scarcely investigated or loosely related to Nicaraguan realities, the new administration put all its weight into punishing the Nicaraguan regime. Barely two weeks had passed since it took office when Secretary of State Alexander Haig, in private, claimed before the Honduran Foreign Affairs Minister that the US had "absolutely firm evidence of massive Cuban intervention in El Salvador via Nicaragua" and that

---

314. "Royo: situación 'muy seria' si Reagan gana," *La Prensa* (Managua), 8 October 1980, p. 3.

315. "Belicismo de Reagan nos amenaza," *La Prensa* (Managua), 1 December 1980, p. 1.

316. Everingham, *Revolution and the Multiclass coalition*, p. 175.

317. "Socialcristianos ante el triunfo de Reagan," *La Prensa* (Managua), 12 November 1980, p. 5.

President Reagan would "take whatever steps are necessary to terminate it."[318] Later in March, in public, he said that a "communist strategy" for the "takeover" of Central America had been completed with the "seizure of Nicaragua".[319]

At high levels of the Reagan administration, objective reasoning or respect for Nicaraguan sovereignty were not part of the formulation of policy regarding Central America. No attempt at undertaking a dialogue with the Sandinistas had taken place when the CIA presented proposals for a broad programme of covert actions and President Reagan instructed his government to provide "all forms of training, equipment and related assistance to cooperating governments throughout Central America" to counter "foreign-sponsored subversion and terrorism".[320] By October, the first US-Honduran military manoeuvres took place, intended to threaten Nicaragua and, by November, White House advisor Edwin Meese appeared on TV saying the United States could place a naval blockade or could intervene through a third country to depose the Sandinista government.[321]

The United States adopted an aggressive posture toward Nicaragua despite the evidence showing the viability of a distinct approach. In Nicaragua, powerful institutions such as the private sector, the Catholic Church, independent labour unions, the press, and independent political parties offered alternatives to the FSLN. Policies designed to intimidate the FSLN could have the opposite effect, inclining Nicaragua to the Cuban orbit and thwarting efforts to moderate the political direction of the Sandinista government. Initially, the Reagan administration chose a two-faced policy. In public, it expressed concern for the prospects for political pluralism, respect for human rights and peace in Nicaragua. In private, though violating the Neutrality Act, it encouraged the formation of paramilitary training camps on US territory for launching counter-revolutionary attacks against the GNR and instructed the formation of paramilitary groups on Honduran soil.[322] The Reagan administration sought to find a legal basis for its

---

318. NSA 1991, Document No. 0001266. Memorandum of Secretary Haig's Conversation with Honduran Foreign Minister Elvir, Secret cable No. 030214 from the secretary of State to the American Embassy in Tegucigalpa, dated 5 February 1981.

319. NSA 1991, Document No. 001292. "Press Guidance, March 19," Unclassified Cable No. 071375 from the Secretary of State to the American Embassy in Managua, dated 20 March 1981.

320. NSA 1991, Document No. 001280. "Covert action proposal for Central America," Secret-Sensitive Memorandum for the Secretary from R. C. McFarlane, dated 27 February 1981; NSA 1991, Document No. 001287, Report of the Congressional Committee Investigating the Iran-Contra Affair, "Finding pursuant to Section 662 of the Foreign Assistance Act of 1961, as Amended, Concerning Operations Undertaken by the Central Intelligence Agency in Foreign Countries, Other Than Those Intended Solely for the Purpose of Intelligence Recollection," Secret document, The White House, dated 9 March 1981.

321. Pedro Joaquín Chamorro Barrios, "EEUU repite: el bloqueo posible," La Prensa (Managua), 23 November 1981, pp. 1–2.

322. The government explained that training activities of a military nature were not violating the Neutrality Act because these training camps did not involve the illegal use, possession, transfer, transportation, receipt or making firearms or explosives. NSA 1991, Document No. 001332. "[Title Excised]," Confidential cable No. 132061 from the Secretary of State to the American Embassy in Oslo, dated 21 May 1981; NSA 1991, Document No. 001345. "Letter from Assistant Attorney General, D. Lowell Jensen, to the Honorable Michael D. Barnes,

Nicaraguan policy in the Inter-American Treaty of Reciprocal Assistance (Rio Treaty, signed in 1947). However, it found it very unlikely that it would get the necessary two-thirds majority at the OAS.[323]

The GNR attempted to amend Nicaraguan relations with the Reagan administration in order to improve the ground for the consolidation of the revolution. Before Reagan took office, the FSLN offered the incoming administration help releasing the American hostages taken by the Revolutionary government of Iran.[324] The FSLN faced a fragile economy and launched efforts to attract private investments and maintain a positive international image. In this sense, it invited an influential NGO, the Council of the Americas, to send a mission to help the GNR write a new investment code. Likewise, the GNR made the effort to negotiate with the United Fruit Company the terms for staying in Nicaragua. The GNR, in particular, was worried about Washington's allegations of GRN-FSLN support for Salvadoran guerrillas and the possible cut off US aid. The Nicaraguan regime's plans for 1981 were built on such tenuous grounds that any blow as such, according to Junta member Sergio Ramírez, "could bring the whole house down."[325] The Nicaraguan government was anxious to discuss their uncertainties about the direction of US-Nicaraguan relations and, in this light, the GNR gave particularly warm receptions to congressional delegations visiting Nicaragua.[326] After this threat, state-owned media support for the Salvadoran insurgents decreased markedly in the hope that this signal helped to assure better US-Nicaraguan relations.[327] Subsequently, FSLN leaders refrained from issuing public statements favouring revolution in neighbouring countries. Failure to get positive signals from Washington led the GNR to voice its protests before the Organisation of American States, the United Nations, and the Non-Aligned Movement.

Inside the Reagan administration, an isolated effort took place to reach a negotiated agreement with the Sandinistas, making sense out of the evident difficulties posed by the approach followed regarding Nicaragua. In August 1981 Assistant Secretary Thomas Enders met GNR members to gauge prospects for improving US-Nicaraguan relations. At this point, the US government seems to have seriously considered following the diplomatic tract. While the State Department prepared specific proposals for discussion, the Secretary of State imparted

Chairman of the US House Subcommittee on Interamerican Affairs," dated 24 June 1981.

323. NSA 1991, Document No. 001403. "Nicaragua and the Rio Treaty," Confidential Memorandum from L/ARA-K, Scott Gudgenn to Mr. Braibanti, dated 2 November 1981.

324. NSA 1991, Document No. 001249. "Demarche on Hostages," Limited Official Use Cable No. 00102 from the American Embassy in Managua to the Secretary of State, dated 9 January 1981.

325. NSA 1991, Document No. 001250. "Conversation with Junta member Sergio Ramírez," Secret Cable No. 00103 from the American Embassy in Managua to the Secretary of State, dated 9 January 1981.

326. NSA 1991, Document No. 001256. "CODEL Studds-Edgar-Milulski in Nicaragua," Limited Official Use Cable No. 00288 from the American Embassy in Managua to the Secretary of State, dated 20 January 1981.

327. NSA 1991, Document No. 001272. "Support for El Salvador Insurgency in Soviet, Cuban and Nicaraguan Media," FBIS Analysis Report, dated 10 February 1981.

instructions to lower the tone of statements about the government of Nicaragua and to refrain from making public declarations about these efforts.[328] On 31 August, Enders asked the GNR for a demonstration of good will. On 8 September the US government moved against exile camps and, later, the Sandinistas initiated a strategy of concessions to maintain the momentum of diplomacy. In October, as President Reagan met with President-elect de la Madrid of Mexico, 106 Congressmen urged the White House to back a Mexican-Venezuelan initiative to ameliorate the tension in Central America. Later, on 1 April 1982, the State Department contacted the government of Nicaragua to express its willingness to reach an agreement on issues of concern to both countries. Talks would address the arms flow toward Salvadoran guerrillas, the regional arms race and Nicaraguan fears of suspected US destabilisation efforts. To deal with these topics, the State Department suggested issuing a formal joint statement committing both countries to the principle of non-intervention and to agree on a process and a period for reaching mutually agreed objectives. The OAS, the State Department observed, could be called upon to provide for an effective verification of the agreements.[329] Yet hard-liners inside the Reagan administration boycotted the effort. Enders did not get anything through the administration that resembled anything like a negotiation and, on 16 November, the National Security Council instead approved a covert action programme against the government of Nicaragua.[330]

Neither Congress nor the American public fully backed the Reagan administration's strategy toward Central America. In December 1982, Congress took away some foreign policy prerogatives from the Executive and enacted the Boland Amendment. This barred funding of any activities designed to provoke the overthrow of the government of Nicaragua or a military exchange between that country and Honduras that would "justify" greater US involvement. To avert the congressional ban, the administration chose to pursue its objectives through "covert" activities. The Nicaraguan opposition to the FSLN was nor large nor combative enough for the Reagan administration. Thus since December 1981 it decided to take actions to create paramilitary groups that were to be funded, trained, and supplied to fight the government of Nicaragua.[331] To get it through Congress, the administration argued these actions were aimed at "facilitating the efforts by Nicaraguan democratic leaders to restore the original principles of political pluralism, non-alignment, mixed economy, and free elections to the Nica-

---

328. NSA 1991, Document No. 001373. "Relations with Nicaragua," Secret cable No. 224207 from the Secretary of State to All American Republics diplomatic posts, dated 22 August 1981.

329. NSA 1991, Document No. 001482. "Eight point peace plan," Confidential cable No. 093251 from the Secretary of State to the American Embassy in Managua, dated 8 April 1981.

330. David Ryan, *US-Sandinista diplomatic relations: voice of intolerance*, (Basingstoke: Macmillan, 1995), pp. 18, 22, 37; Pezzullo, Oral History Program.

331. NSA 1991, Document No. 001539, Report of the Congressional Investigating Committee Investigating the Iran-Contra Affairs, "Proposed Covert Action Finding on Nicaragua," Secret action memorandum from Donald Gregg for William P. Clark, National Security Council, dated 12 July 1982.

raguan revolution."[332] Among its stated aims were forcing Nicaragua to respond in "hot pursuit" actions across its borders and thus strain its diplomatic relations with its neighbours; to eliminate civic liberties, and to decrease internal and external support for the regime.[333]

Inside Nicaragua, initially very few actors welcomed the overtly interventionist and aggressive policy of the Reagan administration. The opposition to the FSLN rejected the cut-off of US aid, fearing that increased hardship on top of an already floundering economy would drive the GNR to eliminate freedom of the press and civil liberties and harass a business sector that still controlled sixty percent of the economy.[334] Though, at this time, *La Prensa* had taken distance from the FSLN, for example, it openly criticised Secretary of State Alexander Haig's "interventionist" and "threatening" statements and asked for "respect" toward Nicaraguan sovereignty.[335] Opposition leaders rejected the warpath taken by the Reagan administration. The exceptions were most former National Guard members based in Honduras who saw in US policy an opportunity for them to get back to power.[336]

With US financial and logistic support, former National Guard members created a paramilitary force that in time grew in capability to confront the Sandinistas. The United States, first covertly, and later overtly, paid for their training, maintenance, and supply. The insurgency, nicknamed Contras after being called Contrarrevolucionarios (Counter-revolutionaries), forced the GNR to divert large economic resources to military expenditures. The "Contras" inflicted significant losses on the Sandinista regime. At times, the GNR lost effective control of border areas in northern and southern Nicaragua. The economy experienced losses, direct and indirect, valued at several hundred million dollars. The Contras followed Washington's instructions. Though it remained a force composed of former National Guard officers and enlisted men, for US domestic and international public opinion consumption the Contras were led to adopt "civilian" leaders. Since the Contras owed its existence to the generous funds provided by

---

332. NSA 1991, Document No. 001414. "Finding pursuant to section 662 of the Foreign Assistance Act of 1961, as Amended, Concerning Operations Undertaken by the Central Intelligence Agency in Foreign Countries, Other than Those intended Solely for the Purpose of Intelligence Collection," National Security Council, drafted in July 1982.

333. According to former CIA agent David MacMichael, testifying before the World Court at Le Hague. NSA 1991, Document No. 002560. "ICJ Nicaragua case-Second Day," Limited Official Use Cable No. 06231 from the American Embassy in The Hague to the Secretary of State, dated 13 September 1985.

334. NSA 1991, Document No. 001409. "Nicaragua: conditions and US interests," Issue Brief of the Library of Congress, Congressional Research Service Report IB80013, prepared by Nina Serafino, updated 19 November 1981.

335. Pedro Joaquín Chamorro Barrios, "Los problemas de los nicaraguenses los resolveremos los nicaraguenses," *La Prensa* (Managua), 12 November 1981, p. 1.

336. Former National Guardsmen based in Honduras, with Tegucigalpa's aquiescence, began to undertake sporadic actions against the Sandinista Army. US Embassy's initial instructions on these incursions were to neither "condone" nor "encourage" them, but by local standards, not rejecting these armed actions altogether could be interpreted as if the US was prepared to support them under the right circumstances.

the Reagan administration, it easily mismanaged its resources and developed an excessive and expensive bureaucracy on Honduran soil.

Reagan's policies allowed the GNR to portray itself as caught between the destabilising forces of the Left and Right. The GNR remained firm in its basic orientation, pursuing a comprehensive land reform that gave unused and idle land to peasants, mostly in the form of co-operatives. It also confiscated the properties of exiles, staying away from endorsing the anarchic seizure of businesses and farms.[337] Yet, excesses were indeed committed. Government-sponsored thugs sometimes threatened the population. In any case, the actions brought about by Reagan's foreign policy made it easier to justify the establishment and the extension of states of emergency when confronting hostile acts from the counter-revolutionaries. At the same time, Reagan's foreign policy made it more difficult for Nicaraguans to engage in meaningful dialogue between themselves. Those to the Right could be accused of collaborationism if they chose to engage in talks with the GNR and fail to be invited to join a future government formed under the umbrella of the United States. Those in the government found that no matter how hard they tried to bring opposition leaders to the negotiating table, none of them could command the role of interlocutor.

Hardly a model of democracy, Nicaragua did enjoy a large degree of pluralism. The GNR was far from showing an unswerving commitment to the evolution of an authoritarian Marxist state. The FSLN avoided a complete crackdown on the opposition, either because it waited for the right circumstances or because it sought to present a pluralistic façade to its allies in Latin America and Western Europe. Whatever the reason, the private sector, independent political parties, labour unions, and the Church continued to operate, albeit with some restrictions that were understandable for a country that was undergoing a war sponsored by a foreign power. The government owned two of the three newspapers and both TV channels, confiscated from Somoza's estate. Yet despite some temporary closing and a practice of censorship that augmented with the increase in Contra hostilities, most of the time the independent newspaper *La Prensa* continued to report news as it saw it. The Council of State, gathering Labour, Business, Peasant, Church, and Political Party representatives, allowed discussions to take place before taking important decisions. Though the Council may have provided a pluralistic façade to the Sandinistas, it also served to give exposure to opposition leaders who consistently pointed out flaws in GNR policies.

The Sandinistas had been profoundly affected by the perception that the United States was largely responsible for the continuation of the Somoza dynasty. In adopting an intolerant, aggressive policy toward Nicaragua, the Reagan administration deepened the FSLN's mistrust of the United States and their desire to seek Cuban and Soviet Union support to counterbalance Washington's influence. The development of bilateral Soviet-Nicaraguan relations, however, remained low-key. US delays in extending aid gave way to an increase in Soviet

---

337. NSA 1991, Document No. 001354. "Fernando Chamorro seeks Asylum in Costa Rica," Confidential cable No. 03059 from the American Embassy in Managua to the Secretary of State, dated 14 July 1981.

bloc aid and delegations to and from Nicaragua. Moscow increased economic and military aid, yet it remained reluctant to defray the cost of "another Cuba" in the Americas.

The Reagan administration oversimplified the events and was uninterested in the facts, unless they could be isolated and used to show it was on the right track with respect to Nicaragua.[338] However small this Eastern-bloc presence may have been even in relation to the aid provided by other Western countries, the Reagan administration repeatedly portrayed Nicaragua as a Communist State that defied the peace of the hemisphere. The presence or absence of democracy in Nicaragua was the rhetoric instrument that allowed the government of the United States to promote a policy aimed at overthrowing a government it did not control.

To gather public support, the White House undertook a propaganda initiative under the National Security Council called "Public Diplomacy."[339] This meant increasing the rhetoric against the government of Nicaragua, presenting the FSLN as a national security threat, and painting a better picture of the counterrevolutionaries than was warranted by their merits. The strategy included programming speeches, TV appearances, and other measures where these could have the greatest potential impact on the audience, for example, such as just before Congress voted on the aid packages to the Contras. Success in this "public diplomacy" effort was deemed essential because "our ability to gain public support for our Central American policy will contribute immeasurably to our ability to achieve the substantive objectives of that policy."[340] Nicaragua was of "strategic importance" to the United States, because it bordered the Caribbean, which Reagan considered "the lifeline to the outside world."[341]

Beyond the United States

The Nicaraguan regime could not have endured such an obstinate US policy had it not been for the political and financial backing it received from multiple international sources. Early on, as bilateral talks did not seem to work, the GNR voiced its protests to multilateral bodies such as the Organisation of American States and the United Nations, from where Nicaragua frequently received moral

---

338. Congress identified weaknesses in US intelligence performance on Central America in 1982. This included the occasional oversimplification of events, suggesting that "the environment in which analytic thought and decisions occur" had been under pressure "to reinforce policy rather than to inform it." NSA 1991, Document No. 001598. "US Intelligence Performance on Central America: Achievements and selected instances of concern," US House of Representatives, Permanent Select Committee on Intelligence, Subcommittee on Oversight and Evaluation Staff Report, dated 22 September 1982.

339. NSA 1991, Document No. 001625. "NSDD-77 on Public Diplomacy," Memorandum for Charles Hill, NSSD Executive Secretariat, Department of State, dated 14 January 1983.

340. NSA 1991, Document No. 001750. "New Coordinator for Public Diplomacy for Central America," Limited Official Use cable from the Acting Secretary to all American Republic Diplomatic Posts and all OECD Capitals, dated 5 July 1983.

341. NSA 1991, Document No. 001683. "Central America: Defending Our Vital Interests," Address by President Reagan before a joint session of Congress, April 27 1983.

and political support. Throughout this period, the international environment turned favourable for the Sandinistas. Between 1981 and 1982, Socialists took power in France, Spain, Sweden, Greece and Austria. In Latin America a leftist coalition governed Bolivia and, as transitions toward democracy took hold, governments started to assert themselves in the international arena, taking distance from Washington in several issues but in particular on Nicaragua's right to self-determination. In January 1983, Mexico, Colombia, Venezuela and Panama formed the Contadora Group to promote a negotiated solution to the Central American imbroglio, precisely in response to the increase of regional tensions provoked by Reagan's policies. In 1984, the new governments of Guatemala and Costa Rica, who had backed the Reagan administration's efforts against Nicaragua, took distance from the Reagan administration. Inside the United States, the American public increasingly took to the streets to remind their authorities that they did not wish to be led to "another Vietnam." The United States cut off aid and enacted economic sanctions against the Sandinistas, but other countries in Western Europe, Latin America, the Non-Aligned world and the Soviet bloc increasingly came to the rescue.

Of these, the Contadora Group was the most effective in providing a buffer against what seemed an unavoidable path to war. Contadora had been formed in January 1983, building upon previous Latin American experiences to negotiate and express, outside the OAS framework, common positions regarding issues of concern to Latin America.[342] It stressed the need for dialogue, recommended removing the East-West prism used by the Reagan administration to interpret events in the region and underlined the socio-economic roots of the Central American conflict. Later the undertaking encompassed measures in the areas of demilitarisation, non-intervention, self-determination, and democratisation, and was to be applied to all the Central American countries. Thanks to the regional consensus-building efforts in favour of peace carried out by the Group, it put additional constraints on the Reagan administration from embarking on a region-wide conflagration that would have put the incipient Latin American democracies at stake. Instead, the Reagan administration worked to dissuade Central Americans from engaging in a series of negotiations that would have provided legitimacy to the Sandinista Government. Reaching an agreement under Contadora's auspices would have implied ceasing support for the Contras and dismantling US military bases in El Salvador and Honduras. Contadora received the backing of US allies in Western Europe and important segments of the US Congress and media, obliging the Reagan administration to portray its policies as being consistent with the Group's aims. Thereafter, the Reagan administration was compelled to adopt a semblance of moderation to gain Congressional and US public opinion's support or acquiescence for its isthmian policies.

While Contadora worked to present a viable framework to negotiate a lasting peace, another regional event altered the ground for political decision-making

---

342. The creation of the Union of Banana Exporting Countries (UPEB), the Panama Canal negotiations, and the creation of the Latin American Economic System (SELA) are among the most relevant regional experiences.

in Nicaragua. In October 1983, the United States invaded the small island of Grenada in the Caribbean, thwarting a Marxist-led coup against the government of Maurice Bishop. The United States used the protection of US citizens as a pretext for the military intervention. Most importantly, the invasion signalled Washington's determination to use force unilaterally to deal with regimes that defied US pre-eminence in the region. In particular, the GNR's anxiety grew because of the invasion. In the aftermath of Grenada, the GNR's apprehensions reached near-hysterical levels. The government ensured all foreigners were properly documented to make sure the United States could not use the treatment or protection of American citizens as a pretext for an invasion.[343] The proportion of the budget dedicated to defence had declined since 1981, but since this event, it was increased dramatically.[344] In multilateral forums, GRN leaders repeatedly expressed fears of an imminent US invasion, expressed Nicaragua's willingness to negotiate and turned to Contadora with gestures of peace.[345]

The Grenada invasion produced important shifts in Sandinista policy. While the political opposition felt reassured of US support, the Nicaraguan regime engaged in talks with the Church, the political opposition, *La Prensa*, businessmen and non-governmental organisations. The GNR sought to reduce domestic tensions and to reaffirm its commitment to holding elections in 1985.[346] Likewise, the GNR sent back to Cuba some 1200 technicians and athletes and 1000 advisors in the fields of defence, health, education, and culture, while the FMLN, the Salvadoran guerrilla group, sent away its Nicaragua-based personnel to Mexico and Panama.[347] Thereafter, an effort to "correct" the "errors" of the revolution took place in all fields of government policy.

All these international efforts and circumstances provided an alternative path for the Reagan administration to influence the direction of political affairs in Nicaragua in favour of the institutionalisation of democratic procedures and practices. Whatever the motivations, the Sandinistas had frequently and publicly declared their intention to uphold pluralism and had conducted efforts at cre-

---

343. NSA 1991, Document No. 001890. "Registration of foreigners in Nicaragua," Limited Official Use cable No. 05420 from the American Embassy in Managua to the Secretary of State, dated 22 November 1983.

344. Defence expenditures went from 22% of the national budget in 1981 to 18.2% in 1983. The trend was reversed after this event, reaching 24.1% in 1984 and 34.1% in 1985. "Coyuntura: se inicia la recta final," *Envío* 6 (74, August 1987), p. 6.

345. NSA 1991, Document No. 001882. "GRN leaders stress fears of imminent US invasion," Confidential cable No. 05172 from the American Embassy in Managua to the Secretary of State, dated 9 November 1983; NSA 1991, Document No. 001888. "Nicaraguan officials on CIA, Peace, Negotiations," Confidential cable No. 05371 from the American Embassy in Managua to the Secretary of State, dated 19 November 1983.

346. NSA 1991, Document No. 001892. "GRN (illegible) political parties," Confidential Confidential cable No. 05460 from the American Embassy in Managua to the Secretary of State, dated 25 November 1983.

347. NSA 1991, Document No. 001896. "La Prensa on Sandinista Policy Changes," Unclassified cable No. 05508 from the American Embassy in Managua to the Secretary of State, dated 28 November 1983.

ating participatory political institutions—though they did not follow Western democratic models. In addition, relevant non-Sandinista political actors inside Nicaragua had chosen to take part in these interactions. If the aim had been to foster democracy, the US could have supported this process. But the undeclared goal was to preclude the consolidation of a regime it did not control. Therefore, the Reagan administration adopted a deceptive policy designed to overcome the limitations imposed by Congress on the use of funds against a government with which it was not formally at war.

The US Congress became an important limitation on US policy toward Nicaragua. Congress resisted President Reagan's advocacy of more forceful measures in Central America such as military assistance and covert operations. In March 1984, Congress' resistance grew as a result of the discovery that, approved by President Reagan, the CIA had placed magnetic mines in the harbour of the Nicaraguan port of Corinto.[348] Domestically, this discovery also attracted bad publicity for the Reagan administration. This action was rejected world-wide, with the exception of a few US allies, and provoked international calls in support of the rule of international law and of the Contadora process.[349] The Reagan administration, however, did not alter its course. Rather, when the Nicaraguan government took the case to the World Court, the Reagan administration announced it would not accept the jurisdiction of the Court in Central American cases. Most importantly, this action infuriated Congressmen, because it was a clear violation of the Boland Amendment, barring the use of funds, directly or indirectly, for military or paramilitary operations against the government of Nicaragua. This violation of the law merited an inquiry and possibly an impeachment of the President, but 1984 was an electoral year and Reagan was perhaps too popular to undertake such actions without provoking an electoral impact contrary to the political opposition.[350]

Among the measures to overcome this constraint, the Reagan administration appointed a bipartisan commission, headed by former Secretary of State Henry Kissinger, with the declared aim of formulating a policy toward Central America that would have broad support. The creation of the Commission was an element of a public affairs/legislative action plan designed to develop bipartisan support and "the provision of adequate resources" for US policies and to enhance US military presence and capabilities in Central America.[351] In this

---

348. NSA 1991, Document No. 001994. "Special Activities in Nicaragua," Top Secret Memorandum from Oliver North and Constantine Menges for Robert C. Mc Farlane, National Security Council, dated 2 March 1984.

349. After the fact, the United States attempted to justify this act of war as an exercise in its right of self-defence recognised in the UN Charter and in the Rio Treaty. However, no government other than the United States and Central American proxies took this argument seriously.

350. Despite this "infuriation" in Congress, the Reagan administration went on with its covert actions. In September 1984, the public learned that the CIA had prepared an Assassination Manual for the Contras advising the selective use of violence to "neutralise" carefully selected targets.

351. NSA 1991, Document No. 001758. "Central America." Top Secret White House Memo-

sense, Reagan also exploited the alleged Soviet threat to turn Congress' rejection of his aid requests into a political liability, accusing them of provoking a "second Cuba." In view of the difficulties in obtaining appropriations to carry out the Nicaraguan covert action project, the United States sought funds or supplies from third countries. These agreed to provide support to the Contras directly or through Honduras or Costa Rica.[352] To get funds approved by Congress, the Reagan administration argued they were not intended to destabilise or over-throw the government of Nicaragua but to induce it to enter into negotiations with the armed opposition and to cease their support to insurgencies in the region.[353] How did supporting the armed effort against the GNR would achieve that objective was never explained. It also engaged in talks with the Nicaraguan government precisely when Congress considered terminating Contra funding, but it ceased them when it did not serve the Reagan administration's purpose, blaming the Sandinistas' intransigence.[354]

The first Nicaraguan elections

In this context, the electoral process in Nicaragua could not avoid being the sub-ject of external influences and events. Since 1980, the GRN had announced it would hold elections in 1985. In February 1984, due to the increase in hostilities by the Contras, the Council of State resolved to postpone the elections, but the GRN revoked this decision and decided to advance them instead. The elections were re-scheduled for November 1984, precisely two days before the presiden-tial and congressional elections to be held in the United States. This decision sought to diminish the possibility of US military intervention in the last year of the Reagan administration. It also aimed at obtaining a larger international legitimacy for the government if Reagan were re-elected and to lay the ground for an understanding between the United States and Nicaragua in the case of a Democrat winning the Presidency.[355] Despite efforts made by the political oppo-sition, following Washington's instructions to postpone the elections, the GRN remained firm in its intention to hold them on the agreed date.

---

randum for the Honorable George P. Shultz, Secretary of State; Caspar Weinberger, Secretary of Defense; William J. Casey, Director of Central Intelligence, and General John W. Vessey, Chairman of the Joint Chiefs of Staff, dated 12 July 1983.

352. NSA 1991, Document No. 002027. "Supplemental Assistance to Nicaragua Program," Secret memorandum from the Director of Central Intelligence, William Casey, for the As-sistant to the President for National Security Affairs, Robert Mc Farlane, dated 27 March 1984.

353. NSA 1991, Document No. 002037. Secret letter from Robert C. McFarlane for the Honorable Howard Baker, Majority Leader, US Senate, dated 5 April 1984. The legality of the Reagan administration's actions centered on their purpose (avowedly not intended for overthrowing the Nicaraguan government), rather than the recipient's purpose, which was obviously so.

354. NSA 1991, Document No. 002127. "Central America," Secret Minutes NSC/ICS 400616 from the National Security Planning Group Meeting on 25 June 1984.

355. "El proceso electoral avanza entre grandes dificultades: Análisis de coyuntura del 5 de febrero al 5 de marzo," *Envío* 3 (33, March 1984), p. 3-a.

Holding free elections was a new experience in Nicaragua. Since 1983 the Council of State had held sessions to issue an electoral law, where all political parties discussed and agreed the norms that would rule the electoral process and the composition of the Electoral Tribunal. Nicaraguans would choose not only a President and a Vicepresident, but also a National Assembly that would act as a Constituent Assembly until a new Constitution was drafted. The political opposition inside the Council proposed and obtained a political amnesty for all who had left Nicaragua after the revolution. This included those who were involved in armed activities against the GNR, with the exception of former National Guard officers and Contra leaders.

The GNR made an effort to make sure that the political opposition felt confident about the process. It agreed to provide free time on state-owned TV and Radio stations, increased by fifty percent the subsidies for the political campaign, and agreed to incorporate the losing Presidential tickets as members of the National Assembly. It also lifted the state of emergency that had been in place since March 1982 and agreed to allow foreign observers to the elections. However, a segment of the political opposition, not the largest but the most heard by Washington, boycotted the elections.

This segment of the opposition, gathered along the Nicaraguan Democratic Coordinatorship (CDN) and led by former Junta member Arturo Cruz (who had resigned as the GNR's Ambassador to Washington), chose to side with the Reagan administration rather than taking the opportunity to strengthen the democratic process. Few observers, including the US Embassy in Managua, doubted the FSLN would win. The latter was of the opinion that "the experience of undergoing a national election will have a salutary effect on Nicaragua's disjointed opposition and perhaps, the FSLN itself." Yet both the Reagan administration and the CDN worked to debase them.

The CDN conditioned its participation in the elections to the implementation of a series of measures that more resembled its political platform than a list of necessary conditions for holding a free and fair electoral process. They included, for instance, the elimination of the drafting and the holding of a dialogue with the Contras. The CDN's abstention was backed by powerful organisations such as COSEP and the Catholic Church. *La Prensa* abandoned pretended objectivity and campaigned against those presidential candidates who did not abide by the boycott and against the electoral process as a whole. Mediated by the Socialist International, to which the FSLN adscribed, the GNR negotiated with Cruz the CDN's participation in the elections. If Cruz got the Contras to agree to a cease-fire, the GRN would agree to postpone the elections until January 1985 and provide all the electoral guarantees requested by the CDN. The negotiations broke out precisely when it was made public in Washington that Reagan had an advantage of thirteen percentage points over Mondale, the Democrat's presidential candidate.

Neither Cruz nor the Reagan administration had any intention of allowing the Sandinistas to legitimise themselves through an electoral process that the FSLN was likely to win. There was no evidence that Cruz had a popular following, but the Reagan administration portrayed it as the only legitimate opposition to the FSLN. In the six months prior to the elections, the Reagan administration used a combination of diplomatic, military and economic pressures to delegitimise the elections in the eyes of the US public and the world. To provide greater weight to the CDN's boycott, the US Embassy worked to convince other presidential candidates to drop out of the race. Embassy staff made visits to registered political parties to seek their abstention from the elections. According to a Congressional investigation, the CIA made cash payments to press and to urge political parties to abstain from the elections.[356] Independent Liberal Party's presidential candidate Virgilio Godoy (who had served as Labour Minister during the GNR's term in power), for instance, was pressured by the US Ambassador to abandon the electoral contest a few days before the elections. In exchange, the United States offered Godoy the opportunity of leading a future coalition of political opposition parties in elections that would be held later and in which he would have ensured victory.[357] As the elections approached, the Reagan administration invented an international "Mig" crisis claiming Nicaragua was about to import advanced Soviet combat aircraft, to make people forget that Nicaragua was undergoing an electoral process and to portray the FSLN as warlike, not a political party that attempted to obtain popular approval through elections. The FSLN ticket, led by Junta President Daniel Ortega, won by a large majority. However, these results were virtually ignored by the US and Western European press, bypassing the fact that independent international observers noted that the elections were free from major irregularities, showed the existence of political pluralism and a high rate of voter turnout.[358]

Despite Washington's and the CDN's boycott, the elections of 1984 served to provide a greater degree of institutionalisation to the Nicaraguan political process. It meant a step forward toward the transformation of a political system that at times seemed to be based on the FSLN's interpretations of the popular will into a variant of democracy. This process had a positive effect on the FSLN, who learned to become a political party and abide by the rules of the political system. However, it had a negative impact on the opposition, which grew dependent of the United States and remained disjointed in the years ahead. It also worked to lessen the international pressures on the FSLN to hold their 1979 promises. But by no means did it lessen the Reagan administration's resolve to provoke a regime change displacing the Sandinistas. Thus holding the elections, however free and fair, did not reduce the uncertainties of the transition process they were supposed to alleviate.

356. NSA 1991, Document No. 003179. "U.S. efforts to promote democracy in Nicaragua: Choices for Congress on covert and overt aid," US Congress, Arms Control and Foreign Policy Caucus Issue Preview dated 3 August 1989.

357. According to Godoy's Vice-presidential candidate. "La recta final de las elecciones," *Envío* 4 (41, November 1984), p. 4-b.

358. Latin American Studies Association Delegation to Observe the Nicaraguan General Election of 4 November 1984, "The electoral process in Nicaragua: domestic and international influences," (Pittsburgh: LASA, 19 November 1984).

Transition under siege

The Nicaraguan transition not only had to endure all the uncertainties and complexities of a political process led by a group with ambivalent sentiments toward a representative democracy but also adverse acts from the region's major power. The November elections held both in Nicaragua and in the United States could have brought a new start to a process that required nourishing by all the concerned parties, particularly Washington. From the Reagan administration's viewpoint, however, the occasion served to bring the hostilities to new heights. In the post-Vietnam era, direct use of US force in a protracted war was not an option, though it may have been palatable to President Reagan. Hence, between continuing to support the Contras and recognising the existence of a regime it did not control but that attempted to operate within democratic principles, the National Security Council saw no other option than the first.[359]

Among the first measures in this direction during its second term in office, the Reagan administration made sure its Central American allies understood its determination to "prevent the consolidation of Marxist-Leninist rule" in Nicaragua.[360] Publicly, Reagan himself announced in January 1985 his intention to remove the Nicaraguan government "in its present structure," calling the new Nicaraguan government "Communist" and the Contras "freedom fighters" who had fought the Somoza dictatorship.[361] Pressured by western allies and by Congress to reach a negotiated solution in Central America, the Reagan administration's public rhetoric supported Contadora, but portrayed aid to the Contras as needed for strengthening the allies' negotiating position. In practice, it refused to enter into negotiations with the Sandinistas because it assumed that the FSLN was Communist and Communists did not abide by agreements.[362] Negotiations with the Sandinistas would legitimise them and make it more difficult to eliminate them. According to the NSC, previous requests for funding the Contras had been limited, thus creating the belief that the threat to US security was also small. Thus, to be more credible, not only did the perceived threat have to be "reoriented" but also further requests had to be substantially increased[363]

Inside the United States, the "Public Diplomacy" effort against the Sandinistas went on but with a higher level of sophistication, in line with the ad-

---

359. NSA 1991, Document No. 002343. "Nicaragua options," Top secret memorandum from Oliver North to Robert McFarlane, National Security Council, dated 15 January 1985.

360. NSA 1991, Document No. 002356. "Central America trip: Observations and conclusions," Secret Information Memorandum for the President from Robert McFarlane, National Security Council, dated 31 January 1985.

361. Ryan, *US-Sandinista diplomatic relations*, p. 104.

362. According to the US Department of Defense, containment was not possible with the Communist FSLN because Communists had "massively violated the 1953 Korean armistice, the 1954 Geneva accords on Indochina, the 1962 Declaration on the neutrality of Laos, and the 1973 Paris agreements on Ending the War and restoring peace in Vietnam." NSA 1991, Document No. 002758. "Prospects for Containment of Nicaragua's Communist Government," Department of Defense Report, dated May 1986.

363. NSA 1991, Document No. 002343. "Nicaragua options," Top secret memorandum from Oliver North to Robert McFarlane, National Security Council, dated 15 January 1985.

ministration's aim to get funding for the Contras. The "educational campaign" carried out by the White House intended to breed the notion that the Contras were the equivalent of the United States' founding fathers and that the amount of aid requested was so small that it hardly mattered. It also aimed at presenting the Sandinistas as puppets of the Soviets, racist, human rights violators, drug traffickers, and international terrorists.[364] The strategy comprised work by Psychological Operations Personnel from the Department of Defense.[365] It also incorporated "white propaganda" operations such as preparing op-ed pieces for the Washington Post and the New York Times, written by the staff of the Public Diplomacy office but signed by Robelo and Cruz, among others.[366] Since the facts sometimes mismatched the administration's statements, events were "researched" and "reported" to support the administration's case.[367] In sum, it implied giving "information" of whatever the administration thought it was needed to convince Congressmen of the need for continuing to grant aid to the Contras.

To increase the credibility of its allegations, in April 1985 the Reagan administration enacted further economic sanctions against Nicaragua. In the context of the Latin American indebtness issue, the FSLN used the sanctions to plea for national unity and promote the image of Nicaragua being bullied by the United States. Abroad, the FSLN successfully used it to tackle Western and Latin American capitals in search of economic aid. International attention toward the regime increased along the widespread international criticism of the sanctions. The government could not crack down on the internal opposition without downgrading its hopes of western economic and political assistance, despite the fact that some of its most prominent members, such as Archbishop Obando y Bravo, declared their support for the measure. The trade embargo did not produce significant economic disruptions because the Government had substantially decreased Nicaragua's trade relations with the United States.

The Reagan administration may not have achieved the overthrow of the FSLN and the establishment of a regime it would control, but it substantially altered the Nicaraguan government's domestic and international policies and priorities. The Sandinistas had to allocate increasing amounts of resources to fighting

---

364. NSA 1991, Document No. 002394. "Public Diplomacy Action Plan, Support for the White House Educational campaign," Confidential Project Proposal-sensitive document, The White House, Office for Public Diplomacy, dated 12 March 1985.

365. NSA 1991, Document No. 002644. "Denial of detail of personnel by DoD," Memorandum from Otto Reich to NSC-Mr. Walt Raymond, Coordinator for Public Diplomacy for Latin America and the Caribbean, dated 5 January 1986.

366. NSA 1991, Document No. 002396. "White Propaganda Operation," Confidential Eyes-Only Memorandum from Jonathan Miller to Pat Buchanan, Assistant to the President and Director of Communications, dated 13 March 1985.

367. NSA 1991, Document No. 002616. "Nicaragua: telling it like it is," Secret memorandum from Robert Mc Farlane for the Secretary of State, the Secretary of Defense, the Director of Central Intelligence and the Chairman of the Joint Chiefs of Staff, The White House, dated 11 November 1985.

the insurgency, in detriment of other investment programmes.[368] Domestically, US foreign policy obliged the FSLN to be very careful about its actions, because their slightest departure from democratic practice was and could be used against it. For instance, the government suspended civic liberties in October 1985, and justified it as necessary to fight the insurgency. However, it was used by the Reagan administration to substantiate its request for additional funds to the Contras and was sharply criticised by the international press. In the international realm, US foreign policy forced the Nicaraguan government to seek to influence US Congress in their vote on the aid packages for the Contras. As dates for the vote on Contra funding in Congress approached, for example, at least once the government's censorship of La Prensa sharply decreased. After an uproar mounted when visiting Moscow as Congress voted on a Contra aid package, President Daniel Ortega had to be very careful about the political allegiance of the foreign statesmen he chose to visit. To allure international opinion, the Nicaraguan government renounced a substantial portion of Cuban military instructors and declared moratoriums on the acquisition of sophisticated armaments.[369] For years, the FSLN had resisted the opposition's and the Reagan administration's call to negotiate directly with the leadership of the Contras, arguing they would rather do so directly with the government of the United States. To take ground from the Reagan administration's arguments, however, the Nicaraguan government was forced to engage in direct talks with the Contra leadership—though only after it inflicted the Contras large losses and recognising that, as long as Honduras provided them safe haven, they would not disappear.

Naturally, so much attention was put on Capitol Hill regarding the funding of the Contras that Congress became an influential actor in the course of political events in Nicaragua. The Reagan administration invested too heavily in the military option and ignored the work of the civic opposition. Often, US foreign policy did not appear to have clearly defined objectives and seemed to have taken a too visible and bilateral approach. Evidently, the Reagan administration had been obstructing the multilateral diplomatic efforts of the region and had violated Congressional restrictions on the use of Federal funds. The unilateral US policy using armed Contra forces, conducted initially without the full knowledge of Congress and later with only mixed, limited support, had failed, creating a political space for Congress to redirect US policy toward Nicaragua.

Since the inception of the Contadora initiative, many members of Congress favoured it as a peaceful alternative to the confrontational approach followed by the Reagan administration. In the context of the scandals grown out of the mining of Nicaraguan harbours and the preparation and publication of the "Assassination Manual" by the CIA, Congress began to take the formulation of policy in its own hands. In May 1985, Congress barred the Reagan adminis-

---

368. So much pressure was put on the Nicaraguan economy that the annual inflation rate reached 1200 percent in 1987.

369. NSA 1991, Document No. 002376. "GON statement February 27 on the international situation," Unclassified cable No. 01233 from the American Embassy in Managua to the Secretary of State, dated 28 February 1985.

tration from entering into formal or implied agreements with US aid-recipient countries conditioning such aid on providing funds to the Nicaraguan rebels. In July, it declared its support for the Contadora effort and authorised expenses by the State Department for the implementation of an agreement based on Contadora's document of objectives. It also began to investigate improper activities by the CIA and find violations to the Boland amendment.[370] Later, in 1987, it shut down the Office for Public Diplomacy after it found out that it violated the law prohibiting the use of funds for propaganda purposes not authorised by Congress.[371] A report on a visit to the region led by Senators D'Amato and Bird concluded that the United States had not been actively supporting democratic institutions because the administration had focused on pressing all governments to fall behind the policy of destabilising the Sandinista regime.[372] Thus Congress devised measures in support of a long-term policy including support for the civic opposition and the private sector. However, it continued to provide "non-lethal" aid to the Nicaraguan rebels, keeping the Reagan administration's military option alive.

From late 1986 to early 1988, the Reagan administration was further debilitated by a series of scandals. The first was the downing of a C-123 supply plane by the Sandinistas which, despite US denials, was found to be part of a network co-ordinated by Colonel Olliver North at the NSC. Then there was the killing of an American citizen by Contra forces, followed by the findings on the administration's deals with Iran to supply the Contras. In November 1986, Democrats won majorities in both Houses of Congress, thus increasing their ability to work for an alternative approach toward the region.

Within the United States, other circumstances and trends significantly contributed to alter the course of what seemed to be the likely course of events were the Reagan administration been left unchecked. Reagan's policy toward Nicaragua remained unpopular among the American public, some of whom feared they were being led to another Vietnam, becoming very active against Congressional approval of additional funds to the Contras. Church and church-supported groups actively opposed US policy toward Central America, in particular and most effectively by those based in Washington, DC. In addition, the media became wary of the Reagan administration's claims, promptly uncovering embarrasing evidence of its deceptive involvement with the Contras.

A series of circumstances beyond the United States and Nicaragua contributed to improve the international environment for the Nicaraguan transition. As

---

370. The CIA advised Contra leaders on how and when to lobby Congress to obtain appropiations for themselves, contrary to the anti-lobby restrictions in the use of federal funds. NSA 1991, Document No. 002626. "GAO/NSLAD-86-13 Allegation of Lobbying Assistance," General Accounting Office Report, dated 5 December 1985.

371. NSA 1991, Document No. 003031. Letter to the Honorable Jack Brooks, Chairman, Committee on Government Operations, House of Representatives, from the Comptroller General of the United States, dated 30 September 1987.

372. NSA 1991, Document No. 0028.58. "Report on trip to Central American countries, July 5–16," Memorandum from Senator Dick D'Amato to Senator Robert Byrd, US Senate, dated 5 August 1986.

time passed, practically every state in Western Europe (including the Vatican) and Latin America, plus Canada and Australia, among others, formally requested the Reagan administration to desist from the military option regarding Central America. Guatemala, who faced an insurgency with sanctuaries in Mexico, broke the northern Central American bloc that the Reagan administration had built up against Nicaragua, adopting a policy of neutrality toward the Central American conflict. With the administration of Christian Democrat President Vinicio Cerezo, since 1985 Guatemala expanded the policy of its military predecessor of approaching Mexico in relation to Contadora. Efforts by the Contadora Group itself were strengthened with the incorporation of a "Support Group" composed of Peru, Argentina, Brazil and Uruguay, countries who had recently undergone democratic transitions. Later, their work was aided by the addition, despite Washington's protest, of the Secretary Generals of the UN and the OAS.

These international events and the impasse the Reagan Administration went through in relation to funding the Contras provided the ground for Central American Heads of State to follow Guatemala's and later Costa Rica's initiatives toward peace. For the first time since the Nicaraguan revolution, Central American Presidents met with their Nicaraguan counterpart in May 1986 in Esquipulas, Guatemala. Though the United States pressured President Cerezo to make sure nothing emerged from the meeting that Nicaragua could sign, the Declaration—signed by all Central American Presidents—expressed their will to agree to the signing of the Contadora Act and established regular Presidential summits as a vehicle to analyse and seek solutions to the region's most urgent problems.[373] These efforts gained strength in Central America and in the US Congress when in April 1987 President Oscar Arias of Costa Rica reformulated Contadora's proposals. Based largely on Contadora and the proposals by the Democratic leadership in the US Congress, the Arias Plan deferred action on its most difficult provisions (reduction or prohibition of foreign troops, limitation of arms imports, foreign military bases and exercises). It also committed all Central American governments to hold elections, respect freedom of the press and assembly and undertake national dialogues.[374] Though Reagan rejected and boycotted Arias' initiative and those that followed, this plan became the focus of the peace efforts in the region for the following years.

Allowing democratic institutions to evolve

This combination of US and other international influences, along the Contra's continued ineffectiveness, improved the environment for a peaceful transition in Nicaragua. Following the trend initiated with the first Heads of States' meeting at Esquipulas and the Arias Peace Plan, in August 1987 the Central American Presidents met again in Esquipulas to sign a peace agreement requiring each

---

373. Ryan, *US-Sandinista diplomatic relations*, pp. 122–123.

374. NSA 1991, Document No. 002976. "Issue Preview: Congress and the Arias Peace Plan," US Congress, Arms Control and Foreign Policy Caucus Report dated 27 April 1987; "Una propuesta que desarma: análisis de coyuntura del 5 de mayo al 6 de junio de 1986," *Envío* 5 (60, June 1986), pp. 1a–2a.

In the Shadow of the United States

country, within ninety days, to call for a cease-fire, end support for guerrilla forces fighting in the area, and decree a general amnesty, all of which would be discussed within national reconciliation commissions and verified by international observers. The accord also committed governments to hold municipal, legislative and presidential elections within their own constitutional frameworks and timetables.[375] Following the agreement, the Sandinista government created the National Reconciliation Commission, lifted censorship of the press, opened *La Prensa* and *Radio Catolica*, and called for a national dialogue with the political opposition. In January 1988, at a similar meeting held in San Jose, President Ortega announced his government would hold talks directly with the leadership of the Contras. The Reagan administration went on with pressuring its Central American allies to blame Nicaragua for the alleged lack of progress in fulfilling Esquipulas' aims, threatening to curtail aid if, as a result of Esquipulas, Congress cut off funding the Contras.[376] But reconciliation in Nicaragua continued: in March, with Archbishop Obando y Bravo as mediator, and after an offensive that caused more than one thousand casualties to the Contras, government and Contra representatives met in the Nicaraguan town of Sapoa. Not participating in the dialogue with the Sandinistas would have diminished the Contras' leeway in the United States at a time where Congress and public opinion centred their attention on the fulfilment of the peace accords. There Sandinistas and Contras signed an agreement commiting the insurgency to demobilize and the government to decree a general amnesty. It included a petition for humanitarian aid, to be delivered through neutral organisations, to help relocate the Contras to Nicaraguan territory. Encouraged by the Reagan administration, however, hard-liners within the Contra leadership led by Enrique Bermudez disavowed the Sapoa agreements. Despite the progress in reconciliation, up until the last months of its second term the Reagan administration persevered in its effort to provide lethal and non-lethal aid for the Contras.

The international environment in which the Nicaraguan peace process would continue did not clear until the United States held its Presidential and Congressional elections in November 1988. Talks between Sandinistas and Contras broke up in June without agreement, because a faction of the Contra leadership tried to buy time until the November elections. This group expected the victory of the Republican Presidential candidate and Reagan's Vicepresident, George Bush, to improve the prospects for maintaining themselves as a cohesive paramilitary force against the FSLN. Congress, no less disrespectful of Nicaraguan sovereignty, however, took the lead in defining US policy toward Nicaragua. In January, it established conditions to cease funding the Contras such as the abolition of the draft, absolute freedom of the press and the right to strike and the non-discrimination toward Miskito indians.[377] In October, it appropriated two million dollars for the promotion of democracy in Nicaragua, provided its use

---

375. "Esquipulas II: Gran paso hacia la paz," *Envío* 6 (75, September 1987), p. 1.

376. Honduras and El Salvador complied with the Reagan administration's wishes. "Esquipulas III: Jaque a la guerra," *Envío* 7 (80, February 1988), p. 4.

377. "Reagan persiste: se dificultan los diálogos," *Envío* 7 (79, January 1988), p. 2.

was consistent with the Sapoa and Esquipulas accords.[378] But at the same time it provided 27 million dollars in non-lethal, "logistical" support for the Contras, provided the CIA did not participate in its disbursement. The election of Bush did not mean a dramatic policy change. In April 1989 he extended the trade embargo against Nicaragua and continued to fund the Contras. Unlike Reagan, however, Bush sought to conciliate Congress and design a strategy in tune with the regional efforts toward peace. The Bush administration made an effort to stop the demobilisation of the Contras, but Central American Presidents went on with their plans anyway, agreeing at Tela, Honduras, to finish the process by December 1989.[379] This combination of domestic and international circumstances was boosted by the Soviet Union's disengagement from regional conflicts under the leadership of Mikhail Gorbachev. Together, they gave greater room for the peace process and allowed Niaraguan political forces to finally confront their differences without the high degree of external pressures they had endured throughout the decade.

For the Nicaraguan opposition, the road toward building an alternative to the Sandinistas was full of complications. Throughout the Reagan years, the administration's backing of the Contras constrained their range of choices regarding participating in the political process. By paying for and providing political support for the insurgency, the Reagan administration reduced any incentive the Nicaraguan political opposition had to nourish and improve the imperfect political institutions of democracy established by the Sandinistas. By making the overthrow of the FSLN the top (though undeclared) priority of the government, the United States increased the price potential democrats had to pay if they chose to abide by the rules of the game, thus turning them away from the construction of democracy.

At this juncture, those who chose to side with the Reagan administration had to learn to become a political force that could stand on its own feet. As it became evident that the Contras had no chance of winning, they jumped onto the wagon that had been railed by Nicaraguans in the FSLN and the domestic opposition who, despite US policy, helped form the fragile democratic institutions that existed as the peace process evolved. As the United States began to fund internal opposition activities, however, it would take them much longer to detach themselves from Washington and to learn enough political tolerance to sustain a pluralistic political process.[380] Emboldened by Washington's preference

---

378. NSA 1991, Document No. 003142. "Nicaragua: Municipal elections," National Democratic Institute for International Affairs Report, 20 december 1988.

379. "La guerra retrocede: crisis de la política USA," *Envío* 8 (96, August 1989), p. 13–14.

380. According to an August 7, 1988 UPI dispatch, private conservative groups and the CIA funneled more than ten million dollars to defray the cost of internal opposition activities in 1988, with the aim of encouraging them to take a "bolder" approach to test Nicaragua's pluralism. COSEP leader Enrique Bolaños Geyer, for instance, publicly declared his aim of "abolishing the Sandinista system." Both COSEP and the CDN took advantage of the political opening brough about after Esquipulas to make public its desire that the FSLN hand over power to a Junta composed by representatives from COSEP, the CDN, the Contras and "some Sandinistas".

and support, the political opposition, now gathered along the National Opposition Union (UNO), contributed to tense the political environment as the general elections approached. As long as the funds from the United States continued to arrive, the political opposition maintained their unity.

Nicaraguans had a chance to test the existing democratic institutions and procedures with the general elections of February 1990. From the FSLN's standpoint, the delegitimation of the results of the 1984 elections could not take place again. Backed by the results of most public opinion polls, the FSLN was certain of its victory and made sure that the elections were free and fair. Thus they subjected themselves to the view of more than 2,500 observers and provided all the guarantees sought by the opposition. To prevent accusations that the electoral process was not conducted freely, the government changed a law prohibiting the use of foreign funds for political aims. The new provisions allowed foreign donations, provided fifty percent of the funds were channelled to the Supreme Electoral Council.

Despite these advances, the electoral process was not free from US interferences. Throughout 1989, the United States scrutinised all decisions taken by the Nicaraguan government or the Supreme Electoral Council regarding the elections. In addition, not only did the Bush administration fund the campaign of Violeta Barrios de Chamorro, who ran for the presidency under UNO's ticket, but it also made sure that the Contras were still an alternative were the election results to counter its aims. The original Esquipulas trade-off, democratisation for demobilisation, did not come about and the electoral campaign was carried out at the same time that the Contra war went on in rural areas. The FSLN could not hold back the elections nor could it claim that it had ended the war. The US trade embargo would not be lifted if Daniel Ortega were re-elected. So only Chamorro could hold the promise of relief if she were elected to the Presidency, as attested by an invitation from President Bush to the White House on 8 November 1989. By late 1989, peace did not seem to be reaching the region, as evidenced by the Farabundo Martí National Liberation Front (FMLN) offensive against the Salvadoran government in November and the US military intervention of Panama on 20 December 1989.

The war had taken a heavy toll on the Nicaraguans, producing more than 57,000 casualties (of which 29,000 died), twelve billion dollars in damages, and a hyperinflation that contributed to worsen the living conditions of the impoverished masses. These conditions were aggravated by the consequences of Hurricane Joanne in 1988, which provoked damages worth over 824 million dollars, and the economic adjustment programme the government carried out without the blessing of international financial institutions. Despite the war, health, education and other social indicators improved dramatically throughout the ten years of revolutionary government. But in the minds of Nicaraguan voters, the prospects for continuing the confrontation with the United States and the Contras more than offset these achievements. The FSLN had made many mistakes. The control exercised by the Party and the Government over all aspects of ordinary citizens' life, the lifestyles of the FSLN leadership, the sterile confrontation with the Catholic Church and the conduct of the FSLN with respect to its pre-revolution allies created the conditions to strengthen the opposition's bid for power. As a result, Nicaraguans voted massively for Chamorro, voting the FSLN out of office, fifty-five percent for UNO and forty-one percent for the Sandinistas.

Neither Chamorro's coalition nor the FSLN expected this electoral outcome and both forces were unprepared to define rules of the game allowing each other to stay on as important political forces. The FSLN had no guarantees of its survival, and the Contras, backed by the Bush administration, pressed the elected authorities to prolong their existence and be recognised as a legitimate armed force. In the end, conciliatory efforts made by both the new President and the FSLN created the conditions for future stability. Before handing over the government, the FSLN majority in Congress passed a law providing autonomy to the Ministry of Defence and the Popular Sandinista Army (PSA) and cutting in half the size of the armed forces. In turn, Chamorro recognised the PSA as Nicaragua's only armed body and negotiated with the Contras their entrance into a portion of Nicaraguan territory where they could stay while they were incorporated into Nicaraguan life. Yet, contrary to Latin American and European governments and international bodies such as the OAS and the UN, the Bush administration did not contribute to alleviate Nicaragua's polarisation. Given this setting, the first steps toward the transfer of power required the involvement of international mediators such as former President James Carter, OAS Secretary General Joao Baena Soares and the UN's Secretary General's envoy, Elliot Richardson. In time, as incumbent administratrions had no more reasons to justify the prolongation of the Contra war, the characteristics of Nicaragua's democracy and the country's alignment were left to be defined by Nicaraguans themselves. Later, lacking the the US as the sole cohesive factor that had gathered the opposition to the Sandinistas, the UNO coalition fractured itself and President Chamorro was led to rely on the FSLN's near-majority in Congress to provide an effective government.

Reappraising the US in Nicaraguan politics

The Nicaraguan regime trajectory was conditioned by policy choices in the United States and by the way domestic actors handled US influences. The dynastic dictatorship of the Somozas emerged in the context of the Good Neighbour Policy, but it could hardly have endured so long were it not for the ability of the Somozas to wire themselves up in Washington's ruling circles and adapt themselves to what Washington expected.

The revolutionary government headed by the Sandinistas faced a similar setting; their actions were highly constrained by the Reagan's administration decision to curtail their power, yet they were able to reduce Washington's pressures for change only by developing greater ties with European powers, Latin American states and American NGOs that countered US Central American policy. The authoritarian alternative of the right seemed to be swept over by the Revolution, but after Reagan reached the White House it was revived by US policy. The transformation of the Nicaraguan regime was significantly shaped by the FSLN and its international allies' efforts for upholding peace and self- determination, none of which was achieved prior to the enactment of the new institutional foundations that were in place at the time of the first transition election in February 1990. While the government of Violeta Barrios de Chamorro initially depended on US aid and guidance to stay in power, the Sandinistas remained an important and powerful actor. The new regime pended on a difficult equilibrium between domestic and external actors' willingness to sustain it. Democracy in Nicaragua was made possible because of a combination of factors such as the collapse of Reagan's counterrevolutionary policy, the impasse in Nicaragua's civil war and the regional peace process.[381]

---

381. Similar conclusions are offered by Shelley Allerton McConnell, "From bullets to ballots: Nicaragua's revolutionary transition to democracy," PhD Dissertation, Standford University, 1998.

PANAMA

The Canal and the Transition

The root of Panama's experience with military authoritarianism cannot be traced, as in the Dominican Republic and Nicaragua, to an American military occupation, but rather in response to unsettled nationalist grievances against the US control of the Panama Canal. The United States has been a pervasive factor in the evolution of Panamanian politics. Probably in no other country in the Latin Caribbean has US influence been so persistent and overwhelming. With this feature in the background, the study of Panamanian politics offers the opportunity to dwell on the interaction between domestic and international circumstances impinging on regime transitions, but particularly on the effect that alterations of the regional and international orders, and military intervention by the United States, had on its trajectory.

Before the military coup in 1968, Panama had a much higher democratic potential than Nicaragua and the Dominican Republic prior to the onset of their respective dictatorships. Panama enjoyed a fair degree of constitutional rule. Though electoral frauds were committed frequently, new Presidents were elected no later than every four years and had no opportunity to re-elect themselves. Panamanians enjoyed basic political freedoms. Separation of powers existed and organised popular groups frequently challenged and succeeded in altering government decisions. Yet, the political system remained dominated by a few wealthy families and suffered from its ineffectiveness regarding the issue of Panamanian sovereignty over the Canal and the effecting of meaningful social and economic reforms. The Torrijos regime (1968–1978), which adopted an inclusionary orientation, interrupted democracy but achieved a national aspiration by negotiating a new Canal treaty granting sovereignty over the Canal and its adjacent areas and a gradual transfer of its administration to Panama. In 1978, the authoritarian regime launched a transition to civilian rule that remained monitored by the National Guard. However, as it went on, significant changes in the international arena took place, altering the setting in which domestic political events unfolded. These shifts provided the background for the renewal of authoritarian rule, disguised in constitutional forms. The immediate aftermath of the 1989 US military intervention was the restoration of democracy, but its performance was not substantially better than before 1968. In due course, the outcome of the Panamanian trajectory came about because of the intersection of choices and events both in Panama and in the United States.

The United States in Panama's political history

United States-Panama relations have been deeply rooted in Washington's interest in controlling the inter-oceanic Canal. The advantages offered by the isthmus of Panama for the construction of a canal—a tiny strip of land located in the middle of the American continent—made it the target of Washington's recurrent attempts at influencing the course of its political affairs. In the late nineteenth century, the United States made an effort to secure the construction of an interoceanic waterway. It was at this moment that the Nouvelle Compagnie du Canal de Panama (created in 1888, following the failure of the French company to which Colombia had commissioned the construction of the canal) offered to sell its concession to the United States. In January 1903, Washington succeeded in reaching an exclusive agreement with Colombia, by which it was to receive, for a period of 100 years, the concession to build and use an interoceanic route. Due to circumstantial factors, however, the Colombian Congress did not approve of the agreement. Then the Theodore Roosevelt administration in Washington and a group of Panamanians, anxious to reap the profits from the construction of the waterway, manoeuvered to force what was a province of Colombia to become an independent state. Panamanian Conservatives not linked to the Liberal party, which ruled the rest of Colombia, sought and obtained American support to move forward with this project.[382] Through the Hay-Bunau Varilla Convention, signed in November 1903, Washington built the juridical framework it used to construct and exercise effective control over the Canal, as well as to influence Panama's political affairs.

The Hay-Buneau Varilla convention was signed by Philippe Buneau-Varilla, the French promoter-engineer who owned most of the shares of the company, as Panama's Plenipotentiary (though acting on his own). Through this treaty, Panama ceded to the United States, in perpetuity, a territory of ten miles of land and sea, in return for a payment of ten million dollars and an annual rental of $250,000 in gold. The United States also reserved the right to use its police, army, and naval forces, and to build fortifications for the effective control of the land that had been transferred. In exchange, the United States would guarantee Panamanian independence; in practice, the weakness of the new state facilitated Washington to exercise more prerogatives than those reserved to it by the treaty.[383]

From then on, the Canal was a crucial factor in Panama's economic development and repeatedly intruded in its domestic politics. The Canal (owned, operated and defended by the government of the United States) was the country's most important economic asset; Canal operation spillovers generated some two-thirds of its GNP and two-thirds of its foreign exchange. Cutting the country in two, the Canal's magnificence was also a highly visible reminder of the circumstances surrounding the signing of the Treaty, whose provisions seemed

---

382. Panamanian historians claim that Panama enjoyed a fair degree of national consciousness at this time; yet, without the threat of the use of force by the United States it is unlikely that Panama would have become a formally independent state in 1903 or the following decades.

383. A thorough account of this relationship is in John Major, *Prize possession: the United States and the Panama Canal, 1903–1979*, (Cambridge: Cambridge University Press, 1993).

to take most of its benefits away. Panamanians particularly resented the provision authorizing the United States to act "as if it were sovereign" over the Canal Zone and "to the entire exclusion of the exercise by the Republic of Panama of any such sovereign rights, power or authority." This sourness imbued Panamanian politics with an intensity of nationalistic feelings that was continuously exploited by the local élite.

From the beginning of the twentieth century, Panama's relationship vis-à-vis the United States was one of a quasi-protectorate. Washington pressured local authorities to approve a clause in the 1904 Constitution allowing the US to interfere in the new Republic's internal affairs. Indeed, the United States' need to issue payments for the construction of the Canal led Panama to sign the 1904 Washington Convention, making the US dollar the legal currency. The United States also reserved the right to enforce "law and order" anywhere in the country, frequently intervening in situations of crisis.

Unlike Nicaragua and the Dominican Republic, the pervasiveness of US influence did not provide the setting for the emergence of a personalistic military dictatorship. In Panama, the exercise of US influence was fundamentally different. First, the United States government directly controlled the country's main natural resource (and source of wealth). Second, it disarmed the National Police and had the chance to exercise its military power almost freely in the isthmus. Thus, for several decades Panamanians did not have the chance to build an authoritarian option on the basis of a local army. In addition, the United States created an enclave on the banks of the Canal—the Panama Canal Zone— which reduced the autonomy of the ruling élites administrating the state.

The distinct nature of the exercise of US power over Panama had important implications for the type of political regime that evolved. After independence, a handful of the wealthiest families retained control over most of the economy and the country's political affairs as well. For sixty-five years, all Panamanian Presidents but two were members of this small ruling elite. Unlike Nicaragua and the Dominican Republic, no single man or family emerged to control the destinies of the country. If there was a person who could have followed Trujillo and Somoza's steps, he did not find the conditions conducive to that end. The United States monitored and controlled most of the new nation's police and military affairs, in an effort to prevent the political instability often associated with the employment of police forces by one political group against another. In Panama, the establishment of a powerful military establishment did not follow the Good Neighbour Policy. Unlike the Dominican Republic and Nicaragua, Panama was not (formally and totally) occupied for a long period and, since it already had troops stationed in the Canal Zone, Washington did not perceive the need to promote the creation of a strong army. The National Guard that was later created was slow to grow and remained for two decades under the guidance of US forces in Panama and under the leadership of members of the local oligarchy. Free from dictatorial rule Trujillo or Somoza-style, the ruling élite replicated their experience with party politics and elections under Colombian rule. Though they continuously exploited nationalistic feelings, the Panamanian plutocracy resorted to American authorities in the Canal Zone or the State Department to supervise electoral contests and arbitrate political disputes.

Since most Panamanians resented the terms of the Hay-Bunau Varilla Convention, the contractual form of the US presence in Panama remained the key issue in the country's political life. Efforts to change the treaty sometimes produced better provisions for Panama. The 1936 Arias-Roosevelt convention eliminated the Constitutional article that sanctioned American intervention in the isthmus, raised the amount of payments for the use of the Canal Zone and authorized Panamanians to enter this area. Nevertheless, the US Senate did not pass the accord until 1939—just before the outbreak of World War II—when American interests required a relaxation of tensions. Even though the treaty in no way modified the perpetuity clause, for the Senate to pass it Panama agreed to allow American military forces to carry out maneuvers anywhere within Panama, and to grant them the right to take unilateral steps to defend the Canal in the event they did not have sufficient time to consult with Panamanian authorities. In December 1947, at the outset of the Cold War, the United States sought to reach a settlement allowing the military bases that had been unilaterally established in Panamanian territory during World War II to remain. Nevertheless, because of large-scale protests, the National Assembly voted down the proposal. In 1955, the Remón-Eisenhower treaty extended US presence in a military base at Río Hato in exchange for opening the Canal Zone market to a limited number of Panamanian companies, increased to $1.9 million the annual payment to Panama and extended employment benefits to Panamanians. However, such changes fell short of Panamanian hopes for increased revenue from the Canal and for the recognition of Panamanian sovereignty over this asset.

The Canal proved to be a physical infrastructure that permitted the United States to subsidize its foreign trade and to establish in its adjacent areas a military enclave in the heart of Latin America. Panama's political process did not endanger the total US domination of the Canal strip, allowing the United States to set up a colonial enclave that, until 1978, appeared in textbooks as an American overseas possession. Washington paid attention to Panama's political developments, but most of the time the country's oligarchic system posed little threat to Washington's basic interests. The most notable exception was Arnulfo Arias' presidency in 1941, who was rapidly deposed after he seemed to lean toward Germany in World War II.

After World War II, Panama went through a series of transformations that shook the foundation of Panama's feeble political system. Once the war effort ended, widespread social problems became evident. Different groups, bypassing party lines, became active in politics. In 1949, residents of poor neighbourhoods succeeded in obtaining a court ruling protecting them from eviction. In 1950, the President accepted the conditions established by unions protesting price and rent hikes. Under the government of President José Remón (1952–1955), who emerged from the ranks of the National Police, Panama won some a few trade concessions from the United States. With the opening of the Canal market to Panamanian businesses, Panama experienced some degree of industrialization, which would add to the increased activity that had been encouraged by the expansion of the Canal work force during World War II. This, along with a limited import-substitution policy beginning in the 1960s, transformed the country's social structure so that workers and members of the upwardly mobile middle classes entered the political stage. Increasingly, middle-class groups began to organize autonomously, but the oligarchy's family clans did not succeed in channeling popular aspirations in favor of their network.

On top of these social transformations, the Cuban revolution altered the setting for the evolution of Panamanian politics. On the one hand, emerging student and professional groups increased their political activism. On the other, members of the Panamanian plutocracy became aware of the need to effect changes. In 1960, Roberto Chiari, a representative of this "sensitized" sector, assumed the presidency through relatively "competitive" elections.[384] Chiari publicly acknowledged himself to be "probably the last one of that small circle in holding the presidency."[385] Fearful of the perspectives of a revolution inspired in Castro, Chiari promulgated a programme of moderate social reforms. However, despite Chiari's declared intentions, his proposals for agrarian, fiscal and other reforms aborted.

The turning point in US-Panamanian relations came with the widespread, bloody protests in January 1964 over the American presence in the Canal. A group of high school students who tried to raise the Panamanian flag in the Canal Zone was confronted by the American population and the Canal Zone Police and, in the context of the disturbances, some of them were killed. In Panama City, for two consecutive days, nearly one hundred thousand Panamanians—out of a total country population of less than 1.2 million—took to the streets to protest at what they perceived as an aggression. Chiari's government was compelled to sever diplomatic relations with the United States, and did not renew them until Washington agreed to negotiate a new Canal treaty.

Under the administration of Chiari's successor (and cousin of Chiari), Marcos Robles (1964–1968), Panama and the United States held talks to review the administration, use, and defence of the Canal; these talks led to the signing of a draft treaty in 1967, aimed at abrogating the 1903 treaty. Panama would have "in principle" recovered its sovereignty over the Canal Zone and the United States reserved the right to leave as many troops in the isthmus as it deemed necessary. The perpetuity clause would have been replaced by an only slightly less onerous one establishing a term of 100 years. Nevertheless, vigorous popular opposition once again thwarted passage of the proposed treaty.

In any case, in 1968, neither Panama nor the United States was ready to approve new treaties. In Panama, as the May 1968 elections approached, the

---

384. These elections have been praised as the "freest" in the nation's history before 1968, because they marked the second time—the first was in 1932—an opposition candidate won a presidential election and the outgoing government transferred power to the opposition. However, in the Panamanian context, It may be argued that this was facilitated because the outgoing president and the president-elect had close ties in sugar production and distribution, respectively.

385. Quoted in Daniel Goldrich, *Sons of the Establishment: Elite Youth in Panama and Costa Rica*, (Chicago, IL: Rand Mc nally and Co., 1966), p. 36.

controversy surrounding the proposals made it impossible for the National Assembly to tackle the issue. Because of nationalist awareness, particularly after the January 1964 incident, Panama was not ready to accept the new relationship that would have emerged from the Johnson-Robles treaty. Neither was the United States, then deeply involved in Vietnam, prepared to accept a change. Nineteen sixty-eight was a sensitive political year (US elections were to be held in November) for this country as well. During this period, the view of the isthmus of Panama as a hub for the defence of American interests in the Western hemisphere prevailed.[386] Nevertheless, an unexpected political turn in Panama altered the course of events.

The breakdown of oligarchic rule

On 11 October 1968, a group of young military officers deposed President Arnulfo Arias Madrid only eleven days after he took office. Despite the all-out effort by the Robles administration to steal the election, Arias won by a substantial margin. His victory had been made official only after National Guard Commander Bolivar Vallarino insisted on a reasonably honest count of the ballots. Yet, once he assumed power, President Arias chose not to respect the deals he had made with the National Guard to clear the way for reaching Presidential office. The US government, fearing nationalistic outbursts like that of 1964, trusted Arias would obtain the approval of the Robles-Johnson treaties.[387] In 1968, most of the oligarchy came to terms with Arias, who by this time had lost any populist or nationalist inclination.[388] Yet junior officers led by Major Boris Martínez and Major Omar Torrijos, whom Arias had ordered to be transferred overseas, led the coup against the new President. Arias, caught by surprise, fled to the Canal Zone. After the deposed President's hopes for a general strike and widespread opposition did not materialize (rather, members of his coalition and close political collaborators deserted him), he went into exile in the United States.

Initially, the leaders of the coup intended to return to constitutional rule soon after taking power but had no definite plan for its implementation. Thus they persuaded Vallarino's former deputies, Colonels Pinilla and Urrutia, to head the new Junta, but only after a "constitutional" solution had failed to take hold. Arias' First Vice-president, Raúl Arango, was offered the Presidential seat. Influential political parties were receptive to the proposal, as was Arias' rival, David Samudio. But Arango's refusal and subsequent vacillations convinced Junta lead-

---

386. In the House of Representatives, Congressman O. J. Flood asserted that the United States would never give up its supremacy over the Canal Zone. His declaration was supported by 120 Representatives and Senators from both parties, and by various conservative organizations that lobbied to block a resolution in favor of yielding to Panamanian demands. Manuela Semidei,"Panama, les Etats-Unis et la Zone du canal", *Problemes D'Amerique Latine*, vol. XXIX (29 November 1973), p. 8.

387. "Panama: Prospects for Relations with the US," Defense Intelligence Agency's Secret National Intelligence Estimate Number 84-68, dated 28 August 1968.

388. Arias' program for the May 1968 election is in Ricaurte Soler (comp.), *Pensamiento político en Panamá en los siglos XIX y XX*, (Panamá: Biblioteca de la Librería Cultural Panameña, 1988), volume 6, pp. 378-379.

ers that he lacked the strength to maintain himself independent of Arias. Junta leaders also played with the idea of creating a government of national unity, supported by all parties, but they were suspicious of all politicians and thus turned down this option.

To legitimise the coup, the initial cabinet appointees included the president of the Chamber of Commerce, an attorney for a large company owned by one of the oligarchic families, a prominent member of Arias' presidential coalition and the president of the National Association of Cattle Raisers. The make-up of the cabinet reassured the dominant élite and the United States, which cautiously chose to recognize the new government only after receiving assurances that it would abide by international treaties.[389] The civilian cabinet, however, was generally unsuccessful in resisting the demands of the military. Martínez and Torrijos continued to exercise a decisive influence on all political matters. The two officers who engineered the coup shared real power, rather than titular heads Urrutia and Pinilla.

After the Junta failed to arrive at a 'constitutional solution,' it undertook the administration of the government. The coup leaders released a statement announcing the dissolution of the National Assembly, the banning of all partisan activities, and the formation of a provisional junta that reserved legislative powers for itself. They announced the creation of a "Movement for the Restoration of the Republic" whose declared purpose was "revolution without dictatorship and freedom with order." Statements included the "absolute repudiation of communism" traditional among coup leaders in other parts of the continent, a call for the eradication of nepotism and corruption, the separation of the National Guard from politics, the sizing-down of the government bureaucracy, and an announcement of possible general elections after the government apparatus had been "moralized" and "cleansed."[390] The steps taken by the new military government included various small-scale administrative, fiscal, and agrarian reforms. At the same time, the new government repressed all opposition: all political parties were banned, the University of Panama was closed, and unions were persecuted. For this reason, broad civilian sectors, including many groups opposed to the oligarchy, demanded a return to constitutional rule.

Opposition to the regime became a major challenge for the National Guard within a year after it took over. A guerrilla stronghold near the Costa Rican border, and armed resistance, both urban and rural, threatened the new regime. The United States showed its displeasure by suspending military aid. The masses expressed opposition to militarism. But the impression within the barracks that the oligarchy caused troubles, while the masses demanded answers to their grievances, led Torrijos to the conclusion that the population would support the National Guard only if it backed their legitimate aspirations.[391] After sending Martínez

---

389. Humberto Ricord, *Los clanes de la oligarquía panameña y el golpe militar de 1968*, (Panamá: undefined publisher, 1983), pp. 137-138; David N. Farnsworth & James W. Mc Kenney, *US Panamanian Relations, 1903–1978*, (Boulder, Colorado: Westwiew Press, 1983), p. 71.

390. Ricord, *Los clanes de la oligarquía panameña y el golpe militar de 1968*, pp. 137–138.

391. Interview with Marcel Salamín, former Torrijos' advisor, April 2001; see also Thomas L.

into exile, Torrijos began to implement measures to reduce tensions between organized popular groups and the government. Intellectuals, former legislative deputies, labour and student leaders, and several guerrilla leaders were freed and invited to join the government. In this key period, Torrijos succeeded in gaining the support of organized trade unions.[392] In addition, he began to distance himself from the oligarchy by naming intellectuals and other leftist activists to government posts, thereby winning supporters for his reformist programme. Because of the personal relationships Torrijos had built up during his career with officials having positions similar to or lower than his, when the provisional junta tried to send him into exile in Mexico on 16 December 1969, most of the National Guard officers and troops remained loyal to him. Thus Torrijos dismissed Pinilla and Urrutia and granted the titular position of President to a civilian collaborator, Demetrio Basilio Lakas.

The belief that the CIA and the US Army Intelligence unit in Panama had abetted the coup against him compelled Torrijos to find alternative interlocutors with the United States. Torrijos charged Major Manuel Noriega, whom he put in command of the National Guard's intelligence services (G-2), to develop a close relationship with US intelligence services. According to Noriega, Torrijos believed that the National Guard should establish this link to "make sure the Americans would not miscalculate because of too little or wrongly developed information." Noriega was the sole person responsible for communicating US intelligence services about the Torrijos regime's activities and intentions, "to combat rumours and misinformation about our political goals." In time, talking directly to the CIA became "the natural order of things in dealing with the United States." Often, the Panamanian leader used the CIA as a "back channel," in isolation from the US Embassy and the State Department and from Panama's own Ministry of Foreign Affairs.[393]

After power struggles within the National Guard were over, the Torrijos regime adopted a populist, inclusionary orientation.[394] This turn may be partly explained by the social background of the coup leaders. Both commanders whom the National Guard had seen between its creation and 1968 had family ties to the ruling urban oligarchy. Colonel José Ramón Cantera, who was also President

Pearcy, *We Answer Only to God: Politics and the Military in Panama, 1903–1947*, (Albuquerque: University of New Mexico Press, 1998).

392. On Labour Day 1969, for example, unions and local peasants acclaimed Torrijos during a trip he made to the banana-growing region. Rómulo Escobar Bethancourt, *Torrijos: colonia americana No*, (Panamá: M. V. Publishing Co., 1981), p. 95.

393. Manuel Noriega and Peter Eisner, *The Memoirs of Manuel Noriega*, (New York: Random House, 1997).

394. Panama's reformist military regime was not unique in Latin American history. For example, barely a few days before the coup in Panama, General Velasco Alvarado took power in Peru, establishing a government of the armed forces that intended a thorough social and political transformation of the country. During the period of "benign neglect" in US-Latin American Relations (1969–1973), similar military regimes took over in Honduras, Ecuador and Bolivia. These experiences were not unheard of in other Latin American countries such as Chile, El Salvador or Brazil.

of the Republic from 1952 until his assassination in 1955, was a first cousin of President Chiari Remón (1960–1964) who, in turn, was succeeded by his cousin, Marco A. Robles (1964–1968).[395] Commander Bolívar Vallarino, who headed the National Guard until his retirement in 1968, also came from one of the same families. Yet, most of the young officers had no links to the oligarchic clans; due to the presence of the American military bases and the several decades in which Panama had no military of its own, the country's traditional élites had no incentive to cultivate ties with these officials or to encourage their children to pursue military careers.[396] In the 1960s, a growing number of young officers had been trained in military academies, including a small number in Peru, whose military schools were known for their independent, reformist stances.[397]

Seeking to legitimise itself, the new regime established a reform agenda for which it received the backing of intellectuals, the then exceptionally and politically powerful student movement, the socially mobile middle classes, peasants and organized labour. The military government adopted a reformist ideology, nationalized the telephone and electricity industries, and expanded Panama's role as a point of transit for goods and capital, which led to the growth of the international banking centre and of the duty-free zone in Colón. Unlike Trujillo and Somoza, both of whom were more interested in accumulating wealth and power, Torrijos was more concerned with government reforms. However, since Panama's economic development potential seemed to be curtailed by the fact that the United States controlled its most important natural resource—the Canal and its adjacent areas—the Torrijos regime's priorities initially turned to the international arena.

---

395. The Chiari family was one of the approximately twenty families that controlled the majority of industries in Panama. Marco A. Gandásegui, h., "La concentración del poder económico en Panamá." In Soler, Ricaurte (ed.), *Panamá: dependencia y liberación* (San José, Costa Rica: EDUCA, 1974).

396. Torrijos' personal background provides a clue for understanding his reformist orientation and nationalist aspirations. Torrijos was trained as a school teacher. Teachers of his school included many Chilean (mostly from the Popular Front) and Spanish Republican immigrants (hired because Panamanian teachers refused to live in the distant town of Santiago, where the school was located) who projected their political and social values to their students. Later, while receiving training as a cadet at a Salvadoran military academy, Torrijos witnessed the rise and fall of a "revolutionary" military government headed by young military officers. After graduation, as an officer in Panama, Torrijos' commanders entrusted him for several months with the personal security of General Juan Domingo Perón, who had recently been expelled from Argentina, arriving in Panama as an exile.

397. Torrijos, along with other junior officers, received counterinsurgency and military-operations courses in the School of the Americas, located in the Canal Zone. This school was the United States' principal tool for training Latin American military personnel. Many became dictators, but some of them perceived the link between national development and internal security and, when the need arose, used the power of the state to forge inclusionary regimes. If by definition the National Guard was responsible for defending the nation, its US-induced professionalization carried the seeds of its politicisation. The country's main economic resources—the Canal and the banana plantations—were owned by foreigners, and there were few national industries to protect or foreign enemies to fight against. Thus, In 1968 the National Guard was, in essence, structurally inactive, which, given the option, led its officers to seek a redefinition of their role in Panamanian society.

Starting in 1970, the government's foreign-policy objectives consisted of winning US recognition of Panamanian sovereignty over the Canal and the adjacent territory. To show its independence from the United States, the Torrijos regime first cancelled a lease agreement between the United States and Panama for the Río Hato air base and rejected the Robles-Johnson treaties. Perceiving the limited results of previous negotiations on the status of the Canal, Torrijos introduced two innovations to Panama's foreign policy. Firstly, the negotiating process took on national dimensions. Discussion forums were encouraged (in which government policymakers participated), and symbolic anti-American actions were taken, such as the establishment of an "annual anti-imperialist week," the momentum of which diminished only after the signing of new treaties. Secondly, the regime adopted a multilateral approach to the negotiating process. Although the general format of diplomatic relations remained oriented to the Western bloc, Panama soon joined the ranks of the Non-Aligned Movement, signed cooperation and friendship treaties with other countries that expressed their support for the Panamanian cause, and later broadened relations with Cuba and other countries of the Soviet bloc. At each international forum, Panama demanded the "decolonisation" of the Canal Zone (thereby increasing the support from the Third World) and the abrogation of the 1903 Canal Treaties. Torrijos warned that continued US control over the Canal Zone would inevitably result in a new outbreak of nationalist outburst in the isthmus, and that he would lead this violence himself if the United States failed to recognize Panama's unconditional sovereignty over the entire territory.

Torrijos initially intended to return to Constitutional rule within the near future. Apparently, the National Guard Commander believed that the military should not stay in power too long, but used it as an opportunity to effect changes in the electoral system with the aim of preventing corrupt electoral practices. Torrijos appointed independents as Magistrates of the Electoral Tribunal and charged them with the task of revising the electoral laws to democratize the selection of candidates and reduce the possibilities of fraud, for which they consulted the leaders of the previously banned political parties. The second mandate was to hold elections by mid-1970, but this was postponed until 1971. However, early in 1971 the government of the United States agreed to negotiate new treaties with Panama. Believing that a change of government would complicate the negotiations, the Torrijos regime took the decision to postpone them again until the negotiating process was completed.[398]

To be successful in this enterprise, the Torrijos regime laid out the grounds for extending itself in power longer than it had initially envisaged. But to do that it could not, so the chiefs of staff believed, allow any division within Panamanian society that could threaten the regime's ability to work toward the goal of acquiring effective control and sovereignty over the Canal. The existence of an opposition movement, the National Guard staff felt, could weaken their chances

---

398. Interview with Fernando Manfredo, 27 September 1995. Manfredo was among those Magistrates.

of obtaining a new Canal Treaty.[399] Thus, a different institutional framework for the political participation of society would be required, different from the system that had existed until 1968, to which the National Guard attributed most of the history of political instability in Panama. Then the Torrijos regime launched the "New Panama movement," aimed at mobilizing and channelling the support of the masses. Torrijos gave special importance to the creation of grass roots' organizations that might become alternative sources of support. The first such organizations were the health committees, created with the guidance of technicians and sociologists.[400] Later on, the Torrijos regime promoted community-development programmes, reorganized local parishes and encouraged popular involvement in government projects. In this way, the state undertook a series of reforms that would serve for the establishment of a broad coalition with popular, rural, and urban groups. In putting this coalition together, Torrijos gave trade unionism a place in the political arena.[401]

In his relationship with Panamanian businessmen, Torrijos chose to co-opt some individuals and groups opposed to his government by granting them limited concessions. It created the Ministry of Commerce and, through a series of policies intended to broaden Panama's role as an international financial centre and to diversify the country's traditional export base, the government obtained, if not the support, at least the acquiescence of some sectors within the business community. Likewise, Torrijos succeeded in co-opting the reformist wing of the oligarchy by granting firms associated with it to take part in new contracts for the construction of urban housing projects.[402]

The Torrijos regime

Torrijos was the first and only head of state in Panamanian history to make a sustained effort to come into direct contact with the popular classes, through countless public appearances in which he attempted to show his government's accessibility and accountability to popular demands. Aided by Panama's small size (77,800 square km) and reduced population (most of which inhabit the Capital and the western part of the country), Torrijos continuously toured the country urging the population to tell him first-hand about their problems and aspirations. For several years, long lines of persons with demands or who simply wanted to speak to Torrijos personally could be seen outside his residence in the

---

399. Roberto Díaz Herrera, *Las vallas del silencio. Panamá: a los 18 años del golpe militar*, (Panamá: Panamanian Defense Forces, 1986), p. 16.

400. Ricaurte Soler, "Panamá: la autonomía universitaria de 1968 a 1978", *Tareas*, (April–September 1981), p. 71.

401. Starting in 1969, the government encouraged the formation of unions and created the Ministry of Labor and Social Welfare as a separate government entity. It alsodecreed various laws and regulations, including a law enforcing the—long-since ignored—minimum wage. In December 1971, the military government approved a new labor code favorable to workers.

402. Steve Ropp, *Panamanian Politics: From Guarded Nation to National Guard*, (New York: Praeger Publishers, 1982), p. 62.

capital, his house in Farallón beach, or anywhere else he went. Torrijos would listen patiently to and take note of requests for his government to make improvements. He would immediately order local officials and regional National Guard officers to attend to these requests. This contributed to Torrijos' enormous popularity, and the masses came to identify closely with their charismatic leader.

Through the 1972 Constitution, the Torrijos regime set up the institutional framework of government for the following years. On the one hand, It contained temporary mandates that justified the National Guard's role in politics. For example, the delegates to the 1972 Constituent Assembly, elected in their respective parishes, gave the National Guard an active role in all government ministries, by stating that they were to act "in harmony with the public forces." Article 207 named Torrijos as the "Maximum Leader of the Revolution" and head of the government for six years. On the other hand, it also included provisions about the role of the President, the recognition of political rights, the separation of power and the independence of the electoral tribunal, among others, that became the basis for the launching of a transition to democracy once Torrijos' term ended.

Torrijos apparently sought to pave the way for the restoration of democracy in Panama at the end of his self-imposed end of term in power. However, deteriorating economic conditions encouraged the Torrijos regime to launch a partial political opening earlier. Domestically, Panama had experienced high rates of inflation due to the international oil crisis. Abroad, reformist military regimes and governments of the left had been deposed, leaving Torrijos as one of the few remaining reformist military rulers in Latin America. In this context, Torrijos tried to overcome the downturn in the economy by increasing public-sector investment and employment with funds from foreign loans. Torrijos sought to arrest the negative effects of this crisis on workers' purchasing power. This included a freeze on housing rents, which prompted the Panamanian Chamber of Construction (CAPAC) to mobilise its members and paralyse the industry, claiming that the country was "headed toward communism." For the first time since 1968, various organizations got together to mobilize against the government—led by the National Civic Movement, which included the Chamber of Commerce, the Lions' Club, the National Medical Association, and the short-lived Housewives' Association. From 1975, Torrijos set out to restructure those political alliances that gave him greater legitimacy for staying in power. This brought about a widening of his reformist coalition to include representatives of business interests previously excluded from the regime's social base. To maintain the national unity Torrijos sought—deemed as a prerequisite for maintaining stability during the Canal negotiations—the government implemented policies designed to reduce the dissatisfaction of these groups.

By the mid-seventies, international conditions changed in favour of the Panamanian cause. Both international and domestic pressures built up on Washington to relinquish its control over the Panama Canal. Inside the United States, numerous think tanks and other non-governmental organizations of various ideological leanings supported transferring the Canal to Panama. The holding of a United Nations Security Council meeting in Panama City in March 1973 to deal with the issue of the Canal was a success for Panama, as all member countries, except the United States (and Great Britain, which abstained) supported the Panamanian position.

All of these efforts built up and influenced Washington to come to terms with Panama. Washington's strategists felt they had paid too little attention to Latin America; thus reaching new agreements with Panama took on a regional importance, and became an imperative of American policy toward this region. This broad support for Panama finally led the United States to modify its stance regarding the Canal. Three months after the UN meeting in Panama, President Nixon, in a speech to Congress on foreign policy declared that it was time to improve relations between both countries and conclude the negotiations."[403] Hence, in late 1973 (following the coup against President Allende in Chile), the United States made a special effort to conduct negotiations with Panama over the future of the Canal. By 1974, the United States was ready to repeal the perpetuity clause of the Canal treaty. At about the same time, a mission sent to Panama by the Foreign Affairs Committee of the US Congress concluded that if the 1903 Treaty was not replaced by a new agreement between the two nations, American interests throughout Latin America, and especially in the Canal, would be at risk.[404] The agreement signed in February 1974 by Foreign Affairs Minister Juan Antonio Tack and Secretary of State Henry Kissinger represented the possibility of giving a concrete response to Panama's aspirations. The accord proposed eliminating the concept of perpetuity and called for the complete replacement of the 1903 treaty and its amendments with another agreement, placing a limit on American jurisdiction. Yet, the Watergate scandals and President Nixon's downfall delayed the negotiations for the new treaty.

By the mid-seventies, the international order offered new conditions facilitating an agreement. Washington's attention was fixed on the Middle East (the Israeli-Arab conflict); on promoting détente with the Soviet Union—to place stricter limits on the building of new strategic weapons and to find a balance in Eastern Europe through cutbacks in conventional forces—and with China; and on its participation in a Security and Cooperation Conference with its European allies.[405] From 1970 to 1975, the United States continued to be immersed in a military conflict of large proportions in Southeast Asia, as well as in a process of East-West détente that implied, for Third World countries such as Panama, certain degrees of peripheral autonomy.

In this context, the Torrijos regime broadened its margin for negotiation by stepping up ties with its neighbours, with emerging mid-size powers, and with governments of varying ideological orientations. In an attempt to balance the US' overwhelming influence, the Torrijos government embarked on a policy of denunciation of the US and sought the support of the region's governments. Along

---

403. Quoted in John Dinges, *Our Man in Panama* (New York: Random House, 1990), p. 103.

404. International Relations Committee, *A New Canal Treaty: A Latin American Imperative. Report of a Study Mission to Panama, November 21-23 1975*, (Washington: US Govt. Printing Office, 1976).

405. Farnsworth and Mc Kenney, *US Panamanian Relations, 1903–1978*, p. 1.

with other governments in the area—Echeverría's in Mexico, Perez' in Venezuela, Manley's in Jamaica, Velasco's in Peru and Peron's in Argentina—that were also struggling to exercise their autonomy, Panama supported various initiatives in favor of Third World "liberation" movements; in 1975, Panama renewed diplomatic ties with Cuba, a step taken earlier by oil-rich Venezuela.

In addition, strategic considerations also favoured the completing of agreements on the Canal. Firstly, the Canal was becoming inadequate for supertankers and other large ships. American analysts predicted that the existing Canal facilities would become obsolete, for which another interoceanic waterway or an enlargement of the Panama Canal would be required. The issue of how long the US military bases would remain became less important insofar as the construction of a sea-level canal, if carried out, would require fewer workers, less infrastructure and, therefore, fewer areas subject to security controls. If a simpler transportation waterway was being planned, a large-scale American presence was no longer indispensable. For military strategists, the advances made by nuclear technology for military use had reduced the need for conventional forces to defend the Canal. Likewise, studies on the possibility of constructing another interoceanic waterway in a different location indicated that, seen in the light of engineering considerations, probably the best site for constructing a larger Canal was in Panama.[406] In addition, the Southern Command reasoned that the Canal could be effectively defended only through non-hostile means. But because of the strategic defeat in Vietnam, "in great measure... the spirit of the government and the nation was not to wage dirty little wars at some distant corner of the world."[407] Insofar as Panama had succeeded in obtaining large international support, the United States could not formulate a credible, consistent policy toward Latin America until it gave a response to Panama. Washington could not afford not to respond to what by the mid-1970s had become a Latin American demand.

Upon arriving at the White House in January 1977, President James Carter expedited the signing of the Treaties. In August 1977, President James Carter announced that the negotiations had concluded, and in September Torrijos and Carter signed the new treaties at the OAS headquarters in Washington. The provisions of the accords replacing the 1903 Treaty included full recognition of Panamanian sovereignty over its territory, a gradual transition in the Canal administration to Panama, and other parallel accords that included several loans and grants to a total of 345 million dollars. Panama was to receive between fifty and seventy million dollars per year from the Canal's revenues. A parallel "neutrality" accord gave the United States the "right" to defend the Canal indefinitely were its continuous operation to be at risk from third parties.[408]

---

406. James Busey, *Political Aspects of the Panama Canal: The Problem of Location*, (Tucson, Arizona: The University of Arizona Press, 1974), p. 16.

407. This quote is taken from a document reviewing US military doctrine, written in 1986 for the US Joint Army Project on Low Intensity Conflict, "Analytical Review of Low-Intensity Conflict", (Fort Monroe, VA: 1986).

408. Before ratifying the accords, the US Senate passed the De Concini Amendment, thereby reserving for the United States the right to intervene in the Canal Zone "when the continuous operation of the interoceanic waterway is in danger." Panama obtained a Joint Interpretation

The Canal and the transition

The signing of the Torrijos-Carter Treaties in September 1977 marked the beginning of the struggle to gain their passage. In Panama, Torrijos and his negotiators promoted the treaties among the population. Opponents of the treaties
were given free space or time in the newspapers, radio and television, and no
overt efforts were made to silence them.[409] The following month a plebiscite was
held in Panama in which the treaties were approved by a little over two-thirds
of the votes cast, but the US Senate took several months to ratify them. Torrijos
deemed essential to maintain the national unity that had been achieved in order
to avoid any dissent that could be used by opponents of the treaties in the US
and made strenuous efforts to maintain the multi-class alliance that supported his regime.[410] Torrijos was determined to have the treaties approved by the
United States. To President Carter, he privately proposed to relinquish power
if that would help the White House to persuade enough Senators to ratify the
accords.[411] Torrijos was also prepared to bomb the Canal and assume the likely
US reactions if they were not.[412]

The following year was a turning point in Panamanian history. On the one
hand, the US Senate finally ratified the Canal treaties (by a margin of one vote),
though not without substantial lobbying from Panama and a strenuous effort by
the White House. The treaties came into effect later that year, when Panama became formally sovereign over all of its territory. The administration of the Canal
and all of the US defence sites were to be gradually transferred to Panama over a
period of 22 years. In addition, Torrijos' term in power expired. Though he could

---

Accord, which was annexed to the Neutrality Treaty, the terms of which stated that "the
United States has no right, nor shall it attempt to have it, to intervene in the political process
or the internal affairs of Panama." Amendment (a,1) to the Neutrality Treaty. United States,
Department of State, *The Defense and Neutrality of the Panama Canal Under the New Trea-
ties* Special Report No. 37, (Washington, D.C.: Bureau of Public Affairs, Department of
State, 1978), p. 3.

409. Farnsworth and Mc Kenney, *US Panamanian Relations, 1903–1978*, p. 159.

410. Once again, this understanding determined the content and direction of government policies. In November 1977, Torrijos announced that the cost of electricity would be reduced
when the treaties were ratified, that needy children would be given two pairs of shoes per
year, that between one and 1.5 million school uniforms would be given to public-school students, and that textbooks would be sold at cost, among other measures that never material-
ized. Their announcement was most likely a populist effort to raise expectations vis-à-vis the
canal treaty, and thereby diminish the chances of grass-roots' dissent at a crucial moment in
Panamanian history. "Anuncia Torrijos al Pueblo: Guerra contra el desempleo y la pobreza",
La Estrella de Panamá, 2 November 1977, p. 1.

411. In private communications with Carter, Torrijos also admitted that he would seek "a solution
through loud action should every peaceful solution fail." He referred to guerrillar warfare
and breaking the entire Central American region in flames. Taped message sent by General
Omar Torrijos to President Carter through the US Ambassador to Panama, dated 25
November 1977. Transcript provided by former NSC Advisor during the Carter administration, Robert Pastor.

412. Noriega, *The Memoirs of Manuel Noriega*, pp. 45–47; the full story is in Rómulo Escobar
Bethancourt, *Torrijos: colonia americana No*, (Panamá: M. V. Publishing Co., 1981).

easily have obtained another six years as "Head of Government", in the last phase of the negotiations for the Canal treaty the Torrijos regime reiterated the promise that it would unleash a political opening once the accords were ratified (an argument that may have helped Carter persuade Senators to approve the Treaty).

Once the US Senate ratified the Canal treaties, the Torrijos regime extended a political opening leading toward civilian rule. Political parties were allowed to initiate activities and exiles were allowed to return. Aiming to emulate the Institutional Revolutionary Party (PRI) of Mexico, the Torrijos' coalition formed the Democratic Revolutionary Party (PRD), which soon joined the ranks of the Socialist International. Though the opposition played no role in launching the transition, it did take the opportunity afforded to them by the National Guard. Later followed the Christian Democrats, aided by their peers abroad, and supporters of former President Arnulfo Arias (who formed the "Panameñista" Party), in addition to various Liberal Party factions. Most of them participated in the election for Corregimiento Representatives, whose Assembly would choose, according to the 1972 Constitution, the new President, Vice-president, and the members of the new legislative body in October. Supporters of the Torrijos regime easily obtained most of the seats, because it was at the peak of its prestige and because most of these opposition parties, except for the Christian Democrats, had been inactive for ten years. Thus, the Assembly of Corregimiento Representatives endorsed, though not without some arm-twisting by the National Guard, Torrijos' handpicked candidate for the Presidency. Lawyer Aristides Royo, a former Minister of Education under Torrijos and a member of the Panamanian team negotiating the treaties was sworn in as President of Panama, while banker Ricardo De La Espriella was sworn in as Vice-president. Torrijos announced the National Guard would return to the barracks, and from then on kept a low profile in governmental affairs. Continuing as Commander of the National Guard, however, Torrijos remained the "power behind the throne."

With the Canal issue out of the way, the course toward a more democratic political system seemed to fare well for Panama. International conditions were favourable. There was a sympathetic administration in Washington that encouraged respect for human rights and respect for electoral processes. The wave toward democratic transitions had already started in Ecuador and Peru, and the Panamanian regime's most important friends in Latin America were democratic leaders of Costa Rica, Venezuela and Colombia, all of whom had supported the Panamanian cause. With these international conditions in the background, soon after taking over the Royo administration and representatives from political parties agreed to modify the electoral laws and the make-up of the legislative branch. The next President would be elected in 1984 by direct, popular suffrage. In addition, a new legislative Assembly would be formed within two years, only one-third of whose members would be elected directly through the popular vote.

Three factors would hinge on the way the Panamanian transition evolved. First, the evolution of the international arena. If no significant alterations of the international environment took place, external pressures could continue to play a positive role in the furtherance of democracy. Pursuing their own interests, domestic players would have the chance to set up the formal institutions of democracy, at their own pace. Second, the military's commitment to the transition. Under the 1972 Constitution, the National Guard became an autonomous entity. Despite handing power to a civilian, it held substantial power to influence the course of events. In the short term, this commitment would most likely not be maintained if the Chiefs of Staff felt that their main interests were threatened by the transition: their autonomy and the Panamanian government's commitment to respecting the provisions of the Torrijos-Carter treaties. Third, domestic political actors' willingness to participate in the construction of democracy including but beyond setting up and respecting constitutional norms and procedures.

With respect to the latter, Panama's transition had too few democrats to start with. Within Torrijos' inner circle, the charismatic Commander was among the few who favoured launching the transition.[413] Though the Torrijos regime had encouraged mass mobilizations and the participation of organised sectors in government policy and decision-making, by 1978 most of the new generation of political leaders were conditioned to authoritarian rule. The National Guard kept "reserved domains" within the administration. In addition, civilians who participated in the higher echelons of the PRD and the government often requested the National Guard's guidance. From 1903 to 1968 Panama had experienced party politics and elections, but these exercises did not gain enough prestige in the hearts and minds of the population to represent a significant moving force behind democratisation. For example, with the exception of the small Christian Democratic Party, democracy did not figure in the platform of most of the parties and political leaders entering the stage.

Thus the beginning of civilian rule saw a rebirth of traditional political parties with the same leaders, symbols, and forms of discourse reminiscent of the 1960s. Octogenarian Arnulfo Arias, for instance, returned to the country and became the leader of the "opposition." Arias later announced the formation of his "Panameñista Party," which he described as "a circle of influences surrounded by energy, the esoteric force of which is the sign of an inexorable victory." Christian democrats, for example, who are considered to have played a reformist, constructive role elsewhere in Latin America, fell under the leadership of a prominent conservative member of the oligarchy, Ricardo Arias Calderón. Most of his early discourse revolved around the claim that the Royo administration favoured "communist doctrines," partly in response to the new administration's support for the Sandinistas in Nicaragua.[414] Between 1978 and 1984, for example, at no time did the opposition made the effort to establish a modus vivendi with the National Guard in view of furthering democracy. In this context, a positive trajectory of the Panamanian transition would require that the international environment remain favourable and that the National Guard remain devoted to democratisation. But neither of these two endure long enough for the new political institutions to take hold.

---

413. Interview with Marcel Salamín Cárdenas, Torrijos' advisor for ten years. April 12, 2001.

414. Raúl Leis, *Radiografía de los partidos*, (Panamá: Centro de Capacitación Social, 1984), p. 11, 63.

Though the international environment appeared to be warm to the Panamanian regime, there were signs indicating the possibility of a twist. Nearby Central America seemed to be divided over whether exclusionary military dictatorships or reformist civilian or military regimes would dominate the region. According to Dunkerley, after 1968 Torrijos became the "most consistent and serious defender of military reform and nationalism in the [Central American] region."[415] He was particularly active in this sense in El Salvador (Torrijos had graduated from a Salvadoran military school and had several former classmates in the Salvadoran army) and Honduras, but encountered the opposition of Somoza and other right-wing military leaders, who manoeuvred against Torrijos' intentions. During the negotiations for the new Canal treaties, Torrijos learned how external factors become internalized. Thus he sensed that the evolution of the region would affect both Panama's political situation and the United States' commitment to respect the Canal treaties. Consequently, as head of the National Guard Torrijos took bold actions in Central America seeking "a favorable political outcome so that the Panamanian political process would not be adversely affected.[416]

Following this logic, Torrijos unceasingly made efforts to influence regional political developments. In Nicaragua, in addition, dictator Anastasio Somoza Debayle had showed his opposition to the Torrijos regime and to the signing of the Torrijos-Carter Treaty. Thus Torrijos supported the Sandinista National Liberation Front (FSLN)'s struggle against Somoza. Covertly at first, this operation started in 1975, several years before the Sandinistas received the support of broad sectors within the region.[417] The friendly relations between the Sandinistas and Torrijos grew and eventually became public knowledge, so much so that, despite the problems this relationship could have caused for the ratification of the Treaties by the US Senate in 1978, Torrijos did not withdraw his support. This was aided by the fact that the Carter administration perceived Torrijos as a moderating force in the Central American upheaval.[418] Although Torrijos approached El Salvador with similar intentions, he found completely different conditions in that country. The structure of the Salvadoran regime's political and military power was different from that of Somoza's, the rebels' cohesion was precarious, international support for the rebel groups was much weaker, and the chances of the Carter administration allowing another revolution—after those

415. James Dunkerley, "Central America: Collapse of the Military System." In Christopher Clapham and George Philip (eds.), *The Political Dilemmas of Military Regimes*, (London: Croom Helm, 1985), pp. 176-177.

416. Unpublished interview of Guillermo Manuel Ungo, leader of the Revolutionary Democratic Front of El Salvador (FDR), 23 December 1986.

417. The full account is in José de Jesús Martínez, *Mi General Torrijos*, (La Habana: Casa de las Américas, 1988).

418. Telephone interview with former President James Carter, Berkeley, California, March 1986. Published in Giancarlo Soler Torrijos, "No hemos tenido el apoyo adecuado de Washington para el proceso de Contadora. Entrevista a James Carter", *Diálogo Social*, (September 1986), p. 47.

in Nicaragua and Iran in 1979—were minimal.[419] In late 1979, to aid Carter's bid to the White House, Torrijos welcomed in Panama the deposed Shah of Iran, Mohammed Reza Pahvlevi, and later participated in negotiations to obtain the liberation of American hostages prior to the November 1980 elections in the United States. With this aim in mind, Torrijos also played with the idea of trading the Shah for the US hostages, but apparently the Iranian revolutionary regime was not interested.[420]

In 1981, two major events altered the setting in which the Panamanian transition unfolded. The first was Ronald Reagan's access to the White House in January. Not only had Reagan publicly opposed transferring the Canal to Panama, but several of his ideologues had openly criticised Torrijos' alleged leftist orientation and had publicly asked for a "reversal" of his regime.[421] For instance, Jeanne Kirpatrick's famous *Commentary* Article that brought her to Reagan's attention referred to Torrijos as a "tinpot dictator".[422] Recovering US hegemony became the Reagan administration's imperative, giving US foreign policy an unusually offensive character. This implied a reorientation of US foreign policy priorities away from promoting democracy and respect for human rights and toward national security concerns reminiscent of the Cold War. The Reagan administration pledged to respect the Canal accords and adopted a cautious approach toward the Panamanian regime. But the change in US priorities was clear enough; indeed, following orders from Torrijos, in 1981 then-Lieutenant Colonel Manuel Noriega, the National Guard's intelligence chief, met in Washington with the CIA Director to discuss the "problems in Central America" and the ways in which Panama could continue to cooperate with US intelligence.[423] From then on, Noriega worked to forge a closer relationship with the United States.[424]

The second event was Torrijos' sudden death on 31 July 1981. The fall of the "Leader of the Revolution" upset the domestic political equilibrium and the National Guard's commitment toward democratisation. Before disappearing from the scene, Torrijos had been preparing a reorganisation of the National Guard because he distrusted his followers in the chain of command would allow civilians to take hold.[425] At the time of Torrijos' death, nobody had been groomed

---

419. Marcel Salamín, *El Salvador: sin piso ni techo*, (Bogotá: Editorial La Oveja Negra, 1980), p. 68.

420. Interview with former President Ricardo De la Espriella, September 1995. According to former National Security Advisor Robert Pastor, this piece of information was not known in the Carter administration.

421. Santa Fe Committee, "A New Interamerican Policy for the Eighties," Report dated in 1980.

422. Jeanne Kirpatrick, "Dictatorship and Double Standards," *Commentary* No. 68 (November 1979), pp. 34–35.

423. Noriega, *The Memoirs of Manuel Noriega*, p. 65.

424. "Torrijos separated the armies (of both countries), but I have united them even more," Noriega said to Undersecretary of State Richard Armitage in November 1987, as the United States demanded his resignation as head of the PDF. Quoted in Frederick Kempe, *Divorcing the Dictator*, (New York: G.P. Putnam's Sons, 1990), p. 328.

425. Kempe, *Divorcing the Dictator*, pp. 164–165.

for the succession; thus a struggle for power ensued. Sub-Commander Floren-cio Flores took Torrijos' position, but he was soon bypassed by Colonels Pare-des, Noriega and Díaz Herrera, the only officers in whom Torrijos had confided when dealing with political affairs. The political apposition, though exhilarated by the fall of the government's champion, remained badly divided and did not take advantage of the new situation. Royo, arguing that he owed his Presidency to Torrijos, offered the Chiefs of Staff his resignation, but they rejected it on the grounds that it would look like a coup d'etat.[426] In March 1982, the chiefs of staff forced Torrijos' immediate successor, Col. Florencio Flores, into retirement, giving way to the rise of Colonel Rubén Darío Paredes as commander in chief. But Paredes disliked Royo's political leanings and had Presidential aspirations himself. In July, on the first anniversary of Torrijos' death, Paredes forced Presi-dent Royo to resign.[427] Royo, arguing he had a severe sore throat that impeded him from performing his duties, did not defend his office and accepted a post as Ambassador to Madrid. Vice-president Ricardo De la Espriella was swore in as President but the State Department did not comment on this event. Instead, soon afterwards President Reagan congratulated the new President and offered financial and technical assistance.

Throughout Royo's term in office, Torrijos had remained the figure that maintained his reformist coalition in power by the force of his own leadership qualities. Royo had kept for himself a large room for manoeuver, but Torrijos had stepped in on critical domestic issues. Key National Guard officers ignored the President and Torrijos continued to second-guess and veto presidential decisions at the request of third parties. Torrijos was always a course of last resort to which Panamanians took their complaints about Royo and his policies.[428] In doing so, Torrijos undermined domestic and international actors' confidence in the transi-tion. Worse so, since Royo performed poorly as President and did not acquire the prestige or the power to rule in his own right. The power vacuum left by Torrijos' death left him even weaker, since his sole significant support disappeared. His quiet acceptance of the National Guard's move could only prove what most ac-tors already observed about the continuing domination of the military.

Royo's forced resignation had long term repercussions for the evolution of the Panamanian transition. The delicate balance between civilians and the Na-tional Guard in the composition of the regime was definitely tilted toward the latter. For instance, whereas Royo's cabinet and the PRD's leadership structure had been selected by the President himself, as soon as Royo left most of these

---

426. Interview with former PRD President Berta Torrijos de Arosemena, July 1995; this piece of information was confirmed with other interviews.

427. The coup against Royo occurred after he showed his intention of continuing the anti-hegemonic foreign policy initiated under Gen. Torrijos. Between Torrijos' death and Royo's ouster from the presidency one year later, Panama publicly stated its opposition to US intervention in El Salvador, criticized the US training of the Salvadoran military, and backed a French-Mexican declaration that recognized, despite Washington's opposition, the Salva-doran rebels' military strength as well as their broad constituency within that country.

428. Confidential Telegram from the American Embassy in Panama to the Secretary of State, dated 8 August 1981.

positions were approved or selected by the National Guard's Commander. Likewise, as De la Espriella was sworn in as the new President, Commander Paredes had warned him to "behave." From then on, every time the Chief of the National Guard felt uneasy about the President, he forced his resignation or manoeuvred the Legislative Assembly turn over the presidential office to a successor. President De La Espriella was forced to resign in February 1984, President Jorge Illueca was almost overthrown a few weeks before the end of his term in October 1984, while Presidents Nicolás Arditto Barletta (1984–1985) and Eric Delvalle (1985–1987) followed.

Throughout most of the eighties, the National Guard's hold on power was legitimated by an odd partnership between Torrijistas, the left, organised labour, university intellectuals, the modern sector of the business community, Western democratic leaders and Washington, who for different reasons connived at the resurgence of military authoritarianism disguised in constitutional liturgies. Within the National Guard (from 1983, it changed its name to Panamanian Defense Forces), Torrijos' successors justified this policy change by the need to safeguard "Torrijos' legacy"—as they interpreted it.[429] The National Guard felt threatened by the arrival of the political opposition to power, most of whose leaders had rejected the Canal Treaties and the Torrijos regime, to whom they were indebted for their new role in Panamanian society. To justify this shift, the Chiefs of Staff argued that the National Guard had initiated a revolution in 1968 which would not be "perfected" until the year 2000, and for which they had to stay as guardians of Panamanian sovereignty.

Mistrusting electoral politics and feeling threatened by the Reagan administration's policy toward Central America, Torrijistas, the left, many university intellectuals and organised labour acquiesced to this turn of events. They feared the alternative was a government that would renegotiate the Canal treaties to extend the presence of US military bases in Panama and dismantle Torrijos' legacy altogether. The modern sector of the business community and political parties linked to it welcomed the regime's economic policy favouring the banking and financial sector of the economy, and dreaded that a return of Arias to power would bring political instability. Western democratic leaders from Spain, Venezuela, Colombia and elsewhere in Latin America maintained good relations with the

---

429. This effort was sanctioned with a written, secret pact signed by Commander Paredes, and Colonels Noriega and Díaz Herrera. Initially, Paredes agreed to retire voluntarily months before the 1984 general elections, in exchange for Noriega and Díaz Herrera help him gain the ruling party's nomination for the 1984 elections and a "clear-cut victory." Thereafter Noriega was to assume the position of commander of the PDF, and was to remain in that position until July 1987. Noriega was then to turn the position of Commander to Díaz Herrera, who would keep it for one year, until July 1988. Paredes left the National Guard in August 1983. Later, sensing his candidacy did not receive the support from the PRD and the National Guard, resigned from his bid to obtain the presidential nomination (a few months later he recanted and was nominated by a small political party). This agreement was disclosed by Díaz Herrera in June 1987 when, in the midst of a breakdown over seeing his personal ambitions being frustrated, he lashed out verbally against his former comrade-in-arms. Copies of this pact are included in Mayín Correa (comp.), *La gran rebelión blanca*, (Miami, Florida: SIBI, 1987).

Panamanian regime. This came partly as a result of the past ties established during the Torrijos years to support the Panamanian cause but also as an effort to preserve Panama's independence vis-à-vis the Reagan administration's policy toward Central America. The Reagan administration, for its part, despite its differences on foreign policy matters with the Panamanian executive, gained the subtle cooperation of the Panamanian military for its strategy toward Central America. The military "cooperation" between the PDF and the United States soon paid off, both for the PDF's ambitions and for the Reagan administration. Commander Noriega allowed the CIA to build installations to train the Nicaraguan Contras, which were to remain secret "at any cost."[430]

Such an odd alliance did not go on without contradictions. Several times the fact that the Torrijistas maintained important positions in government, in particular in foreign policy decision making, prevented Noriega's cooperation with the United States from translating into a greater US military presence in the isthmus. Due to its geographic position, Panama could not ignore the Central American conflict, which threatened to engulf the whole region. Hence, despite the closer ties between the Panamanian military and Washington, the Ministry of Foreign Affairs headed, along with other countries in the region, the efforts to conduct peace negotiations in Central America. In January 1983, Panama (now under President Ricardo De la Espriella), along with Venezuela, Colombia and Mexico, formed the Contadora Group (named after an island off the coast of Panama City where Foreign Ministers of these countries first met), aimed at seeking a peaceful solution to the Central American imbroglio, in opposition to the Reagan administration. During Jorge Illueca's short term in office (February to October 1984), for example, Panama supported Nicaragua's self-determination. As the May 1984 elections approached, Noriega announced that the PDF would take part in the military exercises the United States planned to conduct in Honduras. Nevertheless, after the Ministry of Foreign Affairs turned down the American invitation, Noriega recanted.[431] President Illueca also refused to sign an agreement prepared by the US Southern Command and the PDF aimed at extending the operations of the School of the Americas on Panamanian soil, which was to expire just days before the end of Illueca's term in office. For this reason the PDF sought to have the Legislative Assembly oust Illueca, but instead got the Assembly to name a brother of Noriega's as an advisor to the President, who was given the task of tracking Illueca's moves.[432]

The May 1984 elections thus did not constitute a test of domestic and external actors' commitment toward Panama's democratization. Rather, it became an opportunity to renew this "marriage of convenience", giving further ammunition for the PDF to extend its hold on power. The candidate of the opposition, octo-

430. Bob Woodward, *Veil: The Secret Wars of the CIA*, (New York: Simon & Schuster Inc, 1987), p. 233.

431. María Eliana Castillo, "Después del canal: nuevos desafíos en la política exterior de Panamá." In Heraldo Muñoz (comp.), *Las políticas exteriores latinoamericanas frente a la crisis*, (Buenos Aires: Grupo Editor Latinoamericano, 1985), p. 293.

432. Ibid, p. 291.

genarian Arnulfo Arias, threatened to dismiss the entire structure of the PDF if he won.[433] Commander Manuel Noriega sought to find a presidential candidate amenable to both the Reagan administration and Torrijistas. He offered it first to Fernando Manfredo, a former Minister of Commerce and Industries under Torrijos and then the Sub-administrator of the Panama Canal Commission, the entity in charge of the administration of the Canal.[434] On his refusal, they offered it to Nicolás Ardito-Barletta, a former Minister of Planning under Torrijos and then the World Bank's vice-president for Latin America, who also seemed to be supported by the State Department.[435] The PDF deemed Ardito-Barletta an asset because he had also been a student of Secretary of State George Schultz at the University of Chicago. Thus during the electoral process the PDF committed fraud against Arias. The political opposition remained badly divided, momentarily united by the Christian Democratic Party's efforts to present a common ticket for the election. Yet it did not gather mass support equivalent to the kind it had received through the ballots.

The differing aims of the actors supporting the renewal of authoritarian rule meant that the contradictions and political instability went on. Arditto-Barleta had a very difficult time appointing the members of his cabinet, and sometimes his only chance of showing he was the President was to appoint as Minister of Health the person who had been designated by his allies as Minister of Foreign Affairs and vice-versa. Technocrat Ardito Barletta was unable to bring about any consensus in government policies among those who backed his candidacy. Once he tried to wield his scant power by naming an independent commission to investigate the assassination of Hugo Spadafora, the PDF twisted the arm of the Legislative Assembly to grant him a "leave of absence" and swear in Vice-president Eric Delvalle as President of the Republic. Spadafora had been Vice Minister of Health under Torrijos and had joined the anti-Somoza struggle in Nicaragua, before finally supporting the Contras' Southern Front. Several months before his death he had publicly accused Noriega of involvement in drug trafficking. The White House expressed its irritation with Ardito Barletta's ousting by cancelling the flow of aid. Despite the United States' opposition to Barletta's ousting, Noriega refused to be budged. US Ambassador Everett Briggs asked Noriega not to do it, while NSC advisor Néstor Sanchez warned him that, if Ardito Barletta were dismissed, "it woud never be forgiven by the State Department."[436] Noriega could have used his influence to prevent the President's dismissal, but everyone in the government coalition was lined up against Ardito Barletta anyway. To avoid a falling out with his mentors in Washington, Noriega carried out a sustained effort to portray himself as being in line with US regional security concerns.[437] Subsequently, Panama adopted a low key approach to the

---

433. Noriega, *The Memoirs of Manuel Noriega*, p. 116.

434. Interview with Fernando Manfredo, August 1995.

435. According to Noriega, "that was what the Americans wanted." Noriega, *The Memoirs of Manuel Noriega*, p.117.

436. Noriega, *The Memoirs of Manuel Noriega*, p. 122–123.

437. Thus he told a biennial meeting of the Inter-American Defense Council—as Latin

Central American peace process. In addition, President Delvalle and Noriega hired a public relations firm in Washington to lobby the Reagan administration in their favour.

In the context of the Central American crisis, the Reagan administration could not afford to lose Noriega as an ally. Though his contributions to the United States' low intensity war in Central America might be questionable, the question of who would succeed Noriega if he departed and what impact this would have on the PDF and the governments' orientation had no definite answer at this moment. Noriega's second-in-command Colonel Díaz Herrera, for example, was seen by the State Department as a leftist. Thus the Reagan administration initially sought a conciliatory position to prevent its relationship with Panama from deteriorating into possibly risky extremist positions. For instance, in September 1986, forty-six senators voted against a bill submitted by Senator Jesse Helms requesting that the CIA investigate the PDF's role in drug trafficking. An aide to Assistant Secretary of State Abrams explained to the House Select Committee on Narcotics "we do not believe that our interests will be well served by adding public speculations over this matter."[438] In September 1986, CIA Director Casey and National Security Advisor Colonel Oliver North countered the charge that Noriega had cooperated with traffickers shipping drugs to the United States. North reportedly hired an advertising agency to reduce the effects of the anti-Noriega campaign, after the Panamanian strongman promised to devise a plan to assassinate the entire Sandinista leadership in Nicaragua. Senate hearings on Panama were carried out anyway, called by Senator Jesse Helms. Assistant Secretary of State for Inter-American Affairs Elliot Abrams made an effort to convince Helms not to hold the talks because he felt that "it is not the adequate moment" since Noriega had promised to cooperate with the US effort against the Nicaraguan government.[439] Abrams added that the administration was not ready to "classify Panama as a democracy," but that it was necessary to realize that "no dispute has taken place over the presence of US military forces" with Panamanian authorities; the Reagan administration had "a great respect for the Panamanian government and its civilian and *military* leaders."[440] However, the State Department quietly undertook actions to prepare the setting for aiding the Panamanian opposition to the controversial General. In the first months of 1987, Panamanian business leaders were invited by the National Democratic Institute to the Philippines so that they would become familiar with the process that led to the ousting of dictator Ferdinand Marcos, and the State Department

---

American countries, including Panama, carried out efforts to bring about peace in Central America—that the peace negotiations in the region were futile because the "grave communist threat" had to be faced first. Quoted in Dinges, *Our Man in Panama*, p. 293.

438. Ricardo Urrutia, "Panamá: Las crecientes tensiones con Estados Unidos." In Heraldo Muñoz (comp.), *Las políticas exteriores de América Latina y el Caribe: continuidad en la crisis*, (Buenos Aires: Grupo Editor Latinoamericano, 1986), pp. 414, 417.

439. Dinges, *Our Man in Panama*, pp. 287-288.

440. Emphasis added. Ricardo Urrutia, "Panamá: las crecientes tensiones con Estados Unidos," pp. 412-413.

transferred diplomatic officer John Maisto from the US Embassy in Philippines to Panama.

Changing international and domestic circumstances

From 1986, the pillars sustaining international order started to change, forcing the United States to progressively reassess its foreign policy priorities regarding the rest of the world. Premier Mikhail Gorbachev's "new thinking" altered the Soviet Union's domestic and foreign policies, aimed at a restructuring of the country's economy. The relaxing of tensions brought about by the changes in the Soviet Union redefined the hypotheses on which US strategic plans had been based. Washington was freer to move to the back burner one of the main conventional scenarios of its Cold War's grand strategy: the possibility of a confrontation with the Warsaw Pact in Western Europe. This led the United States to reevaluate conventional warfare and to foresee that the setting of future confrontations would be in the Third World. Politically, the issues of democracy promotion and the war against illegal drug trafficking climbed on Washington's foreign policy agenda.

Throughout the eighties, Panama slowly reacquired its importance within the United States' global projection of power. At the beginning of the decade, the United States increased its intelligence gathering capabilities in the country. US installations in the isthmus became capable of monitoring all of Central America and much of South America. According to Palmer, the Panama Canal itself was no longer vital, but "in a wider context... the area formerly called the Canal Zone continues to be an important strategic site for the support of activities, in situations of crisis, affecting the national interest anywhere in the Caribbean basin or South America." But these installations were scheduled to close, according to the Carter-Torrijos treaties. Yet the loss of base rights in the Canal Zone could translate into "tangible and intangible costs which might not be acceptable for the United States... (since) as [the] nation and as [the] people want to stay as a superpower."[441] With this objective in mind, General John Galvin, in a farewell speech before being transferred from his position as head of the Southern Command to head of the NATO in 1986, stated that the United States might hand over administration of the Canal to Panama ten years ahead of time (31 December 1989) in exchange for Panama allowing some of the main American military bases to remain until 2015.

To move in this direction, the United States required a different set of interlocutors in Panama. Not only Noriega sometimes got out of hand, but the PDF's raison d'etre was built on the supposition that it would replace the US armed forces in its role of defending the Canal from external threats. Noriega's apparent corruption could be undervalued for some time, but these plans required strategists to think in the long term. In any case, in the event that a reformulation of the Canal treaties was indeed proposed by Washington, Panama's counterpart would have to be legitimate in the eyes of Panamanian and international public

---

441. Gral. Bruce Palmer, *Intervention in the Caribbean: The Dominican Crisis of 1965*, (Lexington, Kentucky: The University Press of Kentucky, 1989), pp. 174–175, 181.

opinion to have a greater chance of success. Because these considerations, American political analysts and military strategists maintained that Treaty changes were required. For example, in March 1987 Assistant Secretary of State for Legislative and Intergovernmental Affairs J. Edward Fox said in a letter to Senator Jesse Helms that "when the Carter-Torrijos treaties are renegotiated, we will have to bring up to discussion the issue of prolonging US military presence in the Panama Canal beyond the year 2000" and that "steps will be taken to resolve" these needs.[442]

The United States possessed a set of strategic and logistic facilities on Panamanian territory that—in accordance with the Carter-Torrijos Accords—had to be unequivocally transferred by the end of the century. The United States maintained in Panama the headquarters of the Southern Command and the Southern Army, charged with US defense south of its borders. According to General Fred Woerner, head of the Southern Command until September 1989, of the Southern Command's leading objectives, that of defending the Panama Canal was among the last priorities. According to Woerner, the Southern Command's objectives were, in this order: to guarantee American national interests in Latin America, for which reason it was assigned the task of supporting counterinsurgency operations in El Salvador; to ward off Soviet, Cuban, and Nicaraguan influence; to carry out Washington's foreign policy objectives; to increase US military influence in the region; and, among others, to defend the Panama Canal.[443] To extend its military, logistic, and intelligence capacity, the United States also placed in Panama sophisticated systems in support of these objectives.[444]

In addition to these strategic changes, two unexpected events in 1987 triggered the break in the marriage of convenience sustaining military authoritarianism. First, CIA Director William Casey died in early 1987. Since 1981, Casey had been Noriega's main interlocutor within the Reagan administration. These ties appeared to Noriega so strong that he believes Casey had the power to defend him and, because of his death, his opponents in Washington were able to take the upper hand.[445] Second, the PDF's Sub-commander in chief, Colonel Roberto Díaz Herrera, retired in June. During a nervous breakdown, a few days later he accused Noriega of a series of crimes, including rigging the 1984 elections, and involvement in Spadafora's and Torrijos' deaths, among others (he

---

442. At the moment, there were no formal negotiations between the two countries, although within the inner circles of the President's office and the PDF, such an intention was expected. A reprinted version of this letter is in Nils Castro, *Objetivos Estratégicos de Estados Unidos en Panamá*, (San José, Costa Rica: Comité de Solidaridad con Panamá, 1988), pp. 21, 22–23.

443. General Fred Woerner, "The Strategic Imperatives for the United States in Latin America", *Military Review* vol. LXIX, no. 2r3 (February 1989), p. 22.

444. Among others, an electronic communications command and control centre was set up on Panama's Galeta Island. There the Pentagon built a submarine platform equipped with an electronic espionage centre for gathering intelligence information. The island's geological and magnetic conditions facilitated these operations as did no other place in the world. See Castro, *Objetivos Estratégicos de Estados Unidos en Panamá*, pp. 9–11.

445. Noriega, *The Memoirs of Manuel Noriega*, p. 66.

thought he might be next).[446] Coming as this did from someone belonging to Noriega's inner circle, the charges against Noriega elicited rounds of protests from prominent members of Panamanian business organizations, who formed the "Civilist Crusade." The Crusade's activists bypassed political party lines and included most of the white-collar workers from the urban financial and banking centre in downtown Panama City. Though at first Panamanians everywhere participated in the protests, the Crusade did not elicit the backing of large segments of the population, who distrusted the business leader's aims. Yet they did bring a substantial amount of international attention onto the controversial military leader and on the nature of the Panamanian regime. This was particularly acute in the United States, where most opinion leaders criticised US ties with the PDF's Commander.

With so much international attention on Noriega's alleged drug dealings, the Reagan administration ended its defence of the PDF Commander. Domestic considerations also made it hard for the Reagan administration to maintain its former relationship with the controversial General. Republicans had lost control of both Houses of Congress since the November 1986 elections and the Iran-Contra Scandals were still making news.[447] At this time, Reagan had lost control of the Central American policy. Thus, from June to December of that year, Noriega and representatives of the United States conducted negotiations, seeking a way out for the Panamanian military leader. After these negotiations failed, American federal prosecutors in February 1988 charged Noriega with involvement in drug trafficking. Precisely at a time when a "Latin American" initiative to find a political solution to the crisis gained strength—headed by the former presidents of Costa Rica, Colombia, and Venezuela, Daniel Oduber, Alfonso López Michelsen, and Carlos Andrés Pérez, respectively—Abrams pressured President Delvalle to take steps to oust the Panamanian "strongman." However, the ploy failed when, at Noriega's insistence, the Legislative Assembly convened and impeached the President on hastily prepared charges of "treason against the country." Following constitutional procedures, Delvalle's Education Minister, Manuel Solís Palma, was thus named "Minister in-Charge-of the Presidency."

Following Delvalle's dismissal, who went into exile in the United States, the Reagan administration imposed sanctions on Panama. The sanctions deprived the Panamanian state of the resources it needed to maintain a minimal investment program with which to improve its failing economy. The United States eliminated aid programs, excluded Panama from participating in the Caribbean Basin Initiative, and reduced Panama's sugar quota for export to the United States. In addition, all payments derived from the Canal operations were held back, as were payments from American companies for public services, and income-tax refunds owed to Panamanians employed on the Panama Canal Commission. All Panamanian government funds deposited in American banks were frozen. It also with-

---

446. Díaz Herrera, however, had no proofs for most of these charges but for the rigging of elections, in which he participated. Interview with Roberto Díaz Herrera, July 1995.

447. These circumstances are narrated by Theodore Draper, *A very thin line: the Iran-contra affairs*, (New York: Hill and Wang, 1991).

held recognition of the Solis Palma administration and continued to recognize Delvalle as the legitimate President of Panama. These measures were supposed to eventually provoke a greater repudiation of Noriega, possibly strong enough for its domestic interlocutors to gain enough strength to depose the dictator. And they almost did. In March 1988, several PDF Colonels made an effort to oust Noriega, but the coup was thwarted by forces loyal to the controversial General.

By mid 1988, the State Department and the Pentagon differed on how to deal with Noriega. Abrams proposed that Noriega be abducted and brought to the United States to face drug-trafficking charges and that a parallel government be established in Panama, on an American base in the former Canal Zone. For the Pentagon, the conditions were not yet ripe for an armed incursion, since this would have required a large increase in the number of troops stationed in Panama, to protect American citizens living there.[448] To carry out Abrams' plan it would have been necessary to know Noriega's precise whereabouts which, despite the Pentagon's logistic and intelligence equipment installed in their bases in Panama, were not easy to ascertain. In addition, the Pentagon also feared the reaction of the governments and peoples of Latin America to a resurrection of American interventionism as well as the real possibility that, faced with an attack on that scale, Noriega would have been tempted to take hostages from the American population living in Panama. The general aspects of this position were consistent with the Pentagon's post-Vietnam determination not to use American troops for foreign-policy objectives, especially when the objectives were less than clear.[449] A military intervention in Panama under these conditions would not have resolved the United States' short-term concerns over the government that would replace Noriega. Between a highly bellicose and ideological State Department and a highly pragmatic Defense Department there was a momentarily insurmountable rift over US policy vis-à-vis Panama.[450]

In light of this impasse, the White House sought a deal with Noriega. Before Delvalle's dismissal, Washington had set into motion a plan to force Noriega out of power. In May, when it was clear that the sanctions had not immediately led to popular uprisings against Noriega, Washington made a second attempt to negotiate his departure. According to Kempe, the White House sent an envoy with an offer that included a twenty-million-dollar bribe, which would be transferred through a Colombian bank linked to the laundering of drug money.[451] The plan also called for the lifting of sanctions against Panama, recognizing President Manuel Solís Palma, while Noriega was to announce his retirement in a grandiose ceremony on 12 August, his fifth anniversary as commander of the PDF.

The year 1988 was an electoral year and thus the Reagan administration had to be cautious in handling Noriega in order to avoid harming the Republican bid

---

448. Kemp, *Divorcing the dictator*, p.423.

449. Richard Halloran, "US Troops to Go Slowly Into Panama", *The New York Times*, 12 May 1989, p. A8.

450. "Fracasó el Bloqueo Económico y Político a Panamá: W. Crowe", *Excelsior*, 17 October 1989, pp. 2-A, 27-A.

451. Kempe, *Divorcing the Dictator*, pp.439–440.

for the Presidency, which by mid 1988 seemed to falter. To counter criticism that he was negotiating with Noriega, Reagan stated his opposition to extraditing the General on the grounds that such an option would be a violation of the Panamanian Constitution, and that he was pursuing the best path since force should not be used, so as to avoid a "body count"—in clear reference to the Vietnam syndrome.[452] Noriega was to seek asylum in Spain, and Washington was to grant him immunity from prosecution and would not, according to the plan approved by the White House, oppose his return to Panama to run for the presidency in 1989.[453] Although Noriega agreed to the terms of the Reagan administration's plan, it did not materialize because mid-level Panamanian officers pressured the General not to make concessions to what they felt was manoeuvering that would eventually lead to greater capitulations.[454] Noriega stood still hoping the pressures against him would subside after a new President was elected in the United States in November. The White House put forward no further initiatives, while Noriega worked to strengthen his grasp on power.

The apparent intention of many influential Congressmen to obstruct the implementation of the Panama Canal treaties increased tensions between the two countries and augmented the regime's fears about reaching a deal with the Reagan administration. On 4 March 1988, for instance, Senator Jesse Helms proposed to Congress that the President inform the Panamanian government of the United States' intention to suspend the implementation of the treaties if necessary for defending "the supreme national security interests of the United States"—particularly any provision of the accords calling for the withdrawal of military personnel stationed in the isthmus or for the closing of any military bases on the banks of the Canal, "unless Noriega is extradited in thirty days."[455] Later a group of congressmen headed by Republican Congressman Philip Crane introduced a resolution proposal in both houses of Congress calling for the Canal treaties and all related legislation to be repealed.[456]

Under these conditions, another electoral process was most unlikely to generate legitimacy to either contender or produce a democratic outcome. Yet it had to be carried out to fulfil the Constitutional mandate. Again, Noriega imposed

---

452. Kempe, *Divorcing the Dictator*, p. 434.

453. Kevin Buckley, *Panama: The Whole Story*, (New York: Simon & Schuster, 1991), pp. 140–145.

454. This fear was underlined by a confidential State Department document, written on 27 October 1987, stating that "Noriega is not the only problem," not even the most important one. The document explained that If Noriega left and the group of Noriega's inmediate inner circle took power, things could worsen. "Their access to power must be blocked. They must be isolated." The US State Department Document titled "Thoughts on a Panamanian Political Solution" was leaked to the Press and is quoted in "Panamá: intervención y soberanía", *Coyuntura Centroamericana* no. 6-7, February-March 1988, p. 21.

455. *Congressional Record*, 4 March 1988, pp. S1949-S1951.

456. These congressmen also expressed their concern over the fact that neither the Treaty nor its amendments include any legal provision giving the United States the right to "keep defense forces or enter into Panama... to defend the Canal beyond the year 1999." *Congressional Record*, 10 August 1988, p. S11476.

the candidates from the pro-government coalition for the May 1989 elections. A partner of Noriega's in various companies was anointed as the PRD's candidate for president; a brother-in-law of Noriega's as candidate for first Vice-President; and a former Ambassador to Washington as candidate for second Vice-President. Since the octogenarian leader had died a year earlier, the opposition named Guillermo Endara, a former private secretary of Arias, as their choice for the presidency. This occurred only after Arias' widow rejected the candidacy (possibly blackmailed by Noriega's thugs) and the US Embassy pressured the rest of the opposition leaders (who had no confidence in Endara) to present a common ticket for the election. The Bush administration channelled some ten million dollars to aid the opposition's bid. This money was used to instruct electoral officials, to train contingents in Panama as well as in Costa Rica and Venezuela at institutes belonging to Christian Democratic parties and, during the electoral campaign itself, to up the ante offered by pro-government candidates for votes—up to one hundred dollars a piece. According to President George Bush, the US intention was not so much to achieve a solution to the Panamanian crisis through the ballot box, but to "force Noriega to take straightforwardly fraudulent measures."[457] Members of the House Select Intelligence Committee judged this policy as being contrary to the stated objective of supporting Panamanian democratisation.[458]

By holding elections, the Noriega regime hoped to abate expectations for change, giving domestic and international legitimacy to Noriega's ally and granting an extension to the PDF's continuing role in the administration of government. None of the major actors was interested in the purity of the electoral process. Both the government and the opposition bought votes and judges, coerced freedom of information—for which the opposition used American networks stationed in Panama—and spent huge sums of money (state funds in the case of the government and foreign funds in the case of the local opposition). Noriega and his allies were convinced that their candidate would win without resorting to fraud; hence, they proceeded with the decision to hold elections, despite the overwhelming evidence of US meddling.[459] However, the size of the electoral defeat suffered by the PRD was so large and international attention so acute that the PDF proceeded to annul the results of the elections..

Between May and September, Latin American governments sought to mediate through the offices of the Organization of American States. Most Latin American countries expressed their preference for an arrangement allowing for a

---

457. Stephen Engelberg, "US Officials Say Senators Balked at Noriega Ouster", *The New York Times*, 24 April 1989, pp. 1A, 11A.

458. Stephen Engelberg, "C.I.A. funnels Aid to Noriega's Elections Foes", *The New York Times*, 23 April 1989, p. 11A.

459. Jorge Ritter, *Los secretos de la Nunciatura*, (Bogotá: Editorial Oveja Negra, 1990), 127. The possibility of defeat in the elections had been foreseen by lower-ranking members of the PDF's intelligence command, but they chose not to make use of their reports, so that Noriega's electoral defeat would contribute to a restructuring of the army (later on, after receiving evidence of the participation of intelligence personnel in favor of opposition candidates, Noriega dismissed several intelligence officers).

"national solution," through sharing power with the opposition, even if this meant accepting an annulment of the May elections, which the opposition rejected outright. They also coincided, through an OAS resolution, in condemning Noriega for "abuses in the crisis and in Panama's electoral process [which] could trigger an intensification of violence with the consequent risks for the lives and safety of persons."[460] According to a Latin American diplomat, "the idea is to reaffirm our solidarity against Noriega to show that we are assuming an increasingly more serious attitude, and [to show] that the situation is not simply one of Noriega against the United States."[461] In any case, the OAS mediation effort was not conclusive. Noriega was reluctant to leave his position of commander in chief and the opposition, who had been receiving the guidance of US Embassy personnel throughout the campaign, refused to enter into negotiations.[462]

On 1 September 1989 Solis Palma's term in office expired. To fill this vacuum, the Noriega regime chose Comptroller Francisco Rodríguez as President of the Republic. But Rodríguez had no other source of support than the PDF nor did he enjoy the conditional endorsement of several Latin American countries that had initially chosen to condemn US interventionism stronger than Panama's military authoritarianism. Noriega used it as an opportunity to create the conditions where an understanding could be reached with the White House.

Cornered by the United States, Noriega desperately attempted to cut a deal with his adversaries in Washington. Noriega ordered President Rodríguez to renegotiate the agreements governing US military bases. Rodríguez announced in a UN conference on 3 October that he was willing to renegotiate American military bases in the isthmus, and offered Panamanian territory as a operations base for a multinational force to fight drug trafficking.[463] Then Noriega initiated another round of talks with State Department envoys in order to find a political exit for himself. Noriega also sought conditions that would allow him to negotiate with the United States: he secretly had himself tried by the Panamanian Supreme Court on the same charges that had been filed against him in Florida, in an attempt to use the universal principle that no one can be tried twice for the same offence.[464]

In Panama, most analysts speculated on how and when Washington would find a way to reach a settlement with Noriega, the US' old "Man in Panama."[465]

---

460. "México y la resolución de la OEA sobre Panamá", *El Día*, (México, D.F.), 25 May 1989.

461. John Mc Clintock, "Comenzaron a presionar a Panamá E.U. y sus principales aliados de América Latina", *Excelsior*, 29 October 1989, pp. 36A, 38A.

462. Interview with former President Manuel Solís Palma, September 1995.

463. "Ofensiva de Panamá para evitar el aislamiento político", *Excelsior*, 28 October 1989, pp. 2-A, 21A.

464. Ritter, *Los secretos de la Nunciatura*, p. 174.

465. This is based on evidence described by several authors, most notably that of Dinges, *Our Man in Panama*, and Kempe, *Divorcing the Dictator*; their research lead to the conclusion that there was a clear link between Noriega and the CIA for not less than two decades. Neither of these two authors, however, explores the possibility that Noriega's alleged relationship with international drug trafficking could have been a product of his apparent ties to the CIA.

Most local observers believed Bush would resume the cordial relationship Washington had established with the Panamanian military under its controversial leader. The relative failure of Bush's predecessor in the White House, Ronald Reagan, vis-à-vis the Panamanian crisis in mid-1987, and vis-à-vis the Central American crisis, encouraged the Noriega regime's political strategists to trust President Bush to show moderation regarding the impasse in the isthmus. As head of the CIA in the Ford administration (1974–1977), Bush had been Noriega's counterpart during the last phase of the Panama Canal Treaty negotiations.

The Panamanian government anticipated a negotiated solution that would not force it to capitulate to Washington. To increase the likelihood of this outcome, during the 1988 US electoral campaign Noriega made an effort to aid the Republican's bid for the Presidency. He did so by ensuring that his own figure did not become a source of polemics in the Presidential race, by refusing to give Bush's Democratic rival, Michael Dukakis, potentially damaging information on Bush, and by providing money to Bush's electoral campaign.[466] In Panama, Noriega manipulated government-controlled newspapers in favour of his purported enemy, both during the presidential campaign and the brief interim between Bush's victory in November 1988 and his inauguration in January 1989.

These efforts were answered in kind in Washington, though for different aims. In May 1988, leading Pentagon and State Department officials ordered the head of the Southern Command in Panama, Gen. Fred Woerner, to reduce the risk of a conflict with the Panamanian military until the end of the electoral race in the United States. The purpose of this policy was to avoid a situation in which the Republican administration's mistakes would be made public, since Bush, as Vice President under Ronald Reagan, was intrinsically linked to that administration.[467] In fact, Bush's electoral victory was applauded by Noriega's closest advisors, who hoped that sooner or later the more cautious groups of the Republican administration would prevail. Not only Noriega's inner associates but most international observers expected the Bush administration to refrain from implementing unilateral measures, allowing a greater room for manoeuver for the Noriega regime.

Yet US-Panamanian relations follow a dynamic of their own. Though not independent of international conditions, relations between the two countries have been largely conditioned by the strategic importance of the isthmus as the host territory of the Canal and as the site where generations of American soldiers, officers and their families lived while they were stationed on Panamanian soil. The situation in Panama was special for the United States because "we have a large community here and we have a vital interest in the Canal.[468]" Thus the question of who was in power in Panama and under what kind of regime (in the end, to whom the United States would hand over the Canal) bypassed other considerations Washington might have in dealing with the Noriega regime.

---

466. Kempe, *Divorcing the Dictator*, p. 60–61.

467. Kevin Bucley, *Panama: The Whole Story*, (New York: Simon & Schuster, 1991), pp. 162–163.

468. US Southern Army Chief Marc Cisneros, interviewed by Itzel Velásquez, *El fin de la tregua: Crónica de la invasión norteamericana a Panamá*, (México City: Editorial Diana, 1996), p. 100.

The Bush administration sought to remove Noriega from power, but also wanted to ensure that the successor regime would be in line with US concerns. Led by Major Moisés Giroldi—who had put down a prior coup attempt against Noriega in March 1988—on 3 October 1989 junior officers attempted a coup; they expected to depose Noriega and to force Noriega's staff into retirement. Giroldi had been in contact with American military and CIA officials before launching the coup. As an initial measure of support for the rebels, a US Army contingent blocked some access roads from PDF central headquarters in Panama City, thereby temporarily immobilizing the Panamanian military units stationed in Fuerte Amador (located near central headquarters, where troops loyal to Noriega had been assigned). Nevertheless, the United States removed these obstacles a few hours later, when the mutinous soldiers had not yet taken control of the situation.

The Bush administration did not consider Giroldi trustworthy and chose not to cooperate fully with the insurrection which, if successful, would have removed Noriega from power with little or no bloodshed. General Collin Powell, appointed head of the Joint Chiefs of Staff only a few days before the attempted coup, advised Bush not to aid the rebels for "to get rid of Noriega had to be something that would be done through an American plan, not a half-baked coup with a half-baked leader."[469] The White House considered supporting the Panamanian uprising, but ruled it out because it felt uneasy with the rebel leadership.[470] For this reason, Gen. Marc Cisneros, head of the Southern Army, based in Panama, chose to block the aid that had been promised to the junior officers by delaying a meeting with rebel emissaries while the operation was under way.[471] Any solid US support, even on a small scale, would have led to an overwhelming victory for the rebels. Noriega's departure would have left a political and military leadership in place that could not be guaranteed to fully cooperate with the White House. For the Pentagon, the plan to overthrow Noriega had to be more ambitious: the offensive against the PDF would be total, and would include the apprehension of the entire PDF chiefs of staff and the installation of a civilian leadership opposed to Noriega in the Panamanian presidency.[472] Thus Noriega easily subdued the junior officers; Giroldi and his followers surrendered and were later executed.

After the failed coup, Noriega strengthened his hold on power. On 15 December, he had the Assembly of Representatives (whose members had been appointed by Noriega) give him extraordinary powers, purportedly to allow him to face the situation created by the Reagan administration's sanctions, which were still in effect. He was also granted the title of "head of government", thereby emulating a similar law the 1972 Constituent Assembly had passed for Torri-

---

469. Bob Woodward, *The Commanders* (New York: Simon & Schuster, 1991), p. 121; "Powell first US Black President?" *Star & Herald*, 22 August, 1990, p. 1, quoting a cable from the Spanish News Agency EFE transmitted from Los Angeles, California.

470. Andrew Rosenthal, "US Considered Aid to Panama Rebels", *The New York Times*, 5 October 1989, p. 1A.

471. Buckley, *Panama: The Whole Story*, pp. 201–204.

472. Powell's statements in interview with Woodward, *op. cit.*, p. 133.

jos. In his speech to the Assembly, Noriega stated that "Panama is in a state of war because of the situation created by the United States." According to Ritter, Noriega's proclamation was intended to "give a façade of popular acclaim to an investiture whose only purpose was to give him immunity." Noriega's thinking in naming himself head of the government was that "the United States has deposed many chiefs of state, but it had never kidnapped one."[473] By late December 1989 it was so evident that Noriega had no intention to leave power that President Rodríguez, who sought to establish the conditions for returning to Constitutional rule, got ready to announce his resignation.[474]

Yet by late 1989 the Bush administration sensed it did not have the time to continue to negotiate with the Panamanian dictator on his own terms. According to the Panama Canal Treaties, the US administrator of the Panama Canal Commission had to be replaced on 31 December by a Panamanian citizen proposed by the government of Panama but approved by the US Senate. But US Congressmen had no interest in handing in the Canal "to a crazy like Noriega."[475] With this concern in mind, a group of Congressmen proposed an amendment to the treaties "to make sure that there will be a democratically elected government in Panama before a new Panama Canal Commission administrator is appointed."[476] Congress did not get to vote on the amendment. But were the US Congress to disapprove Panama's choice, Noriega would be provided with further political ammunition against the Bush administration and the United States could be regarded as violating international treaties by the rest of the world. Failing to recognize Panamanian authority over the Canal administration would, instead, have legitimised Noriega, who had argued that the United States sought to depose him as a first step in repudiating the Canal treaties.

The other available options for attaining the proposed objective were also discarded. The sanctions had not lessened Noriega's willingness to remain in power, and were ineffective because Panama's International Financial Centre continued to receive foreign exchange. It was not feasible to use counterinsurgency warfare— that is, to arm, finance, and give logistical support to a force such as the Contras in the effort to overthrow Nicaragua's Sandinistas. The amount of time it would have taken this type of an irregular army to become effective was excessive: it had taken the Contras ten years to become a threat to the Nicaraguan regime. In addition, the counterinsurgency training of Panama's armed forces made it unlikely that an irregular army would have any degree of success in the short term. Moreover, the nations of Central America were making great strides in achieving peace, and the US Congress's apparent unwillingness to finance irregular military groups made the administration reluctant to go this route.

---

473. Ritter, *Los secretos de la Nunciatura*, p. 166.

474. Rodríguez scheduled announcing his resignation at a breakfast on 20 December, but did not made it public because prior to that morning the United States began its massive military intervention in Panama. Interview with President Francisco Rodríguez, August 1995.

475. Robert Pear, "Canal pacts: U.S. Looking at Dire Results", *The New York Times*, 10 May1989, p. 11.

476. *Congressional Record*, 19 July 1989, pp. S8238-S8241.

The United States military intervention

On 20 December 1989 President Bush ordered a massive military intervention of Panama. To justify the scale of the intervention, the White House explained that its aims were, in this order, to safeguard the security of the Panama Canal and the integrity of the Torrijos-Carter treaties; to capture General Noriega and bring him to the United States on drug trafficking charges; to protect the lives and property of American citizens living in Panama; and restore democracy to that country. Though the security of the Canal and the integrity of the Canal Treaties were not really in danger, nor were the lives and properties of US citizens, the Bush administration presented the invasion as a comprehensive and praiseworthy operation that was justified in order to get the "bad guy" in Panama.[477] Later, General Cisneros was more specific: The US invasion was not to capture one man, but to "completely neutralize the PDF."[478]

US military intervention in Panama was a decision aimed at attending US strategic concerns over the orientation of the Panama Canal's host regime. According to Watson, it was also carried out to show domestic and international constituencies that the administration was seriously tackling the drug problem. In this regard, the invasion was the "only" option, for a failure to do so would have meant "a great loss for [American] global and regional prestige."[479] It was facilitated by the presence of more than ten thousand US troops who were already stationed at US military bases on Panamanian soil, many of which were familiar with Panama City's streets, and by the considerable infrastructure in place on US bases. But also by the fact that Noriega had no legitimacy in the eyes of the Panamanian population and the international community.

The effectiveness of the United States' military intervention was enhanced by the fact that Noriega's forces offered little resistance. Noriega and his staff underestimated the likelihood of an invasion and failed to prepare their troops to face an attack, despite the abundant evidence that an invasion was imminent.[480] The United States had disseminated disinformation to deceive Noriega and his

---

477. The White House named this operation Just Cause to summarise its objectives and expected consequences in a simple phrase because the idea of justice has a strong appeal in American political culture. The tactic of choosing a phrase or concept to symbolize the purposes of the armed intervention succeeded in increasing both military effectiveness and the support of the US population. Hence, the strength of the phrase was found more in its ability to be cloaked in deep-seated elements of political culture than in its capacity to denote the motives that led Washington to order the invasion. American military doctrine refers to this type of situations by pointing out that "terms express what policymakers want conflicts to be, and not the true atmosphere in which United States' armed forces will have to operate." John M. Gates, "Problemas del desarrollo de la doctrina", *Military Review* (spanish american edition) vol. LXVIII, No. 8, August 1988, p. 7.

478. Velásquez, *El fin de la tregua*, p. 100.

479. Bruce Watson, "Introduction." In Bruce Watson and Peter Tsouras, *Operation Just Cause: the U.S Intervention in Panama*, (Boulder, Colorado: Westview Press, 1991), p. xii.

480. "Desde Washington se le dio la alerta a Noriega", *La Prensa* (Panama City), 11 January 1990, p. 2-A.

commanders regarding the objectives of the military invasion.[481] Some members of Noriega's staff submitted false reports, denying the imminence of the invasion, since they expected the United States to carry out a surgical strike; they hoped that Noriega's ousting would allow them to seize power.[482] Noriega had infiltrated the US Embassy in Panama, but the United States had infiltrated his most loyal forces. The Panamanian defeat stemmed not only from the more sophisticated weaponry used by American troops: before the Panamanian regime was defeated militarily, it had been defeated politically.

Panamanian democracy was thus born linked to the evolution of US strategic considerations, not as a result of domestic struggles for democratisation. As a result of the intervention, Noriega was taken to US soil to face drug trafficking charges and his Chiefs of Staff were forced to retire. The PDF vanished, most of its troops being absorbed by the new police force. With it, the only national institution with the possibility and will to defend an authoritarian alternative also disappeared. The United States could not occupy the country and take over the administration of the Panamanian government nor extend the presence of its troops too long without damaging its image worldwide, at a time when it proclaimed to be the leader of the emerging "New World Order." The invasion was rejected by most Latin American governments, but the Bush administration claimed that the deployment of US troops in Panama had been a last resort.[483]

The "democratic" option came by default. The alternative with less chances of causing further instability in Panama, the one assuring a rapid extrication of US forces and the most legitimate for US policy-makers, was to install the apparent winners of the May 1989 elections. Endara, Arias-Calderón and Ford, who headed the ticket that ostensibly won the elections, were brought onto US military bases on Panamanian soil a few hours before the outbreak of hostilities. There they were instructed on the incoming military operation, swore in as President and Vice-Presidents of Panama, and formally "requested" (but most likely were induced to do so) the military incursion.[484] The official tally of the fatal victims was put at over three hundred and several hundred casualties, the majority of which were civilians not related to the PDF or Noriega.

In practice, the United States assumed the reins of public administration. Endara's claim to power was based on the provisions of the 1972 Constitution, but the US Embassy became the real power broker in the country. American troops replaced the Panamanian police forces while they were trained to undertake their new role, while American officials at the US Embassy initially coordinated most

---

481. Carmen Lira, "Panamá: el rostro oculto de una invasión", Supplement of the Mexican daily *La Jornada*, 24 September 1992, p. 2; Noriega (1997), *The Memoirs of Manuel Noriega*, p. 8.

482. Michael Gordon, "Panama Alerted to Attack, General Says", *The New York Times*, 27 February, 1990, p. 15A.

483. For example, with a vote of twenty in favor, one against, the OAS had passed a resolution asking the United States to withdraw its troops from Panama.

484. Andres Oppenheimer, "Participant: Secret Pact Made Over Inaugural Sit", *Miami Herald*, 27 December 1989, p. 1.

of the administration of the new government. The US Army undertook a public communications campaign aimed at legitimising itself before the population and probably to provide the background for extending the presence of its troops in the isthmus beyond the year 1999, as mandated by the Canal Treaties. For instance, they carried out many of the public activities formerly carried out by the PDF, such as road and hospital repairs and "civic" actions programmes in rural areas and participated in forums to show the benefits of US forces remaining in Panama. Calling themselves a "Military Support Group," they shared administrative tasks in the ministries, particularly in the areas of Government (Interior), Education, Health, and Public Works.

The new regime's poor performance prevented the new government from consolidating itself. Unemployment and crime rates rose. The Endara regime sought revenge against his predecessors. The new President set out to dismiss thousands of government employees who had worked under previous administrations, black-listed them so they would not be hired by private businesses, and replaced them mostly with political appointees. Social and political instability and human right violations remained high. As the President of the National Human Right Commission (CONADEHUPA), Olga Mejía, denounced, "in the country there is a systematic violation of human rights.... The authorities put together files with false witnesses and convict defendants even though they have no evidence."[485] Within a year of taking office, professional associations, the Church and Endara's former allies for the 1989 elections deserted the new President. Aided by his own lack of leadership qualities, few took President Endara seriously.[486] The Endara administration was hardly a champion of integrity and democracy. Nearly all the prominent members of the Endara administration were presidents of banks considered by the Drug Enforcement Administration of the United States to be notorious launderers of drug money.[487] Discontent with Endara reached the Bush administration and the US Southern Command in Panama, some of whose members took part in a failed coup attempt against the Panamanian President, led by former PDF officers not linked to Noriega.[488] Disenchantment with Endara remained high throughout his administration, not only in Panama but also in the United States.[489]

---

485. Fernando Martínez, "Refuta Endara la acusación", *La Jornada*, 30 July 1991.

486. "Panama likes democracy but wants something else too", *The Economist*, 2-8 February 1991, p. 39.

487. "Drug Arrests Disrupt CIA Operation," *The New York Times*, 14 January 1990.

488. In December 1990, the former head of the Public Force, Col. Eduardo He.rrera Hassán— who had been under arrest since August 1990 for alleged links to plans to overthrow Endara—escaped from a top-security prison and led a police uprising against the government. According to Panamanian judicial and intelligence sources, at least four high-ranking American military officers supported the rebellion. The uprising was put down with the intervention of American troops. Vilma E. Figueroa, "Implican a cuatro oficiales de E.U. en complot contra Guillermo Endara", *La Prensa*, 26 April, 1992, p. 1A.

489. For example, the House Ways and Means Committee Chairman expressed its dismay over the "instability of Panamanian democracy and over the fact that drug trafficking and money laundering has increased and is at a worse level than before US forces captured Noriega."

Endara's inability to sustain itself and the continuing social and political instability led both the Bush administration and the Panamanian government to conclude that it was not the appropiate time to open negotiations to extend the permanence of US troops in Panama beyond the term mandated by the Torrijos-Carter Treaties.[490] Not that the United States lost interest. A joint resolution introduced in both Houses of Congress on 21 March 1991 asked for the renegotiation, "on the basis that the Panama Canal is a vital strategic good for the United States and its allies." The request was also grounded on the observation that friendly and cooperative relations existed between both countries, that the region had a "recurrent history of unstable governments which defy the operational future of the Panama Canal" and that Panama had dissolved its security forces and had no other force able to defend the Canal from "potential aggressors."[491] Even after the fall of the Berlin Wall, the Pentagon had no interest in leaving Panama. Because of budget constraints and the relaxation of tensions with the Soviet Union, in 1991 the Pentagon submitted a programme to close one-third of its bases overseas, but then it did not call for a single base to be closed in Panama. Southern Command Chief General George Joulman said that although there was no significant military threat to the United States in the world, the "transition from bipolarity to multipolarity" required a reevaluation of conventional military forces in general, for which reason US forces should remain on Panamanian soil.[492]

In turn, Panamanian democracy, and the future of US military installations in Panama were left to follow their own course. George Bush was defeated by Democratic contender Bill Clinton in the 1992 elections. The new US President felt no need to continue meddling in Panamanian affairs, least of all interfere in the Panamanian electoral process in 1994, where forces previously linked to the PDF won the majority of votes. In the United States, subsequent budgetary and strategic considerations led Washington to the conclusion that, though maintaining a base or two on Panamanian soil would be appropriate, it could live without them. In Panama, once the business and the political élite realized the economic potential of such sites, demand for the US to leave US troops in Panama decreased substantially over time. It is not by chance that the first time Torrijos' and Arias' followers sat down to negotiate matters of interest for the nation took place in the year 2000, after the last of US troops left Panamanian soil and the administration of the Panama Canal had been finally transferred to Panama.

Fernando Martínez, "Preocupa al Congreso de EU la inestabilidad panameña", *La Jornada*, 19 April, 1991, p. 29.

490. "La inestabilidad en Panamá no permite negociar: Linares", *La Jornada*, 21 June 1992, p. 42; "No estamos hablando sobre bases después del año 2000", *Canal de Panamá Hoy*, (CELA's bimonthly bulletin, December 1992).

491. *Congressional Record*, 21 March 1991, pp. S3930 and H2015.

492. Fernando Martínez, "Beneficiosa…"

The Panamanian experience

The struggle for democracy in Panama meant an opening to the participation of political parties and holding free elections. The new political system, mass-based, would be 'disciplined' by the National Guard to avoid the 'disorder' of past democratic experiences prevalent until the coup of 1968. New political forces associated to the National Guard sprang out and became predominant under authoritarian rule, and remained so after new rules of the game were established in 1978. The new political system was different in several aspects: the expanded role of the state, the political arbitration of the National Guard, the participation of the masses, and most importantly, the new terms for Panama's relationship with the United States once the Canal Treaties began to be implemented. After Torrijos' death and the Reagan administration's enticement to get Panama's support for its Central American policy, the National Guard's Chiefs of Staff changed their minds about transferring power to a duly and freely elected government and took steps to remain in control. The opposition found little domestic or US support for their efforts to foster clean elections, but neither did they make a serious effort at getting it; as most organised social forces felt more threatened by the opposition, whose political platforms excluded any social or economic benefits for the population, than by the authoritarian forces, who claimed to follow Torrijos' steps. Authoritarian forces remained in control of the transition; to preserve their fundamental interests they disguised their ascendancy under constitutional forms. In time, increasingly larger areas of government policy became reserved domains of the military. Once Noriega's ascendancy became evident and the United States intervened to prevent the political situation went out of its control, Panama's armed forces were disbanded. As a result, the emerging democracy was born with no major domestic obstacle to further democratisation but with the problem of a national identity that remained pending. Power was handed over to the groups who ostensibly won the May 1989 elections, but no new rules of the game were established as both the US and the new government reestablished the existing constitutional forms.

Like in the Dominican Republic and Nicaragua, the evolution of Panamanian politics cannot be understood without appraising the role of the United States or the way domestic actors handled US influences. The fact that the United States held direct political and physical control over the Canal became the single most important political issue in Panama's history as an independent nation. Confronting Washington's rights over the inter-oceanic waterway became an important instrument for gaining legitimacy. Yet, the highly asymmetric relationship meant that being perceived as being able to "handle" the Americans became an important leverage over rivals. Both conditions, in turn, contributed to retard the development of a political environment conducive to the institutionalization of democratic procedures and practices. The sequence of events in neighboring countries was also relevant, in particular the Central American imbroglio, but also the political openings and transitions in South America. The two issues influenced decision-makers in Panama and in the United States and had an impact over the country's regime trajectory.

CONCLUSIONS

Latin Caribbean Regime Transition in Comparative Perspective

The democratisation of the Latin Caribbean is late by hemispheric and world standards because the political evolution of the states in this sub-region persistently underwent US influences that were contrary to this purpose. In more than a century of involvement in the Latin Caribbean, the United States constructed a sphere of influence that for most of its history remained unstable and conflict-prone. Aiming at maintaining its ascendancy over the area, US pressures for compliance with its preferred values—where democracy was not among its priorities—made more difficult domestic actor's efforts toward constructing or improving democratic institutions and practices. This sub-region's different course resulted from the continuous exertion of US power that, through time, deviated the political configuration of these states from those of Latin America.

The cases included in this book pertain to cases of US imposition where the outcome of regime trajectories was distorted by the exercise of US power. The United States is an unavoidable source of influence for the sub-region's political processes. Regime changes in the Latin Caribbean underwent the constant and direct participation of American decision-makers; yet, the United States did not sustain efforts at fostering democracy throughout all phases of the regime trajectories studied in here.

In this concluding chapter, the impact of US influences upon Latin Caribbean regime trajectories will be discussed in more detail. Proceeding from the ideas laid out in the introduction, first I will discuss the ways in which the United States directly distorted the trajectories of regime transitions. Secondly, to appraise the complexities of US ascendancy, I will evaluate the way in which local actors took into account US and other international influences in their calculations and strategies. To further the understanding of these issues, third I will show how the broader regional order and the sequence of events in neighbouring countries affected the outcome of transitions and vice versa. Finally, building from the findings of this research, I will discuss its implications for the understanding of the role of the United States and for the body of theories that have been used to explain processes of democratisation.

Proposition one: US power distorted Latin Caribbean regime trajectories, without being sufficient to determine their outcomes.

The United States distorted Latin Caribbean regime transformations at the most important conjunctures of their trajectories. To begin with, the three dictatorships may be said to have been unwitting offsprings of US policy towards the Caribbean Basin. Somoza's and Trujillo's were by-products of US policy during the first three decades of the twentieth century, when the United States sought to preserve the area's stability and its use as an inter-oceanic route exclusive of foreign encroachments. Noriega's grew out of US policy in the eighties, a time when Washington was concerned with the course of the Nicaraguan revolution and required allies that supported its policy against the Sandinista government and guerrilla movements in the area.

The beginning of these transitions was facilitated by the fact that Washington changed gears regarding its intended aims for the Latin Caribbean. Though the Kennedy administration feared Dominican events repeated those in Cuba, it had abandoned supporting the Trujillo dictatorship as a way to halt the appeal of the Cuban revolution. The Kennedy administration was also ready to embrace either Trujillo's heirs or a successor government, but local actors pressed to further the liberalisation of the Dominican regime. Similarly, in Nicaragua, the Carter administration sought to avoid a military victory by the FSLN, but US intervention was widely opposed by domestic and regional political forces. Moreover, the Carter administration was distracted with the Soviet Union's invasion of Afghanistan and with the course of the Iranian revolution. Regarding Latin America, it was keen on upholding its policy of promoting respect for human rights, for which the Somoza dictatorship was no longer useful. Washington sought to prevent the military victory of the FSLN, but nonetheless approved the beginning of a new era without Somoza. In Panama, the beginning of the transition was made easier because administrations in both countries had developed a working relationship over the course of the negotiations for the Panama Canal Treaties. At the onset, neither of these transitions was perceived by Washington to significantly threaten the international balance of power.

The outcome of these transitions is a feeble and unfinished democracy that had the chance to be improved only after some time elapsed, domestic actors gained confidence in themselves, with some inducements from other democratic powers, and the hegemonic power lifted its reservations about the trajectory of these political transformations. Washington carried out policies aimed at eroding the power of authoritarian regimes in the Dominican Republic, Nicaragua and Panama, channelling public opinion against authoritarian forces and in favour of opposition élites and increasing the regime's costs of staying in power. However, due to the historic association between the United States and these dictators, the lack of US overt actions against them sometimes were interpreted by domestic protagonists as support for authoritarian rule. Most times the authoritarian forces were identified with the United States and an important part of the struggle by democrats was geared toward gaining legitimacy in Washington. Associated to these external influences, the authoritarian forces preserved some strength once the transition began. Domestic actors performed the con-struction of democratic norms and practices, but these remained limited until the hegemonic power lifted its veto to the political participation of the groups it had opposed.

The United States shaped transition outcomes by determining what "domes-tic" actors could do at strategic moments. During the tenure of the Council of State in the Dominican Republic, Council members could not extend their time in power unless they were willing and able to bypass Washington's command in this regard. This 'veto' initially benefited the forces that had most to gain from the process of democratisation, the PRD and the UCN. Later, the United States did not accept any formula that excluded the Panamanian opposition from pow-er after the general elections of May 1989 were nullified and so it lessened the legitimacy of the caretaker Francisco Rodríguez government. The Nicaraguan transition is full of examples of this kind: due to Washington's obsession with ejecting the Sandinistas from power, Nicaraguan political institutions and prac-tices were so strongly scrutinised by the international community that the gov-ernment could not afford to deviate too much nor for too long from standards of political behaviour set by external influences.

Washington's 'vetoes' were effective insofar as they remained credible. Its imperative to eject the Trujillos out of the Dominican Republic was successful because it backed it by sending ships that could be seen at a distance from the Dominican Capital when the 'wicked' uncles attempted to regain power as Ram-fis Trujillo left. Later Washington vetoed coup d'etats against the Bosch govern-ment and it made sure that all actors were certain that the United States would not tolerate a government change by force. Yet, domestic actors knew best: On the one hand, coups d'etat had been successful in other Latin American coun-tries and the United States had not been able to reverse them. On the other, most powerful actors ascertained that many Americans in and outside of the US government did not like Bosch or his attitude toward Communists. Thus, if they held fast the United States would have to accept the coup as a fait accompli, and so it proved.

US intervention as a whole made these trajectories more prolonged and contested. The US supported, materially and politically, groups which otherwise would have had very little chance of maintaining themselves as real options. In the Dominican Republic this was true of Wessin's forces during the civil war; in Nicaragua, this was particularly true of both the US-funded paramilitary groups that fought the FSLN, made of former somocistas, but also of the UNO coali-tion that defeated the Sandinistas in the general election of 1990. This was also done by undermining forces that otherwise might have had more chance of suc-ceeding, such as the PRD in the Dominican Republic, the FSLN in Nicaragua and the PRD in Panama. Second, it imposed limits to the political behaviour of élites during the transitions. Once the United States chose new interlocutors the rest of the political spectrum had a constrained range of choices: taking sides with Washington by supporting US-endorsed leaders or openly disagreeing with US interlocutors, taking sides with the groups which the US government had been noticeably opposing. This meant that to improve their chances of being a recipient of US aid and support, politicians had the incentive to accommodate to US priorities, to the detriment of working domestically to establish a national agenda for democratisation and improving the environment for the building and nourishing of democratic institutions. Once electoral processes were carried out, successor regimes were left dependent on US aid and guidance, undermining their legitimacy as independent governments and their ability to work with domestic groups for the formulation of policy. Since the quality of the democratic governance was not among US priorities, the task of improving the institutions of democracy was left for subsequent administrations.

Due to the Latin Caribbean's vulnerability, Washington's misconceived assessments affected the course of transitions. This was particularly evident in Washington's perception of the Constitutionalist forces in the Dominican Republic as Communist-infiltrated, or in its view of Giroldi's forces as no different than Noriega in Panama, both of which implied that, once the United States acted to prevent their success, a more peaceful and autochthonous course toward democracy was not achieved.

The United States affected the outcome of transitions depending on the form of involvement it chose to pursue and the aims of its interventions. When it resorted to military force, it had more power to work for its policy objectives. In the Dominican Republic, once Washington sent troops to halt the quarrel in Santo Domingo, it remained as the final arbiter of the political process for as long as its troops stayed in the country. In Panama, it achieved the reformulation of the armed forces, significantly lessening their power and ability to put obstacles to furthering democracy, but also on their capacity to veto any future government's attempt to extend the US military presence in the country beyond the terms negotiated in the Canal Treaties. The indirect US involvement through measures that increased the regime's cost of staying in power, such as in Panama before the military intervention and in Nicaragua throughout the evolution of the transition, did not bring major normative or institutional rearrangements in part because they were not among Washington's aims. In both cases, however, the United States indirectly contributed to heighten the animosity between government and opposition élites, since the latter were perceived by government forces—and many times behaved as such—as instruments of US intervention.

US hegemony may be said to have been exerted with similar intentions throughout the sub-region, but the ways in which it was applied was also a function of the specific conditions prevalent in the countries under study. For example, in the Dominican Republic and Nicaragua, US relations were channelled mainly through the US Embassy. Therefore, many times US Ambassadors had the potential to define the policies and actions carried out in regarding the country undergoing regime change and many twists may be attributed to the perceptions of US diplomats. But in Panama, the network of formal and informal ties between the Panamanian élite and US diplomatic, military, intelligence and Canal authorities made the definition of US policy—and Panamanian expectations of their relations with the United States—much more complex and difficult to discern.

The trajectory and outcome of these transitions cannot be understood without appraising the impact of US influences in general, but by no means they determined the course of events. In the Dominican Republic, the Kennedy administration sought to stop the plans to assassinate the Generalissimo in the immediate aftermath of the Bay of Pigs fiasco, but local actors went on anyway and accomplished their goal. Washington was also interested in supporting the formula of Trujillismo without Trujillo, but this option lost the chance of being implemented as Trujillo's eldest son Ramfis voluntarily and unexpectedly resigned and left the country. The United States fully backed the Bosch government, but it was not sufficient to prevent its downfall, unless it had chosen to back its policy with the same material inducements it was prepared to use to prevent the encroachment of communist influences. The sort of exclusionary democracy that emerged in 1966 was not in Washington's initial agenda, but was the least most international actors expected after the Constitutionalist uprising a year earlier. In Nicaragua, the Reagan administration sought a military defeat of the Sandinistas, but the FSLN's strength and international support, on the one hand, and the President's own domestic limitations, on the other, precluded this outcome. In Panama, the United States sent troops in 1989 to, among others, reform the military and leave out a force that would be in charge of preserving stability, but local actors had a different idea and created a small police force instead.

Yet, the projection of US power was not sufficient to override the legacies of the past. The sum of external and domestic circumstances favourable to democratisation was not enough to bypass Dominicans' inexperience with democratic institutions and practices. Democrats were scarce in the Dominican Republic; most political actors preferred to work outside institutional channels to achieve their goals and very few valued the newly acquired institutions. The utter lack of political liberties for so long under Trujillo made the cause of democracy a highly difficult and possibly improbable task. The return of authoritarian rule once Bosch was deposed and the establishment of a mildly authoritarian presidential system under Balaguer seem in accordance with this condition. Not that this was the only possible outcome. Democratisation required sustained commitments from the most powerful actors but this did not take place. Nicaragua had a more "liberal" trajectory due in part to the fact that the Somoza regime had adopted constitutional forms and allowed for some political participation of the opposition. Once the Sandinistas took over, most of the 'domestic' opposition's struggle was geared toward rendering effective the country's constitutional provisions and liberties, a project the ruling Sandinistas came to view as a concession to the Carter administration. A similar story was followed by Panama. Civilian rule before Torrijos had not brought about a flourishing democracy. By the time the transition was launched the group in power had built a significant populist coalition that did not have democracy among its objectives. In this context, the political opposition's demand for upholding democracy found few listeners in the military.

Proposition two: Domestic actors altered their calculations and choices to take into account the likely reactions of the hegemon.

The United States was an important actor in the trajectory of the regime transitions studied in this book, but its influence depended greatly on domestic actor's willingness and susceptibility to be affected by them. Given the power differential and the historical legacies of US relations with the sub-region, the rest of international influences had to compete with those from the United States. To have a better chance of being effective these lesser influences had to aggregate themselves, building coalitions, recurring to the norms and principles sustained by the hegemonic power, and sometimes making the effort to influence policy-makers in Washington.

The actions, calculations, choices and strategies of the actors involved took into account not only the influence purposely exerted by the hegemonic power, but also expected US reactions, as interpreted by them. Most times, since they were accustomed to a pattern of behaviour from the State Department or Washington in general, domestic actors believed that they "knew better" the intricacies of Washington policy-making and that they could get away with what they were doing. For example, domestic actors were keen observers of the set of circumstances in which the hegemonic power found itself. They did not expect major policy changes from Washington when presidential campaigns were being carried out or when particular US Presidents confronted a domestic or international crisis. This reassured them and made them feel they could take greater risks, since Washington would most likely avoid deviating from the course of action being followed at the moment. But they did expect them when a new administration was expected to come in. Trujillo thought he could expect a better relationship with the United States with the arrival of Democrats to the White House in January 1961; Somoza waited for the US electoral campaign in 1980 to define a new US President with whom he could find a better bargain. The Sandinistas were very keen on the 1984 and the 1988 elections in the US and paid great attention to the political equilibrium between Republicans and Democrats in Congress. So did Noriega, who hoped his former boss at the CIA, George Bush, would come in his aid. In this light, the political equilibrium between Democrats and Republicans in Congress and their approval or disapproval of US foreign policies became relevant for the course of political events, since they could hold the key for the success of their strategies. In turn, this invited actors pursuing regime changes to attempt to influence policies in Washington, given the weight they had on the evolution of their own countries.

Washington's interest in controlling the course of political events invited domestic actors to seek to involve the United States in support of their cause. In the Latin Caribbean, not only did dictators maintain dialogues with the United States, aiming at maintaining its backing, but also did the domestic opposition, who sought guidance and legitimacy to become the new rulers, albeit under real or apparent democratic norms and practices. Domestic actors' will to seek and receive external guidance and support for their activities made the course of transitions highly subject to foreign, but particularly American, influences. In the three cases, the United States remained as the grand elector whose stated or unstated choices were taken into account by domestic actors and the population at large.

The three dictators skilfully turned US influence in their favour at precise political conjunctures in which Washington sought interlocutors in their respective countries and where they could have lost their chance to gain or stay in power. The three dictators were also willing and able to withstand domestic and international pressures against their regimes. They had plenty of experience handling Washington's attitude changes and in circumventing occasional US attempts at curtailing their ties to the US power structure. At times, the international tides against dictatorships increased their pace and scope, forcing the United States to take measures to disassociate itself from these rulers aiming at maintaining its global leadership role vis-à-vis democratic allies. Dictators felt they knew how to handle politics in Washington very well and that they had contributed to help the United States preserve its international ascendancy so much that they could stay in power until the winds flowed in their direction again. But this did not happen. They failed to interpret the trends going on around them and to adopt the changes that would have been required of them to halt or alleviate the pressures against the continuation of their rule.

Dictators developed ties to the Washington's power structure and used them to their advantage every time an agency or another of the US government disapproved of them. Trujillo and the Somozas exhibited and cultivated several links to the US Defense and foreign policy community, Congress and business, while Noriega concentrated them with the US intelligence and defence establishment. Perhaps this is why both Trujillo and Somoza were more effective in circumventing the official US policy line against them. In times of trouble, these bonds were helpful in softening the impact of US policies against them, but also to make believe their domestic detractors, with some degree of success, that they were powerful enough to outwit the White House, reducing the opposition's incentive for gathering mass support for their cause. In time, the Sandinistas' lack of these connections worked against their efforts to stay in power and forced them (and their supporters within the United States) to carry out measures to entice the US Congress, the media and US and international public opinion to their side. In the Dominican Republic, Nicaragua and Panama, the legacy of past US involvement also meant that the domestic opposition had little incentive to gather mass support for the purpose of overthrowing the dictatorship, since all they needed was for the US to come in their aid to effect the regime change. The US so many times intervened to shape the political configuration of these states that, even when it followed a policy of non-intervention, all important actors remained incredulous.

As a result, unlike transitions elsewhere, domestic mobilisations or inter-party or intra-elite negotiations did not provide important moving forces behind the regime breakdown phase of the transition. The masses mobilised themselves during the trajectory of transitions in the Dominican Republic and Panama, but they remained secondary in the unfolding of events. In the Dominican Republic, the leader of the Constitutionalists, Francisco Camaño, rallied the masses against the continuity of authoritarian rule. Washington officials interpreted his apparent naiveté as a sure sign that Communists could control him and thus they halted his ascendancy. In Panama, they mobilised themselves at the start of the widespread protests against Noriega, yet their most important leaders felt they had little to gain if the opposition reached power and thus remained still throughout the course of events.

Domestic actors could not leave Washington's demands, commitments and agenda of concerns out altogether. This approach became an integral element of the strategies pursued by both authoritarian rulers and actors seeking regime transformations. This posed distinct dilemmas for the actors involved. If they felt they were object of foreign pressures, they could attempt to remain firmly in control of power, cede to opposition and US demands and lose control over the transfer of power, or to formulate a pact with the opposition in search of an acceptable way out of power. Whether the authoritarian forces opted for one or another depended on a combination of their pre-existing ties with Washington's power structure; their sense of mission; their evaluation of their own strength vis-à-vis society and their perception of the opportunities afforded by the international arena. The better they felt in relation to one or a combination of these categories, the less likely they would undertake a peaceful transfer of power and, instead, they attempted to remain firmly in control. Trujillo, Somoza and Noriega felt they knew Washington better or had more powerful friends than the officials formulating US policies. Trujillo believed he had saved his country from self-destruction and Somoza felt there was no better alternative to him in his country. Noriega's career happened in a military institution that directed the country's effort at getting the Canal back from the United States and firmly believed that a similar leading role should continue, while the FSLN felt it had to remain as the vanguard of the revolution that deposed the Somoza dynasty. Trujillo, Somoza and Noriega felt contempt for the opposition disregarding them as real options, concentrating their efforts instead on negotiating with Washington officials a way to stay in power. The international arena offered few opportunities for these dictators, but they nonetheless made the effort to exploit them. As a result, Trujillo did not attempt to extricate himself from the Dominican Republic. Somoza and Noriega played with the idea of negotiating a way out of power with their detractors in Washington, but dragged on until they no had a say in the formation of a future government.

US intervention posed a different dilemma for the antiauthoritarian élites. They were sometimes divided over the desirability of further US intervention. Being perceived as instruments of a foreign power could work against them in the eyes of the population, but receiving the political and material support from abroad also helped them achieve their cause. Yet, the more they saw that the United States was willing to put pressure and use force to lead them into power, the more they refrained from negotiating with government forces. The more they perceived being supported by the population, the more they were likely to pursue a strategy that left out the authoritarian élites.

In addition, the form of US involvement altered their options. The room for action for the élites in power was greater when US intervention was indirect and prolonged than when it was direct, limited and overwhelming. If a military intervention took place, strategies by former authoritarian forces took into account whether the new political institutions would assure them of the option of participating in the political process and on the time US troops took to pacify the country (the more it took, the more some groups could try to take advantage of the weakness of the new institutions). As the new democratic institutions gained strength, the former authoritarian forces adapted their political strategies to the new conditions. The new democratic leadership was then prone to ostracise the previous government élite, but as the political game continued, this practice was likely to subside. Democratic prospects thus rested on the strength of the new institutions and the effect of other domestic factors such as leadership styles, public opinion, mass pressures, organisational capacity and the continuity of a positive international environment.

Having to cope with a regional order structured from without, domestic actors engaged in cost-benefit analysis of regime change based on the opportunities and constraints offered by the external environment. There were variable arrangements between domestic circumstances and external influences that fostered or discouraged actors from taking steps towards or away from democracy. For instance, the combination of external and domestic circumstances prevalent between 1961 and 1962 encouraged actors to undertake the construction of democratic institution and practices in the Dominican Republic, as Trujillo and his heirs fell. During this time, however, the flexible approach by Luis Somoza in Nicaragua was enough to get by the external pressures. The opposite happened in Panama from 1981 onwards, when both external and domestic circumstances tilted the trajectory of the transition away from democracy.

For illustrative purposes we could say that there is a level at which pressures mount up: a transition threshold at which external and internal circumstances and events stimulate leading actors to take steps toward or away from launching the transition. At one end of the spectrum, the positive influences outweigh the negatives (opportunities outweigh constraints). Most actions to further democracy have a good chance of being effective because both domestic actors and the international environment are supportive. If this combination continues, in time the existing democratic institutions have a good chance of taking root. Through a period, these positive influences add up, contributing to strengthen the conditions for the emergence of democracy. In the Dominican Republic, this took place between the disappearance of Galíndez in 1956 and Bosch's election in 1962. In Nicaragua, these pressures mounted up from the earthquake of 1973 until 1979, when the trend in favour of democracy started in South America.

At the other end of the threshold, negative influences outweigh the positives (constraints excel opportunities): No matter how hard domestic or external actors work to further democracy, the crafting of institution building has very little chance of succeeding. This is a process-driven situation: the sum of individual influences contrary to democratisation reaches a point in which efforts toward a positive regime transformation have little, if any, chance of being effective. Democrats did not disappear from the Dominican Republic after Joaquin Balaguer took over the Presidency in 1966, but they did not had the opportunity to work toward making effective the existing constitutional institutions until the late seventies. In Panama democrats existed throughout the eighties, inside both the opposition and the government's camp, but structural conditions did not allow them to emerge. The same can be said about Nicaraguan democrats, who had no other choice than taking sides with the FSLN or with the US-funded opposition, or stay home until better opportunities arose.

Between these two extremes, there is an equilibrium point where negative and positive influences roughly balance each other. At this point, an otherwise minor circumstance (i.e., rumours, bad leadership) may tip the balance for or against democracy: What, for example, could have been the trajectory of the Dominican transition had President Bosch negotiated with the military the enactment of an anti-communist policy that would not be so different from the one he was about to implement? The negative regional influences would most likely have continued, but had Bosch survived the coup subsequent events might have provided a better democratic outcome. Being at this equilibrium point, a better leadership by the Dominican President would have given Dominican democracy one more chance. A similar story may be told about President Aristides Royo of Panama. Royo was forced to resign in 1982. Having the prestige of being the person whom the late leader Omar Torrijos had chosen for this position, and enjoying a certain amount of respect from the international community, he could have confronted the military, reached an agreement with his detractors and stayed in power. Had he chosen this course of action, his successors in the Presidency would have had found at least a better chance of confronting the occasional whims of incumbent military leaders to force the resignation of Presidents later in 1984, 1985 and 1987.

Proposition three: The set of domestic/international interactions propelling each regime transition is also conditioned by the broader regional order and the sequence of political events in neighbouring countries.

Latin Caribbean regime transitions may be seen as expressions of specific regional orders. During the regime breakdown phase and the evolution toward a new form of government, these transitions embodied the influences coming from the surrounding regional environment; the resulting regime added up to or detracted from the regional balance of power between authoritarians and democrats. If the outcome was in line with the regional order, it had a greater chance of survival than if it went against it, unless its leaders found extra-regional sponsorships that allowed them to remain against the current or got away with setting up a political system largely isolated from external influences. As a result, regime transitions themselves affected the region's composition. The outlook of the Latin Caribbean in the nineties as an area made by mostly democratic states is highly different from its perspective as a sub-region mostly made up by dictatorships; the outcome of regime trajectories turned them that way. The regional order became an integral part of the phenomena; because of both geography and the sub-region's power structure, events in one country were not independent from other events in time and space. It altered how actors pursued their goals. For example, in the eighties the FSLN believed that if a similar revolution took place in El Salvador, the Reagan administration would have to face a fait accompli and establish a pragmatic relationship with Central America that would have allowed them more room for manoeuvre in its domestic and foreign policy decisions. However unreasonable (this occurrence might have triggered further US intervention against the FSLN), this expectation did provide incentives to local Nicaraguan actors to aid their Salvadoran counterparts, but not enough to become the official policy line of the Sandinista government.

In addition, the impact of the regional order on regime trajectories was both inner and outward directed. The route in which it operated was not necessarily a straight line between the countries exerting influence and those undergoing political change. US policies (among other relevant international influences from the US and elsewhere) had a direct impact in the trajectory of regime change, but also Latin Caribbean actors influenced particular aspects of the policy. They also attempted to tip the scale in neighbouring countries toward individuals or groups of similar political charasteristics, with the aim of altering the regional balance of power in their favour.

This implies that the dynamic of transition trajectories would have been different at different conjunctures of the evolution of the international and regional orders. Even if we took for granted the 'structural' rivalry between the Soviet Union and the United States, the Cold War went through several turns and proceeded through distinct phases, each of which brought about different sets of priorities and policy choices by the hegemonic power. The regional and international conjuncture at which the Dominican democratic experiment went through in 1963 was one of the least auspicious it could have endured: Worldwide, not only East-West tensions had revived, but regionally, tensions had been considerably heightened with the Soviet Union's attempt to install a Missile Base in Cuba. Had the Bosch government taken over at a different conjuncture, say, earlier in the post-Cuban revolution scenario, the Dominican transition might have had at least a better chance at enduring these negative tendencies. The same can be said about the US military intervention in 1965; had this Constitutionalist uprising happened earlier, perhaps soon after Bosh was overthrown, it might have had a better chance at succeeding because Washington would possibly have favoured it. The turn of the Cold War in 1981, partially spurred by the new administration in Washington, also had profound repercussions in transition trajectories in the sub-region. Without this turn, the Panamanian and the Nicaraguan regime transitions would have had a better chance at reaching a democratic outcome sooner, at least without the cost in human lives this turn had throughout Central America but particularly in Nicaragua and El Salvador.

The regional order was also relevant because in times of change, the United States sought to adjust to the new constellation of forces and to consolidate its dominant position, while local élites struggled to gain recognition for their efforts to achieve power. The hegemonic power's concern with security altered negatively the prospects for democracy in the states within this sub-region. Searching for security through control was charasteristic of US policy towards the Latin Caribbean during the Cold War and this had enormous negative implications in the processes of regime transformations. In the sixties, particularly after the Cuban revolution and the Missile Crisis, the United States made the exclusion of Communism a top priority. The new Dominican democracy under Juan Bosch (1963) and later the constitutionalist uprising could not cope with this imperative and thus gave way to authoritarian alternatives. In the eighties, the Reagan administration's obsession with rolling back the Nicaraguan revolution and wiping out leftist guerrillas gave a greater weight to Latin Caribbean armed forces in the running of government, undermining the emerging democratic institutions.

Changes in regional and global contexts offered different opportunities for actors seeking to effect or to prevent regime transformations. Trujillo, Somoza and Noriega understood well the changes in the world's constellation of forces and in the orientation of new administrations in the White House and used them to their advantage. After the Cuban revolution, most Dominican and regional actors believed and acted to make sure that Trujillo's days were over. Following the failed Bay of Pigs invasion and the Cuban Missile Crisis, rightists were emboldened in their attempts to cut short the Dominican democratic experiment. In Panama, the opposition gathered it would be very difficult for them to reach power given the apparent alliance between the National Guard and the State Department for the 1984 elections.

The nature of the regime and the domestic struggles to change them also altered the regional environment. This has had circularity implications, for not only the regional order affects regime transitions, but also regime transitions alters the cohesiveness and unity of the regional order. In this sense, transitions are regional processes because they are causally related over time. Each transition is, at least partially, a function of the intersection of choices within which the previous transition unfolded. The Cuban transition towards a revolutionary regime is partially a function of the intersection of choices in Washington and Guatemala that led to the downfall of the Arbenz government in 1954; the Dominican transition (1961–1966) is a function of the intersection of choices related to the Cuban revolution, and so is Nicaragua. Panama's and other Central American transitions are partially a result of the intersection of choices in Nicaragua and the United States within which the Nicaraguan transition evolved.

In this sense, it can be said that regime transitions had 'forward effects': they were episodes partaking in the transformation of the regional order. Could the Dominican transition in the sixties happen the way it did without the background of the Cuban revolution? How different would the form and content of democratic institutions in much of the sub-region have been had Guatemala's democratic experiment between 1944–1954 survived and proceeded towards consolidation, allowing it to join Costa Rica in the construction of a zone of peace? To say the least, the sub-regions' history would have been diametrically different, possibly less conflict-prone and likely more prosperous.

Saying that Latin Caribbean transition trajectories were conditioned by a regional order is to say that it was a force altering (promoting or preventing) what would have been the "natural" course of events. It is a proposition about what actors would have done had this regional power arrangement not existed. Political processes may also be seen as resulting from contingencies; thus, the possibilities are endless. This is en even more difficult speculation for this area, because the legacies of the exercise of US influence are deeply rooted in the history of the sub-region's political configuration and consciousness. Most dictatorships can be traced directly or indirectly to US policy. Without US influence, maybe they would have existed at different historical conjunctures, but probably not have endured so long nor would have grounded themselves so strongly. Most likely political instability would have continued, but domestic struggles would have had a chance to evolve and mature without a large degree of foreign intervention. Even if we accepted Trujillo's and Somoza's dictatorships as given, US non-interference in the breakdown and transition phases of these countries' trajectories could have meant that domestic political actors would eventually have had to build among themselves the political norms and institutions in which they would have to live. Possibly, this would necessarily not have taken between one or two decades longer than for its South American neighbours.

The onset of these regime transitions could hardly have taken place the moment and way they did were it not for the combination of regional pressures and events taking place at the time. In the case of the Dominican Republic, this is evident in the moment chosen by domestic actors to actively pursue the overthrow of the dictatorship and the killing of the Benefactor, a time when Trujillo was pointed out as an outcast and had lost the support of the United States. Their outright rejection of Trujillismo without Trujillo occurred as detractors increased their assertiveness following the Cuban revolution. This also holds true for Nicaragua, where the armed struggle against Somoza grew in size and strength as the dictator saw a reduction in his external sources of support and other sub-regional actors were determined to provoke the demise of the last heir of the Caribbean tyrants that ruled the sub-region between the 1930's and 1950's. Panama's political opening would most likely not have taken place if the Carter administration had not reached a suitable agreement with Torrijos over the sovereignty and administration of the Panama Canal. Later, many domestic actors in Panama acquiesced to living under an authoritarian regime as long as Washington came to terms with it; they mobilised themselves mainly when General Noriega, like his Nicaraguan and Dominican counterparts, was publicly deprived of his external backing.

Transitions in these countries began against the background of international or regional events that gave greater impetus to the trend against dictatorships and prompted Washington to alter the fundamental strategies regarding the sub-region. Of the range of external circumstances encircling the Trujillo regime, for example, no other had so much impact as Fidel Castro's access to power in Cuba on 1 January 1959. If ahead of this time there was—arguably—a mixture of domestic and international circumstances that might have allowed the Trujillo regime to survive, the arrival of the Cuban revolution made it utterly implausible. It was the single most important event in the sub-region's history. It had the effect of agitating the area's already turbulent waters.

The Dominican transition trajectory coincided with and received inputs from the unfolding Cuban revolution, but most importantly, from the interpretation Washington leaders had on this event and local actors' awareness and use of these perceptions. Before Castro's access to power in January 1959, the Dominican opposition played a passive role; thereafter, they were emboldened. Washington firmly believed that the Cuban revolution threatened its ascendancy over the sub-region and that, to avoid a repetition of Castro's rise to power and to get regional cooperation against the Cuban revolutionary regime, it should foster democracy and strengthen the region's military forces. To get Washington's attention, domestic actors seeking power used US fears about an imminent—though unsubstantiated—Communist takeover to get Washington's backing. In the context of the weakness and inexperience of Latin Caribbean civilian power structures and the priority the United States gave to excluding the influence and participation of the Left, the policy of strengthening the military eventually worked to the detriment of furthering democracy. The most powerful elements of the Dominican power structure were uninterested in upholding democracy and found several opportunities to undermine it by using, with Washington's initial reluctance, the alleged external threat of a Communist takeover to crack down not only on the Left but also on aspiring democrats.

The beginning of the Nicaraguan transition began with the revolution in 1979. Again, this event could hardly have taken place the way it did were it not for the regional backing accrued to the FSLN and the regional leaders' pressures on Washington to prevent it from exercising a hegemonic role. The revolution sparked the regional discord that later shaped and constrained its own course. This circumstance momentarily removed the emergence of authoritarian alternatives of the Right. The fact that Washington had a constructive vision of the challenges ahead could have aided the Sandinista regime to maintain a reasonable degree of political pluralism, since authoritarian alternatives of the Left did not count on foreign sponsorships. The Carter administration was interested in promoting respect for human rights and in establishing a new relationship with Latin America, for which signing the Panama Canal Treaties in 1978 had been a good start. The radicalisation and apparent over-confidence of the Sandinistas, followed by changing circumstances in the United States—the election of Ronald Reagan in November 1980—altered this trajectory. The United States was 'sucked' in by the revolutionary situation in Central America. The Reagan administration had come to power with the aim of rolling back the advance of Communism in Central America and sought to provoke the forceful overthrow of the Sandinista government. The regional conflict that ensued involved armed challenges to the regimes in neighbouring El Salvador and Guatemala. Thus, the Nicaraguan trajectory was turned into a stage for the Cold War, and its fate was not decided until the latter took definite turns at the end of the eighties.

In Panama, major political turns coincided with changes in US attitudes toward Panama's demand for complete sovereignty and control of the Canal. The transition commenced in 1978, once the most powerful local actors perceived that the major impediment for institution building, US sovereignty and control of the Panama Canal and its surroundings, would disappear, following the Canal Treaties signed between President Carter and General Omar Torrijos. The Carter administration made the signing of the new Canal Treaties a showcase for improving US-Latin American relations. Though no overt pressure on Torrijos was made, the Carter administration and Torrijos' most important regional allies (the Presidents of Colombia, Venezuela and Costa Rican democracies) expected Panama to follow their course once the Canal negotiations were over and privately talked to Torrijos about it. The military launched the political opening at the peak of its power, offering a six-year long transition to democracy. Yet, unfolding events in nearby Central America provided inputs for the Panamanian transition, offering incentives for the military to resume authoritarian rule. The Panamanian trajectory was truncated when local military leaders used Washington's concern with the Central American conflict for their own purposes, undermining the process of democratisation to preserve their fundamental interests. Later diffuse civil protests and divisions within the power structure led to the resumption of open authoritarian rule in February 1988.

Explaining Latin Caribbean regime trajectories

The three cases included in this research and the discussion of the three propositions in this concluding chapter provide ample evidence to challenge mainstream views about the role of the United States in Latin Caribbean regime trajectories. Conventional explanations among members of the Washington policy-making and academic community contend that US determination and encouragement accounts for the attainment of democratic institutions in Latin America before, during and after the Cold War. According to Lowenthal, for example, "there is a broad bipartisan agreement in Washington... that fostering democracy in Latin America—and elsewhere, for that matter—is a legitimate and significant goal of US policy and that the US can be effective in pursuing that aim."[493] Evaluating the general impact of these policies, scholar (and former US National Security Advisor) Robert Pastor argued that "US foreign policy has helped and harmed Latin American democracy... on balance, it helped more."[494] Huntington, for example, argued that the lack of democracy in the Caribbean Basin before the Cold War stemmed from the discontinuity of US intervention—thus more intervention would have brought more democracy to the sub-region.[495]

---

493. Abraham Lowenthal (1991), "Preface." In *Exporting Democracy: The United States and Latin America*, (Baltimore and London: The Johns Hopkins University Press, 1991), p. vii.

494. Robert Pastor, "Promoting Democracy Pushing on the Pendulum," in *Whirlpool: US Foreign Policy Toward Latin America and the Caribbean*, (Princeton: Princeton University Press, 1992), p. 200.

495. According to Huntington, "US intervention accounted for the greatest democratic successes in the Caribbean Basin during the early part of the [twentieth] century, while local factors

Yet, the findings of this research point out the inaccuracy of these observations. During the Cold War, the United States was ineffective in fostering democratic institutions in the sub-region. Even when the White House made the promotion of democracy an explicit foreign policy goal, its efforts in the direction of preventing the influence of the Left and in the maintenance of order were detrimental to this aim. Indeed, the United States at times implemented policies that contributed partially with the democratisation of its Caribbean neighbours, adapting itself to the trend already taking place in the sub-region. Most times, not only because of the lower priority given to democratisation but also because of the regional order that US policies left behind, US influence was contrary to this purpose. This research does not provide evidence to conclude that further US intervention would have translated itself into more democratisation; rather, it seems to be the case that, under the normative understandings in which the United States projected its power in the sub-region, the more it intervened, the more it impaired the construction of a political process conducive to democratisation.

Studies by Herman and Kegley, Meernik and Peceny have found that states that were the target of US military interventions were more liberal than before the intervention. However, by defining "before" as one year prior to the events and "after" as ten years later, they disregard the extent to which US actions encouraged the coming to power of authoritarian regimes in the first place, made more difficult the struggle toward democracy, or set the stage for undermining the quality of democratic institutions adopted after US intervention.[496] Regarding the Latin Caribbean, the findings of this research point out that the United States adapted itself to the democratising tendencies within the sub-region and was not precisely the main actor furthering this process. In the fifties, the sub-regional and regional tendency toward liberalisation and democratisation had already started when Washington—fearing another Cuba in their hands—decided to back the efforts of selected aspiring democrats in the Dominican Republic. Taking into account the regional context—of which US attitudes were undoubtedly important but were not the sole factor—Dominicans prepared themselves and became active in the construction and testing of new rules of the game. In fact, many of the most important events in the Dominican regime trajectory were spurred by decisions and actions taken by Dominican actors. Under Kennedy, the United States finally made a consistent effort to support the sequence of events leading toward Dominican democratisation, but it refrained from fully backing this process once their perceptions of the Communist threat in this country increased and powerful Dominican actors turned their back on Constitutional rule. In Panama, US

---

spawned the dictatorships that ruled in the aftermath of those interventions..... When American intervention ended, democracy ended." Samuel Hungtington, "American ideals vs. American institutions," *Political Science Quarterly*, vol. 97, no. 1, (1982), p.27.

496. Margaret Herman and Charles Kegley, "The Use of US Military intervention to Promote Democracy: Evaluating the Record," *International Interactions*, vol. 24, no. 2 (1998), pp. 91–114; James Meernik, "United States Military Intervention and the Promotion of Democracy," *Journal of Peace Research*, vol. 33, no. 4 (1996), pp. 391–402; and Mark Peceny, "Forcing them to be free," *Political Research Quarterly*, vol. 52, no. 3 (September 1999), pp. 549–582.

administrations one after another were satisfied with the military's involvement in politics. In Nicaragua, the Reagan administration's actions were geared toward toppling the Sandinista regime, not at fostering democratic practices and institutions. The United States was not at the forefront in the establishment of democracy in these two countries. If some variant of democracy did emerge after US intervention, it was because domestic actors were already struggling for this aim and because the US could not openly impose dictatorships without endangering its prestige worldwide.

These findings also challenge the school of thought portraying US-Latin Caribbean relations as a by-product of the one-dimensional nature of US imperialism. Regarding Central America, for example, Walter LaFeber has stated that the United States became the "leading protector of the status quo in the twentieth century."[497] Likewise, Robinson argued that the promotion of 'polyarchical' regimes by the United States is just a way to maintain its ascendancy in world affairs.[498] Certainly, with the temporary exception of the Kennedy administration, the United States was not at the forefront of social change and democratisation in the sub-region. However 'unilateral' and 'self-serving' US policies may have seemed, regime transformations in this sub-region are not merely the results of the foreign policy needs of the hegemonic power. Political processes in the area a result of the asymmetric bargaining between actors in the United States, the country under consideration and other actors in the sub-region. For example, the United States did not create long-lasting dictatorships in the Latin Caribbean; it contributed to lay out the terrain in which they were born, but it was Latin Caribbean dictators' skilful handling of US influences what made them so enduring. US policies toward the sub-region were, in general, constrained by Washington's power structure; but in this process, sub-regional actors made substantial contributions to define the form and content of US policies.

Within similar radical interpretations about the role of the United States regarding the promotion of democracy in the third world, Gills, Rocamora and Wilson put forward the notion that the new democracies are just a façade to "cloak new forms of authoritarianism, repression and conservatism" that legitimise the status quo.[499] Certainly, the quality of democratic regimes that were born at the end of the Latin Caribbean regime trajectories could have been better, but to attribute this result to the United States alone is to put aside the limitations of domestic actors who pursued this goal. The cases studied here show that the quality of democratic institutions did improve with time, after the United States refrained from intervening in the sub-region's political processes.

This book also provides ground to replicate Lars Shoultz' findings that US policy toward Latin America has been guided by the need to protect US security,

---

497. Walter LaFeber, *Inevitable Revolutions: The United States in Central America*, (New York and London: WW. Norton & Company, 1983), p. 13.

498. William Robinson, *Promoting Polyarchy: Globalization, U.S. Intervention and Hegemony*, (Cambridge: Cambridge University Press, 1996).

499. Barry Gills, Joel Rocamora and Richard Wilson (eds.), *Low Intensity Democracy, London and Boulder*, (Colorado: Pluto Press, 1993), p. 5, 7.

the desire to accommodate the demands of US domestic politics, and the drive to promote US economic development.[500] US security understandings were instrumental in the formulation of policy toward the Caribbean Basin and these notions guided its actions in the sub-region. Following Shoultz, this research also shows what domestic actors did in order to influence US domestic politics to their advantage: among others, appearing cooperative so that US policy shifts did not mean loosening their ties with Washington's power structure and their ability to stay in or seek power.

Mainstream International Relations theories cannot fully explain the evolution of Latin Caribbean regime changes. Though a power-political understanding of this sub-region has been necessary to comprehend these political processes, realism's emphasis on relations between sovereign states provides little insight about the outcome of Latin Caribbean regime trajectories. As shown throughout the case studies, these processes evolved under conditions of limited sovereignty; besides, outcomes were significantly conditioned by domestic actors' subjective evaluations about the role of the United States and by the sequence of events in neighbouring countries. Neither is the traditional 'difussion' approach sufficient: While it is true that impulses across state borders contributed to these results, it does not explain why Latin Caribbean democratisation is late by western world standards.

To explain Latin Caribbean regime trajectories satisfactorily, it was necessary to shift to the region as the terrain within which the most important political interactions occurred. It meant giving integrated consideration to the local, regional and global levels of analysis, combining both macro and micro approaches. To appraise the impact of international influences we systematised them so as to expose the mechanisms whereby they influenced domestic political processes. The regional subsystem—the Latin Caribbean's regional order—was not just a higher-level factor; it was active at any level, influencing not only individuals but also societies at large. International influences were mediated by the regions' construction, but actors in the region also had the ability to affect the external environment. In this sense, the regional order was not the cause of regime transitions; rather, it affected the way in which actors interacted in their pursuit of their goals. It was also necessary to incorporate the United States' state structure, as Zakaria has said in relation to the world role of the United States.[501] The outcomes of these regime transitions were significantly shaped by decisions taken at the different levels of the state structure in Washington.

Trascending traditional conceptions of the international system, Gary Goertz' work on contexts in international politics is particularly helpful. Blurring the sharp distinction between domestic and international "causes," Goertz offers a way to integrate individual, national and regional levels of analysis. The international order is neither the cause nor the effect of regime transformations. Rather,

500. Lars Schoultz, *Beneath the United States: A History of U.S. Policy toward Latin America*, (Cambridge: Harvard University Press, 1998), p. 367.

501. Zakaria, Fareed. *From wealth to power: The unusual origins of America's world role*, (Princeton, New Jersey: Princeton University Press, 1998), p. 187.

it affects how individuals interact and provide meaning to human activities in the way they take into consideration limits in power, existing norms and past choices before undertaking actions.[502] "The context is neither individually necessary nor sufficient, but in conjunction with other factors it explains the outcome or makes it more likely."[503]

Fundamentally, this research has offered ways to understand the process whereby the United States asserted control over the nations of the Latin Caribbean. Following Ikenberry and Kupchan's effort to explore the nature of the shadow that hegemonic nations cast,[504] the case studies included here show that the United States combined both material incentives and substantive beliefs in its exercise of power. The United States' exercise of power involved not only force and the threat of its use but also the projection of norms that were embraced by Latin Caribbean leaders; acquiescence was the result of both coertion but also the socialization of these leaders into the hegemon's notions of the international and regional order. As a result, it may be argued that in no other part of the world has the impact of a foreign power on political developments been greater than in the Latin Caribbean. During the Cold War, this was the observation usually made regarding Eastern Europe in relation to the Soviet hegemon.[505] But US power projection over this area was longer, spanning the twentieth century, independently of situations of the international order; and more effective, because it relied on a recurrent combination of force and other material incentives and the projection of a set of norms which were embraced by leaders of Latin Caribbean nations. Paraphrasing Carter's Secretary of Defense, Zbigniew Brezinski—the Latin Caribbean may have been a sub-region the United States has "dominated as the Soviets [did] in Eastern Europe."[506]

Regime transitions in the Latin Caribbean represent challenges to both International Relation and Political Science disciplines and point out the need to trascend the usual categories used to depict the sub-region's political processes. Further work on these issues acquires renewed urgency considering the ever-possible prospect of political change in Cuba. The United States is not a paramount power, able to control regional affairs as it wishes; though it sets constraints that affect the calculations and actions of the élites involved in political

---

502. For a discussion on how contexts affect outcomes in international interactions, see Gary Goertz, *Contexts of International Politics*, (Cambridge: Cambridge University Press, 1994).

503. Goertz, *Contexts of International Politics*, pp. 3, 93.

504. G. John Ikenberry and Charles A. Kupchan, "Socialization and Hegemonic Power," *International Organisation* 44 (3, Summer 1990), pp. 283–315.

505. This challenges a statement by Michael Burton, Richard Gunther, and John Higley, "Elites and Democratic Consolidation in Latin America and Southern Europe: An Overview." In John Higley and Richard Gunther (eds.), *Elites and Democratic Consolidation in Latin America and Southern Europe*, (Cambridge and Melbourne: Cambridge University Press, 1992), pp. 346–347, who argue that "in no case is the impact of foreign powers on political developments as great as in Eastern Europe." They overlooked the extent to which the United Sates has permeated Latin Caribbean politics.

506. Brezinski's quote referred to Central America and may be found in "Panamá, el Senado de los Estados Unidos y América Latina", *La Prensa* (Panama City), 9 April 1987, p. 3.

change in the area, those constraints have also limited the United States' actions and its ability to shape a peaceful regional order. The United States has been the axis of a regional configuration that historically permeated political change in the area. Therefore, effective support for democracy within its sphere of influence would demand more than single-minded, transient efforts and would require the incorporation of the complex, power-political dimension within which the regional order is based. Given the great asymmetry in power and resources between the United States and its small Caribbean neighbours, and given America's account of itself in fostering democracy, the lessons from this study point out that if Washington is to exercise a 'hegemonic' role in the democratisation process of the states in the Caribbean Basin, it should do so on another sort of understandings.

Sources and Bibliography

Primary sources: United States

All primary US documents on the Dominican Republic were obtained from the General Records (RG59) of the Department of State at the US National Archives located in College Park, Maryland. The documents quoted in this book are listed heretofore following the classification number assigned by the Archives. All the relevant information regarding the documents is also included. Note that the classification system used until 1961 coincides with the documents' chronological order. Starting in 1963 the classification system was changed to one based on the issues contained in the document; therefore, documents dated 1963 and after do not follow a chronological order.

US.NA.RG59.Decimal file 739.00/12-1058. "Indications of political tensions," Foreign Service Despatch No. 225 from Ambassador Joseph Farland, American Embassy in Ciudad Trujillo, dated 10 November 1958.

US.NA.RG59.Decimal files 739.00/10-1860. Confidential Foreign Service Despatch from the American Embassy in Ciudad Trujillo to the Department of State, dated 18 October 1960.

US.NA.RG59.Decimal files 739.00/10-3062. Secret telegram from the US Embassy in Santo Domingo, dated 30 October 1962.

US.NA.RG59.Decimal files 739.00/10-361. "Program for the Dominican Republic," Secret Memorandum of Conversation between Dr. Joaquin Balaguer, President of the Dominican Republic; the Honorable George Ball, Undersecretary of State, and Mr. John Calvin Hill, Consul General in Ciudad Trujillo, dated 3 October 1961.

US.NA.RG59.Decimal files 739.00/11-1661. Secret Telegram from the American Consulate in Ciudad Trujillo, dated 16 November 1961.

US.NA.RG59.Decimal files 739.00/11-1861. Secret Telegram from the Department of State to the American Consulate in Ciudad Trujillo, dated 18 November 1961.

US.NA.RG59.Decimal files 739.00/11-1961. Secret Telegram from American Consul in Ciudad Trujillo, dated 19 November 1961, 1: 39 p.m.

US.NA.RG59.Decimal files 739.00/11-1961. Secret Telegram from the American Consul in Ciudad Trujillo, dated 19 November 1961, 2 p.m.

US.NA.RG59.Decimal files 739.00/1-1262. Secret telegram from the Department of State to the American Consul in Santo Domingo, dated 12 January 1962.

US.NA.RG59.Decimal files 739.00/12-1261. Secret telegram from the State Department to the American Consul in Santo Domingo, dated 12 December 1961

US.NA.RG59.Decimal files 739.00/12-1362. Secret telegram from the US Embassy in Santo Domingo, dated 13 December 1962.

US.NA.RG59.Decimal files 739.00/12-161. Confidential telegram from the Department of State to the American Consul in Santo Domingo, dated 1 December 1961.

US.NA.RG59.Decimal files 739.00/12-2262. Confidential telegram from the Navy Attaché in Santo Domingo, dated 22 December 1962.

US.NA.RG59.Decimal files 739.00/12-3061. Secret telegram from the American Embassy in Santo Domingo to the Department of State, dated 30 November 1961.

US.NA.RG59.Decimal files 739.00/3-1359. Informal Letter by Ambassador Joseph S. Farland in Ciudad Trujillo, addressed to 'Dear Joe,' dated 13 March 1959.

US.NA.RG59.Decimal files 739.00/3-2260. Top Secret Informal Letter from Ambassador Joseph Farland to the Assistant Secretary of State for Inter-American Affairs, R.R. Rubottom, Jr., dated 22 March 1960.

US.NA.RG59.Decimal files 739.00/3-2860, XR 739.11. Secret letter from General Norman Clark to Colonel King, dated 28 March 1960.

US.NA.RG59.Decimal files 739.00/3-760. Confidential telegram from the American Embassy in Ciudad Trujillo to the Department of State, dated 7 March 1960.

US.NA.RG59.Decimal files 739.00/4-2560. Secret eyes-only Memorandum for the files, signed by Assistant Secretary of State for Interamerican affairs, R.R. Rubottom, Jr., dated 25 April 1960.

US.NA.RG59.Decimal files 739.00/5-2060. "Transmitting Memorandum of Conversation with President Betancourt," Confidential Foreign Service Despatch from the American Embassy in Caracas to the Department of State, dated 20 May 1960.

US.NA.RG59.Decimal files 739.00/5-862. Secret telegram from the American Embassy in Santo Domingo, dated 8 May 1962.

US.NA.RG59.Decimal files 739.00/6-1261. Confidential Telegram from the American Embassy in Ciudad Trujillo, dated 12 June 1961.

US.NA.RG59.Decimal files 739.00/6-1360. "Possible Abandonment of Power by Trujillo in the Dominican Republic," Secret memorandum of Conversation between Virgilio Diaz Ordoñez, Dominican Republic's Ambassador to the OAS Council, and ARA-Amb. Dreier and RPA-Mr. Redington, dated 13 June 1960.

US.NA.RG59.Decimal files 739.00/6-1361. Secret Telegram from the American Consulate in Ciudad Trujillo, dated June 13 1961.

US.NA.RG59.Decimal files 739.00/6-1761. Secret telegram from the American Embassy in Ciudad Trujillo, dated 17 June 1861.

US.NA.RG59.Decimal files 739.00/6-2061. "Venezuela: Caribbean Problems," Confidential Memorandum of Conversation between Jose Antonio Mayobre, Ambassador of Venezuela, Dr. Rafael Caldera, President of Venezuela's Chamber of Deputies, and the Undersecretary, dated June 20 1961.

US.NA.RG59.Decimal files 739.00/6-2461. Secret Memorandum from U. Alexis Johnson to the Secretary of State, dated 24 June 1961.

US.NA.RG59.Decimal files 739.00/6-2661. Confidential Memorandum from the American Consulate in Ciudad Trujillo, dated 26 June 1961.

US.NA.RG59.Decimal files 739.00/6-3060. "Views on the political problems in the Dominican Republic and suggestions for possible courses of action by our Government in its future negotiations with the Government of Dominican Republic," Secret Memorandum from Harry M. Lofton, Second Secretary-Consul to Mr. Thomas C. Mann, dated 30 June 1960.

US.NA.RG59.Decimal files 739.00/7-1359. "Political Situation in the Dominican Republic," Confidential Memorandum of Conversation between Mr. Alvin E. Gilbert and Mr. Ernest B Gutierrez, Officer in Charge of Dominican Affairs, dated 13 July 1959.

US.NA.RG59.Decimal files 739.00/7-1459. Secret Informal Letter from Ambassador Joseph Farland to R.R. Rubottom, Jr., Assistant Secretary of State for Inter-American Affairs, dated 14 July 1959.

US.NA.RG59.Decimal files 739.00/7-1661. Confidential Foreign Service Despatch from the American Consulate in Ciudad Trujillo, dated 16 July 1961.

US.NA.RG59.Decimal files 739.00/7-1861. Unclassified Airgram from the Department of State to all ARA diplomatic posts and US/UN, dated July 18 1961.

US.NA.RG59.Decimal files 739.00/7-259. "Venezuela's position on possible COAS action on the Dominican Republic's complaint regarding Foreign Intervention." Confidential memoranda of conversation, Department of State, dated 2 July 1959.

US.NA.RG59.Decimal files 739.00/7-361. "Dominican Republic," Secret Memorandum from RA Stevenson to Mr. Coeer, Department of State, dated 3 July 1961.

US.NA.RG59.Decimal files 739.00/8-1161. Secret Telegram from Ciudad Trujillo, dated 11 August 1961

US.NA.RG59.Decimal files 739.00/8-1161. Secret Telegram No. 307 from the American Consulate in Ciudad Trujillo, dated 11 August 1961.

US.NA.RG59.Decimal files 739.00/8-1457. Letter by John S. Hoghland II, acting Assistant Secretary of State for Congressional Relations to Senator Mike Mulroney, 20 August 1957.

US.NA.RG59.Decimal files 739.00/8-2261. Confidential Telegram from the American Consulate in Ciudad Trujillo, dated 22 August 1961.

US.NA.RG59.Decimal files 739.00/8-2560. Confidential telegram from the American Embassy in Ciudad Trujillo to the Department of State, dated 25 August 1960.

US.NA.RG59.Decimal files 739.00/9-161. Secret Telegram from the Department of State to the American Consul in Ciudad Trujillo, dated 1 September 1961.

US.NA.RG59.Decimal files 739.00/9-2161. Secret telegram from the Department of State to the American Consulate in Ciudad Trujillo, dated 21 September 1961.

US.NA.RG59.POL 1 DOM REP "Dominican political situation." Confidential memorandum of conversation between expresident of the Dominican Republic, Joaquin Balaguer, and Kennedy Crocket, Director of the Office of Caribbean Affairs, and Henry W. Shlaudeman, Chief of Dominican Affairs, dated 21 August 1964.

US.NA.RG59.POL 1-1 DOM REP. "Contingency Plan," Secret Airgram from the American Embassy in Santo Domingo to the Department of State, dated 22 September 1963.

US.NA.RG59.POL 14 DOM REP, XR POL 15 DOM REP. Confidential telegram from the American Embassy in Santo Domingo to the Department of State, dated 26 June 1965.

US.NA.RG59.POL 14 DOMREP, XR POL 15 DOM REP. Secret telegram from the American Embassy in Santo Domingo to the Department of State, dated 14 June 1965.

US.NA.RG59.POL 15 DOM REP. Confidential airgram from the American Embassy in Santo Domingo to the Department of State, dated 15 July 1965.

US.NA.RG59.POL 15 DOM REP. Secret Telegram from the Department of State to the American Embassy in Santo Domingo, dated 13 October 1963.

US.NA.RG59.POL 15 DOM REP. Confidential telegram from the American Embassy in Santo Domingo to the Department of State, dated 1 October 1963.

US.NA.RG59.POL 15 DOM REP. Confidential Telegram from the Department of State to the American Embassy in Santo Domingo, dated 17 October 1963.

US.NA.RG59.POL 15. Secret telegram from the American Embassy in Santo Domingo to the Department of State, dated 4 July 1965.

US.NA.RG59.POL 15-1 DOM REP. "President Juan Bosch of the Dominican Republic." Secret Memorandum from the Executive Secretary, William H. Brubek, to Mr. McGeorge Bundy, the White House, dated 4 June 1963.

US.NA.RG59.POL 2 DOM REP. Confidential telegram from the American Embassy in Santo Domingo to the Department of State, dated 23 August 1963.

US.NA.RG59.POL 2 DOM REP. "The Dominican Situation", Secret Airgram from the American Embassy in Santo Domingo to the Department of State, dated 11 June 1963.

US.NA.RG59.POL 2-1 DOM REP. Confidential Airgram from the American Embassy in Santo Domingo to the Department of State, dated 1 October;

US.NA.RG59.POL 2-1 DOM REP. Confidential Airgram from the American Embassy in Santo Domingo to the Department of State, dated 1 October 1963.

US.NA.RG59.POL 2-1 DOM REP. Confidential Airgram from the American Embassy in Santo Domingo to the Department of State, dated 8 October 1963.

US.NA.RG59.POL 2-1 DOM REP. Confidential Airgram from the American Embassy in Santo Domingo to the Department of State, dated 5 November 1963.

US.NA.RG59.POL 23-7. Secret telegram from the American Embassy in Santo Domingo to the Department of State, dated 2 August 1965.

US.NA.RG59.POL 23-9 DOM REP Confidential telegram from the American Embassy in Santo Domingo to the Department of State, dated 27 April 1965, 2:43 p.m.

US.NA.RG59.POL 23-9 DOM REP. Confidential telegram from the American Embassy in Santo Domingo to the Department of State, dated 25 April 1965, 5:00 p.m.

US.NA.RG59.POL 23-9 DOM REP. Confidential telegram from the American Embassy in Santo Domingo to the Department of State, dated 26 April 1965, 7:59 a.m.

US.NA.RG59.POL 23-9 DOM REP. Confidential Telegram from the American Embassy in Santo Domingo to the Department of State, dated 26 April 1965, 3:39 a.m.

US.NA.RG59.POL 23-9 DOM REP. Confidential telegram from the American Embassy in Santo Domingo to the Department of State, dated 28 April 1965, 12:59 p.m.

US.NA.RG59.POL 23-9 DOM REP. Confidential telegram from the American Embassy in Santo Domingo, dated 29 April 1965, 1:16 a.m.

US.NA.RG59.POL 23-9. "Situation in the Dominican Republic," Confidential memorandum of conversation between Former President Betancourt and President Lyndon Johnson, dated 3 May 1965.

US.NA.RG59.POL 23-9. Confidential telegram from the American Embassy in Santo Domingo, to the Department of State, dated 29 April 1965, 3:54 a.m.

US.NA.RG59.POL 23-9. Confidential telegram from the American Embassy in Santo Domingo to the Department of State, dated 10 June 1965.

US.NA.RG59.POL 23-9. Confidential Telegram from the Department of State to the American Embassy in Santo Domingo, dated 4 May 1965, 4:46 p.m.

US.NA.RG59.POL 23-9. Secret EXDIS Telecon between Deputy Assistant Secretary Mann, Ambassador Bunker and Assistant Secretary Vaughn to the American Embassy in Santo Domingo, dated 29 April 1965.

US.NA.RG59.POL 23-9. Secret Telegram from the American Embassy in Santo Domingo to the Department of State, dated 29 April 1965, 5:13 p.m.

US.NA.RG59.POL 23-9. Secret telegram from the American Embassy in Santo Domingo to the Department of State, dated 4 May 1965, 3:30 a.m.

US.NA.RG59.POL 23-9. Secret telegram from the American Embassy in Santo Domingo to the Department of State, dated 12 May 1965, 8:39 a.m.

US.NA.RG59.POL 23-9. Secret telegram from the American Embassy in Santo Domingo to the Department of State, dated 7 May 1965, 8:48 p.m.

US.NA.RG59.POL 23-9. Secret telegram from the American Embassy in Santo Domingo to the Department of State, dated 5 May 1965, 11:02 p.m.

US.NA.RG59.POL 23-9. Secret telegram from the American Embassy in Santo Domingo to the Department of State, dated 24 May 1965, 3:00 p.m.

US.NA.RG59.POL 23-9. Secret telegram from the American Embassy in Santo Domingo to the Department of State, dated 25 May 1965.

US.NA.RG59.POL 23-9. Secret telegram from the American Embassy in Santo Domingo to the Department of State, dated 24 May 1965, 12:26 p.m.

US.NA.RG59.POL 23-9. Secret telegram from the Department of State to the American Embassy in Santo Domingo, dated 29 April 1965, 11:11 p.m.

US.NA.RG59.POL DOM REP-HAI. Limited Official Use Telegram from the American Embassy in Santo Domingo to the Department of State, dated 30 April 1963.

US.NA.RG59.POL DOM REP-HAI. Secret Telegram from the American Embassy in Caracas to the Department of State, dated 10 May 1963.

US.NA.RG59.POL DOM REP-HAI. Secret Telegram from the American Embassy in Santo Domingo to the Department of State, dated 5 May 1963.

US.NA.RG59.POL DOM REP-HAI. Top Secret Telegram from the American Embassy in Santo Domingo to the Department of State, dated 2 May 1963.

US.NA.RG59.POL DOM REP-US. Confidential memorandum from Assistant Secretary Edwin Martin to the American Ambassador to Rio de Janeiro, dated 4 November 1963.

US.NA.RG59.XR POL DOM REP-US. Confidential letter from the Deputy Undersecretary of Agriculture, James L. Sundquist, to the Deputy Assistant Secretary for Economic Affairs, Jerome Jacobson, dated 1 November 1963.

All primary documents on Nicaragua come from the compilation made by The National Security Archives (NSA), a Washington DC-based non-governmental organization located at the Gellman Library of George Washington's University. US government documents on US foreign policy toward Nicaragua were declassified through the Freedom of Information Act (FOIA), compiled, put in microfiche form and listed under Peter Kornbluh (ed.), *Nicaragua: The Making of US Policy*, Alexandria, VA: Chadmyck-Healy, Inc. and The National Security Archive, 1991. The documents quoted in this book are listed heretofore following the microfiche number assigned by the editors. All the relevant information regarding the documents is also included.

NSA 1991, Document No. 00121. "Political update," Confidential cable No. 02671 from the American Embassy in Managua to the Secretary of State, dated 12 June 1978.

NSA 1991, Document No. 00166. "GON-opposition dialogue," Secret cable No. 03921 from the American Embassy in Managua to the Secretary of State, dated 23 August 1978.

NSA 1991, Document No. 00191. "Ambassador meets Somoza 30 August," Confidential cable No. 04099 from the American Embassy in Managua to the Secretary of State, dated 31 August 1978.

NSA 1991, Document No. 00202. "Nicaragua-OAS consideration," Confidential cable No. 04147 from the American Embassy in Managua to the Secretary of State, dated 5 September 1978.

NSA 1991, Document No. 00205. "Conversations with Somoza: 5 September," Confidential cable No. 04176 from the American Embassy in Managua to the Secretary of State, dated 6 September 1978.

NSA 1991, Document No. 00211. "Conversations with Somoza: 7 September," Confidential cable No. 04197 from the American Embassy in Managua to the Secretary of State, dated 7 September 1978.

NSA 1991, Document No. 00325. "Perceived needs of Nicaraguans for US involvement," Secret cable No. 04609 from the American Embassy in Managua to the Secretary of State and the American Embassy in Panama City, dated 24 September 1978.

NSA 1991, Document No. 000365. "Nicaragua mediation: negotiating instructions," Confidential cable No. 252512 from the Secretary of State to the American Embassy in Managua, dated 4 october 1978.

NSA 1991, Document No. 00366. "Mediation: a difficult road," Confidential cable No. 04858 from the American Embassy in Managua to the Secretary of State, dated 5 October 1978.

NSA 1991, Document No. 00436. "Nicaragua mediation No. 58: proposed talking points for use with Somoza," Confidential cable No. 05273 from the American Embassy in Managua to the Secretary of State, dated 24 October 1978.

NSA 1991, Document No. 00443. "Nicaragua mediation No. 81: Demarche to Somoza," Secret cable No. 05430 from the American Embassy in Managua to the Secretary of State, dated 30 October 1978.

NSA 1991, Document No. 00482. "Nicaragua mediation No. 121: Conversation with Somoza." Secret cable No. 05775 from the Secretary of State to the American Embassy in Managua, dated 11 November 1978.

NSA 1991, Document No. 0050. "Proposed initiatives with Somoza and the opposition," Confidential cable No. 030739 from the Secretary of State to the American Embassy in Managua, dated 5 February 1978.

NSA 1991, Document No. 000548. "Nicaragua mediation No. 203: Somoza's request to USG," Secret cable No. 06297 from the American Embassy in Managua to the Secretary of State, dated 4 December 1978.

NSA 1991, Document No. 0055. "Demarche to President Somoza," Secret cable No. 000621 from the American Embassy in Managua to the Secretary of State, dated 8 February 1978.

NSA 1991, Document No. 00623. "GON wants to make a deal," Secret cable No. 00235 from the American Embassy in Managua to the Secretary of State, dated 15 January 1979.

NSA 1991, Document No. 00626. "Demarche [excised] January 17," Secret cable No. 00285 from the American Embassy in Managua to Secretary of State, dated 17 January 1979.

NSA 1991, Document No. 00630. "The Caracas Caucus," Confidential cable No. 00305 from the American Embassy in Managua to the Secretary of State, dated 19 January 1979.

NSA 1991, Document No. 00634. United States Bureau of Human Rights and Humanitarian Affairs, "Options," Secret memorandum from Mark L. Schneider to Ambassador Bowdler, dated 19 January 1979.

NSA 1991, Document No. 00639. "Nicaragua meeting," Classification Unknown Memorandum from Barbara Bowie to Ms. Patricia derian, dated 24 January 1979.

NSA 1991, Document No. 0064. "Role of US Embassy in Nicaragua," Secret cable No. 041757 from the Secretary of State to the American Embassy in Managua," dated 16 February 1978.

NSA 1991, Document No. 00647. "Coup plotting," Secret cable No. 033931 from the American Embassy in Managua to the Secretary of State, dated 9 February 1979.

NSA 1991, Document No. 00678. "G-12 continues anti-US statements," Limited Official Use Cable No. 01619 from the American Embassy in Managua to the Secretary of State, dated 2 April 1979.

NSA 1991, Document No. 0070. "Item for Ambassador Solaun," Confidential cable No. 01005 from the American Embassy in Nicaragua to the Secretary of State, dated 1 March 1978.

NSA 1991, Document No. 00753. United States Bureau of Human Rights and Humanitarian Affairs Memorandum from Patricia Derian to Brandon Grove, Department of State, dated 12 June 1979.

NSA 1991, Document No. 00765. "OAS action Nicaragua," Secret cable No. 153522 from the Secretary of State to All American Republics diplomatic posts," dated 15 June 1979.

NSA 1991, Document No. 00833. "Somoza-The First Visit," Secret cable No. 02857 from the American Embassy in Managua to the Secretary of State, dated 28 June 1979.

NSA 1991, Document No. 00835. "Talk with Somoza," Secret cable No. 166874 from the Secretary of State to the American Embassy in Managua, dated 28 June 1979.

NSA 1991, Document No. 00836. "The current scene," Secret cable No. 02870 from the American Embassy in Managua to the Secretary of State, dated 28 June 1979.

NSA 1991, Document No. 00846. "Nicaraguan scenario," Confidential cable No. 168715 from the Secretary of State to the American Embassy in Managua, dated 30 June 1979.

NSA 1991, Document No. 00848. "Somoza: The third Meeting," Secret cable No. 02911 from the American Embassy in Managua to the Secretary of State, dated 30 June 1979.

NSA 1991, Document No. 00866. "Somoza: The Fourth Meeting," Secret cable No. 02990 from the American Embassy in Managua to the Secretary of State, dated 5 July 1979.

NSA 1991, Document No. 00873. "Somoza tells Post reporter he made commitment to USG," Confidential cable No. 03035 from the American Embassy in Managua to the Secretary of State, dated 7 July 1979.

NSA 1991, Document No. 00886. "Nicaragua: The National Guard," Secret cable No. 176171 from the Secretary of State to the American Embassy in Managua, dated 7 July 1979.

NSA 1991, Document No. 0093. "Opposition plotting," Confidential cable No. 04609 from the American Embassy in Managua to the Secretary of State, dated 26 April 1978.

NSA 1991, Document No. 00937. "Transition scenario," Secret cable No. 183735 from the Secretary of State to the American Embassy in Managua, dated 15 July 1979.

NSA 1991, Document No. 00961. "GON backs off from agreement," Secret cable No. 03250 from the American Embassy in Managua to the Secretary of State, dated 17 July 1979.

NSA 1991, Document No. 00968. "(Excised) explains attitude of Urcuyo," Secret cable No. 05458 from the American Embassy in Panama to the Secretary of State, dated 18 July 1979.

NSA 1991, Document No. 00100. "Opposition attitudes toward dialogue," Confidential cable No. 02058 from the American Embassy in Managua to the Department of State, dated 4 May 1978.

NSA 1991, Document No. 001249. "Demarche on Hostages," Limited Official Use Cable No. 00102 from the American Embassy in Managua to the Secretary of State, dated 9 January 1981.

NSA 1991, Document No. 001250. "Conversation with Junta member Sergio Ramírez," Secret Cable No. 00103 from the American Embassy in Managua to the Secretary of State, dated 9 January 1981.

NSA 1991, Document No. 001256. "CODEL Studds-Edgar-Milulski in Nicaragua," Limited Official Use Cable No. 00288 from the American Embassy in Managua to the Secretary of State, dated 20 January 1981.

NSA 1991, Document No. 001266. Memorandum of Secretary Haig's Conversation with Honduran Foreign Minister Elvir, Secret cable No. 030214 from the secretary of State to the American Embassy in Tegucigalpa, dated 5 February 1981.

NSA 1991, Document No. 001272. "Support for El Salvador Insurgency in Soviet, Cuban and Nicaraguan Media," FBIS Analysis Report, dated 10 February 1981.

NSA 1991, Document No. 001280. "Covert action proposal for Central America," Secret-Sensitive Memorandum for the Secretary from R. C. McFarlane, dated 27 February 1981.

NSA 1991, Document No. 001287, Report of the Congressional Committee Investigating the Iran-Contra Affair, "Finding pursuant to Section 662 of the Foreign Assistance Act of 1961, as Amended, Concerning Operations Undertaken by the Central Intelligence Agency in Foreign Countries, Other Than Those Intended Solely for the Purpose of Intelligence Recollection," Secret document, The White House, dated 9 March 1981.

NSA 1991, Document No. 001292. "Press Guidance, March 19," Unclassified Cable No. 071375 from the Secretary of State to the American Embassy in Managua, dated 20 March 1981.

NSA 1991, Document No. 00132. Letter from President James Carter to the President of the Republic of Nicaragua, General Anastasio Somoza Debayle, dated 30 June 1978.

NSA 1991, Document No. 001332. "[Title Excised)," Confidential cable No. 132061 from the Secretary of State to the American Embassy in Oslo, dated 21 May 1981.

NSA 1991, Document No. 001345. "Letter from Assistant Attorney General, D. Lowell Jensen, to the Honorable Michael D. Barnes, Chairman of the US House Subcommittee on Interamerican Affairs," dated 24 June 1981.

NSA 1991, Document No. 001354. "Fernando Chamorro seeks Asylum in Costa Rica," Confidential cable No. 03059 from the American Embassy in Managua to the Secretary of State, dated 14 July 1981.

NSA 1991, Document No. 001373. "Relations with Nicaragua," Secret cable No. 224207 from the Secretary of State to All American Republics diplomatic posts, dated 22 August 1981.

NSA 1991, Document No. 001403. "Nicaragua and the Rio Treaty," Confidential Memorandum from L/ARA-K, Scott Gudgenn to Mr. Braibanti, dated 2 November 1981.

NSA 1991, Document No. 001409. "Nicaragua: conditions and US interests," Issue Brief of the Library of Congress, Congressional Research Service Report IB80013, prepared by Nina Serafino, updated 19 November 1981.

NSA 1991, Document No. 001414. "Finding pursuant to section 662 of the Foreign Assistance Act of 1961, as Amended, Concerning Operations Undertaken by the Central Intelligence Agency in Foreign Countries, Other than Those intended Solely for the Purpose of Intelligence Collection," National Security Council, drafted in July 1982.

NSA 1991, Document No. 001482. "Eight point peace plan," Confidential cable No. 093251 from the Secretary of State to the American Embassy in Managua, dated 8 April 1981.

NSA 1991, Document No. 001539, Report of the Congressional Investigating Committee Investigating the Iran-Contra Affairs, "Proposed Covert Action Finding on Nicaragua," Secret action memorandum from Donald Gregg for William P. Clark, National Security Council, dated 12 July 1982.

NSA 1991, Document No. 001598. "US Intelligence Performance on Central America: Achievements and selected instances of concern," US House of Representatives, Permanent Select Committee on Intelligence, Subcommittee on Oversight and Evaluation Staff Report, dated 22 September 1982.

NSA 1991, Document No. 001625. "NSDD-77 on Public Diplomacy," Memorandum for Charles Hill, NSSD Executive Secretariat, Department of State, dated 14 January 1983.

NSA 1991, Document No. 001683. "Central America: Defending Our Vital Interests," Address by President Reagan before a joint session of Congress, April 27 1983.

NSA 1991, Document No. 001750. "New Coordinator for Public Diplomacy for Central America," Limited Official Use cable from the Acting Secretary to all American Republic Diplomatic Posts and all OECD Capitals, dated 5 July 1983.

NSA 1991, Document No. 001758. "Central America." Top Secret White House Memorandum for the Honorable George P. Shultz, Secretary of State; Caspar Weinberger, Secretary of Defense; William J. Casey, Director of Central Intelligence, and General John W. Vessey, Chairman of the Joint Chiefs of Staff, dated 12 July 1983.

NSA 1991, Document No. 00182. "Human rights demarche," Confidential cable No. 218953 from the Secretary of State, Warren Christopher, to the American Embassy in Managua, dated 29 August 1978.

NSA 1991, Document No. 001882. "GRN leaders stress fears of imminent US invasion," Confidential cable No. 05172 from the American Embassy in Managua to the Secretary of State, dated 9 November 1983.

NSA 1991, Document No. 001888. "Nicaraguan officials on CIA, Peace, Negotiations," Confidential cable No. 05371 from the American Embassy in Managua to the Secretary of State, dated 19 November 1983.

NSA 1991, Document No. 001890. "Registration of foreigners in Nicaragua," Limited Official Use cable No. 05420 from the American Embassy in Managua to the Secretary of State, dated 22 November 1983.

NSA 1991, Document No. 001892. "GRN (illegible) political parties," Confidential Confidential cable No. 05460 from the American Embassy in Managua to the Secretary of State, dated 25 November 1983.

NSA 1991, Document No. 001896. "La Prensa on Sandinista Policy Changes," Unclassified cable No. 05508 from the American Embassy in Managua to the Secretary of State, dated 28 November 1983.

NSA 1991, Document No. 001994. "Special Activities in Nicaragua," Top Secret Memorandum from Oliver North and Constantine Menges for Robert C. Mc Farlane, National Security Council, dated 2 March 1984.

NSA 1991, Document No. 002027. "Supplemental Assistance to Nicaragua Program," Secret memorandum from the Director of Central Intelligence, William Casey, for the Assistant to the President for National Security Affairs, Robert Mc Farlane, dated 27 March 1984.

NSA 1991, Document No. 002037. Secret letter from Robert C. McFarlane for the Honorable Howard Baker, Majority Leader, US Senate, dated 5 April 1984. The legality of the Reagan administration's actions centered on their purpose (avowedly not intended for overthrowing the Nicaraguan government), rather than the recipient's purpose, which was obviously so.

NSA 1991, Document No. 002127. "Central America," Secret Minutes NSC/ICS 400616 from the National Security Planning Group Meeting on 25 June 1984.

NSA 1991, Document No. 002343. "Nicaragua options," Top secret memorandum from Oliver North to Robert McFarlane, National Security Council, dated 15 January 1985.

NSA 1991, Document No. 002343. "Nicaragua options," Top secret memorandum from Oliver North to Robert McFarlane, National Security Council, dated 15 January 1985.

NSA 1991, Document No. 002356. "Central America trip: Observations and conclusions," Secret Information Memorandum for the President from Robert McFarlane, National Security Council, dated 31 January 1985.

NSA 1991, Document No. 002376. "GON statement February 27 on the international situation," Unclassified cable No. 01233 from the American Embassy in Managua to the Secretary of State, dated 28 February 1985.

NSA 1991, Document No. 002394. "Public Diplomacy Action Plan, Support for the White House Educational campaign," Confidential Project Proposal-sensitive document, The White House, Office for Public Diplomacy, dated 12 March 1985.

NSA 1991, Document No. 002396. "White Propaganda Operation," Confidential Eyes-Only Memorandum from Jonathan Miller to Pat Buchanan, Assistant to the President and Director of Communications, dated 13 March 1985.

NSA 1991, Document No. 002560. "ICJ Nicaragua case-Second Day," Limited Official Use Cable No. 06231 from the American Embassy in The Hague to the Secretary of State, dated 13 September 1985.

NSA 1991, Document No. 002616. "Nicaragua: telling it like it is," Secret memorandum from Robert Mc Farlane for the Secretary of State, the Secretary of Defense, the Director of Central Intelligence and the Chairman of the Joint Chiefs of Staff, The White House, dated 11 November 1985.

NSA 1991, Document No. 002626. "GAO/NSLAD-86-13 Allegation of Lobbying Assistance," General Accounting Office Report, dated 5 December 1985.

NSA 1991, Document No. 002644. "Denial of detail of personnel by DoD," Memorandum from Otto Reich to NSC-Mr. Walt Raymond, Coordinator for Public Diplomacy for Latin America and the Caribbean, dated 5 January 1986.

NSA 1991, Document No. 002758. "Prospects for Containment of Nicaragua's Communist Government," Department of Defense Report, dated May 1986.

NSA 1991, Document No. 0028.58. "Report on trip to Central American countries, July 5-16," Memorandum from Senator Dick D'Amato to Senator Robert Byrd, US Senate, dated 5 August 1986.

NSA 1991, Document No. 002976. "Issue Preview: Congress and the Arias Peace Plan," US Congress, Arms Control and Foreign Policy Caucus Report dated 27 April 1987.

NSA 1991, Document No. 003031. Letter to the Honorable Jack Brooks, Chairman, Committee on Government Operations, House of Representatives, from the Comptroller General of the United States, dated 30 September 1987.

NSA 1991, Document No. 003142. "Nicaragua: Municipal elections," National Democratic Institute for International Affairs Report, 20 december 1988.

NSA 1991, Document No. 003179. "U.S. efforts to promote democracy in Nicaragua: Choices for Congress on covert and overt aid," US Congress, Arms Control and Foreign Policy Caucus Issue Preview dated 3 August 1989.

NSA 1991, Document No. 0099. "Embassy-Opposition Dialogue," Confidential Cable No. 02057 from the US Embassy in Managua to the Department of State, dated 4 May 1978.

Primary sources: US Government documents, published

Congressional Record. 4 March 1988, pp. S1949-S1951.

Congressional Record. 10 August 1988, p. S11476.

Congressional Record. 19 July 1989, pp. S8238-S8241.

Congressional Record. 21 March 1991, pp. S3930 and H2015.

International Relations Committee. A New Canal Treaty: A Latin American Imperative. Report of a Study Mission to Panama, November 21-23 1975. Washingon: US Govt. Printing Office, 1976.

"The President's News Conference of June 17, 1965," Public Papers of the President of the United States: Lyndon B. Johnson, 1965, vol. II. Washington, DC: USGPO, 1966.

"The President's News Conference of January 15, 1962," Public Papers of the Presidents of the United States: John F. Kennedy. Washington, DC: USGPO, 1963.

"The President's News Conference of October 31, 1963," Public Papers of the Presidents of the United States: John F. Kennedy, 1963. Washington, DC: USGPO, 1964.

United States, Department of State. The Defense and Neutrality of the Panama Canal Under the New Treaties Special Report No. 37. Washington, D.C.: Bureau of Public Affairs, Department of State, 1978.

United States Senate, 94 Congress, 1st. session. Alleged Assassination Plots Involving Foreign Leaders: An Interim Report of the Select Committee to Study Governmental Operations with Respect to Intelligence Activities, An Interim Report. Washington, DC: U.S. Government Printing Office, 1975.

Primary sources: United Kingdom

The primary British documents on the Dominican Republic were taken from the Public Record Office, located at Kew, London. The documents quoted in the book are listed under the PRO's reference code and document numbers. All the relevant information regarding the documents is also included.

UK.PRO.FO371/147947. "Summary Report on political troubles." Confidential Correspondence from Mr. Mc Vittie at the United Kingdom's Embassy in Ciudad Trujillo, dated 16 February 1960.

UK.PRO.FO371/147948. "Interpretation of recent political changes," Confidential correspondence from Mr. Mc Vittie, United Kingdom Embassy in Ciudad Trujillo, dated 8 August 1960.

UK.PRO.FO371/155986. "Wide scale political campaign in USA in preparation for the Presidential election," Confidential correspondence from Mr. Mc Vittie, United Kingdom's Embassy in Ciudad Trujillo, 5 May 1961.

UK.PRO.FO371/155987. "Conversation between Mr. Achilles and Head of Chancery: State Department concerned at reports received from the [US] Consul General," Confidential Correspondence from Mr. Rennie at the United Kingdom's Embassy in Ciudad Trujillo, dated 3 June 1961.

UK.PRO.FO371/155988. "Show of liberalisation by the Balaguer Government," Confidential Correspondence from Mr. Mc Vittie, United Kingdom's Embassy in Ciudad Trujillo, dated 15 June 1961.

UK.PRO.FO371/155989. "Points made in a statement by President Balaguer published in La Nacion," Restricted correspondence from Mr. Harding, United Kingdom's Embassy in Ciudad Trujillo, dated 12 August 1961.

UK.PRO.FO371/155989. "President Balaguer had consultation with US Consul-General about members of Trujillo family who are likely to oppose him", Confidential Correspondence from Mr. Harding, United Kingdom's Embassy in Ciudad Trujillo, dated 15 July 1961.

UK.PRO.FO371/155991. "Echavarria declared his loyalty to Balaguer," Restricted correspondence from Mr. Mc Vittie, United Kingdom's Embassy in Ciudad Trujillo, dated 20 November 1961.

UK.PRO.FO371/155991. "Public correction appeared in 'El Caribe' of a statement made by President Balaguer about exiling army officers," Restricted correspondence from Mr. Harding, United Kingdom's Embassy in Ciudad Trujillo, dated 13 October 1961.

UK.PRO.FO371/155991. "Mr. Rusk's statements about the return to the Dominican Republic of Hector and Arismendi Trujillo," Confidential Correspondence from Sir Ormsby-Gore, United Kingdom's Embassy in Washington, dated 19 November 1961.

UK.PRO.FO371/167994. "State Department's attitude toward recent military coups," Confidential correspondence from Sir D. Ormsby-Gore at the United Kingdom's Embassy in Washington, DC, dated 12 October 1963.

UK.PRO.FO371/167995. "Dominican government has been recognised by certain European governments," Restricted correspondence from Mr. Lockhart, United Kingdom's Embassy in Santo Domingo, dated 1 November 1963.

UK.PRO.FO371/167995. "Possible return to constitutional legality because of American threats to withdraw aid," Confidential correspondence from Mr. Lockhart, United Kingdom's Embassy in Santo Domingo, dated 18 October 1963.

UK.PRO.FO371/173871. "In 1962 the Council of State used Francisco Aguirre to influence a pro-Dominican lobby in the US for a fee of $150,000 dollars a year," Confidential Correspondence, from Mr. Lockhart, United Kingdom's Embassy in Santo Domingo, dated 2 January 1964.

UK.PRO.FO371/179329. "Mr. Lockhart's Valedictory Despatch." Confidential Correspondence by S. A. Lockhart from the British Embassy in Santo Domingo, dated 2 April 1965.

UK.PRO.FO371/179330. "Complete breakdown of law and order," Confidential correspondence from Mr. Campbell, United Kingdom's Embassy in Santo Domingo, dated 29 April 1965.

UK.PRO.FO371/179331. "The State Department has requested any additional material available on the President's statement that the revolutionary movement has been taken over by a band of Communist conspirators," Confidential correspondence from Sir P. Dean, United Kingdom's Embassy in Washington, DC, dated 3 May 1965.

UK.PRO.FO371/179332. "Camaño has been proclaimed President of the rebel provisional government," Confidential correspondence from Mr. Campbell, United Kingdom's Embassy in Santo Domingo, dated 4 May 1965.

UK.PRO.FO371/179335. "Conversation with Mr. Schlaudeman of the State Department: affirms that Wessin's removal was ordered from Washington," Confidential correspondence from Mr. Campbell, United Kingdom's Embassy in Santo Domingo, dated 11 May 1965.

UK.PRO.FO371/179336. "Although Wessin has broken the cease-fire he seems to have incurred US sympathy," Confidential Correspondence from Mr. Campbell, United Kingdom's Embassy in Santo Domingo, dated 13 May 1965.

UK.PRO.FO371/179338. "Mr. Bundy's views on the Dominican situation," Confidential correspondence from Mr. Campbell, United Kingdom's Embassy in Santo Domingo, dated 27 May 1965.

UK.PRO.FO371/179342. "Reports on tape recordings which have been obtained by monitoring radio frequencies used by San Isidro and Wessin-controlled out station during fighting between 25–29 April," Secret Correspondence from Mr. Campbell, United Kingdom's Embassy in Santo Domingo, dated 17 August 1965.

UK.PRO.FO371/179342. "Comments on Mr. Slater's letter of 2 August in connection with Mr. Killick's visit to the Dominican Republic," Secret Correspondence from Mr. Killick at the United Kingdom's Embassy in Washington to Mr. Slater, dated 19 August 1965.

UK.PRO.FO371/179345. "Comments on the growing American disenchantment with Garcia Godoy," Confidential Correspondence from Sir P. Dean, United Kingdom's Embassy in Washington, dated 27 October 1965.

UK.PRO.FO371/179345. "Situation in October 1965," Confidential correspondence from Mr. Bell, United Kingdom's Embassy in Santo Domingo, dated 26 October 1965.

UK.PRO.FO371/179346. "Details of recent coup d'etat at Santo Domingo," Secret Correspondence from Mr. Bell, United Kingdom's Embassy in Santo Domingo, dated 25 November 1965.

UK.PRO.FO371/179347. "An opinion is that Constitutionalists started the recent fighting in Santo Domingo," Confidential Correspondence from Sir P. Dean, United Kingdom's Embassy in Washington, dated 23 December 1965.

UK.PRO:FO371/147948. "Generalissimo Trujillo's awaited speech," Confidential Correspondence from Mr. Mc Vittie at the United Kingdom's Embassy in Ciudad Trujillo, dated 29 September 1960.

UK.PRO:FO371/179345. "Details of meeting with Provisional President," Secret Correspondence from Mr. Bell, United Kingdom's Embassy in Santo Domingo, dated 4 November 1965.

Secondary documents: books, chapters, dissertations and journal articles

Abernethy, David B. "Dominant-Subordinate Relationships: How Shall We Define Them? How Shall We Compare Them?" In Jan Triska, *Dominant Powers and Subordinate States*, pp. 103–123.

Allerton McConnell, Shelley. "From bullets to ballots: Nicaragua's revolutionary transition to democracy." PhD Dissertation, Standford University, 1998.

Ameringer, Charles D. *The Caribbean Legion: Patriots, Politicians, Soldiers of Fortune, 1946–1950*. University Park, Pennsylvania: The Pennsylvania State University Press, 1996.

Atkins, G. Pope and Wilson, Lamar C. *The United States and the Trujillo Regime*. New Brunswick, New Jersey: Rutgers University Press, 1972.

Baloyra, Enrique. "Democratic Transitions in Comparative Perspective." In Enrique Baloyra (ed.), *Comparing New Democracies*. Boulder and London: Westview Press, 1987.

Bartlow Martin, John. *Overtaken by Events: The Dominican Crisis from the Fall of Trujillo to the Civil War*. Garden City, New York: Doubleday & Company, Inc. 1966.

Bethel, Leslie and Ian Roxborough (eds.) *Latin America between the Second World War and the Cold War. 1944–1948*. Cambridge: Cambridge University Press, 1992.

Bosch, Juan. *Trujillo: Causas de una tiranía sin ejemplo*. Caracas: Librería Las Novedades, 1959.

Bosch, Juan. *The Unfinished Experiment: Democracy in the Dominican Republic*. London: The Pall Mall Press, 1966.

Bosch, Juan. *La fortuna de Trujillo*. Santo Domingo: Alfa y Omega, 1985.

Bowman, Kirk S. "New scholarship on Costa Rican Exceptionalism." *Journal of Interamerican Studies and World Affairs*, vol. 41, no. 2 (Summer 1999), pp. 123–130.

Bracey, Audrey. *Resolution of the Dominican Crisis, 1965: A Study in Mediation*. Washington, DC: Institute for the Study of Diplomacy, School of Foreign service, Georgetown University, 1980.

Buckley, Kevin. *Panama: The Whole Story*. New York: Simon & Schuster, 1991.

Busey, James. *Political Aspects of the Panama Canal: The Problem of Location*. Tucson, Arizona: The University of Arizona Press, 1974.

Calder, Bruce J. *The Impact of Intervention: The Dominican Republic during the U.S. Occupation of 1916–1924*. Austin: University of Texas Press, 1984.

Carothers, Thomas. *In the Name of Democracy: US Policy toward Latin America in the Reagan years*. Berkeley, Los Angeles and London: University of California Press, 1991.

Castillo, María Eliana. "Después del canal: nuevos desafíos en la política exterior de Panamá." In Heraldo Muñoz (comp.) *Las políticas exteriores latinoamericanas frente a la crisis*. Buenos Aires: Grupo Editor Latinoamericano, 1985.

Castro, Nils. *Objetivos Estratégicos de Estados Unidos en Panamá*. San José, Costa Rica: Comité de Solidaridad con Panamá, 1988.

Clapham, Christopher and George Philip (eds.) *The Political Dilemmas of Military Regimes*. London: Croom Helm, 1985.

Coe Clark Jr., Paul. *The United States and Somoza, 1933–1956: A Revisionist Look*. Westport, Connecticut, and London: Praeger, 1992.

Córdova Rivas, Rafael. *Contribución a la Revolución*. Managua: Centro de Publicaciones de Avanzada, s.a., 1983.

Correa, Mayín (comp.) *La gran rebelión blanca*. Miami, Florida: SIBI, 1987.

Cottam, Martha L. *Images & Intervention: U.S. policies in Latin America*. Pittsburgh and London: University of Pittsburgh Press, 1994.

Crassweller, Robert D. *Trujillo: The Life and Times of a Caribbean Dictator*. New York: The Macmillan Company, 1966.

Cullather, Nick. *Illusions of Influence: The Political Economy of United States-Philippines Relations, 1942–1960*. Cambridge : Cambridge University Press, 1994.

Chalker Franklyn, Cynthia. "Riding the wave: the domestic and international sources of Costa Rican democracy," PhD Dissertation, University of Pittsburg, 1998, p. 195.

Chester, Eric Thomas. *Rag-Tags, Scum, Riff-raff, and commies: The US Intervention in the Dominican Republic, 1965–1966*. New York: Monthly Review Press, 2001.

D'Agostino, Thomas Jay. "The evolution of an emerging political party system: a study of party politics in the Dominican Republic, 1961–1990," Ph.D. Thesis, Syracuse University, 1992.

Dahl, Robert A. *Polyarchy: Participation and Opposition*. New Haven: Yale University Press, 1971.

Denny, Harold Norman. *Dollars for Bullets: The Story of American Rule in Nicaragua*. New York: Dial Press, 1929.

Di Palma, Giuseppe. "The Central American and the European Experience." In Giuseppe Di Palma and Laurence Whitehead (eds.), *The Central American Impasse*. London and Sydney: Croom Helm and the Friedrich Naumann Foundation, 1986.

Di Palma, Giuseppe. *To Craft Democracies*. Berkeley, Los Angeles, Oxford: University of California Press, 1990.

Diamond, Larry. "Introduction: Persistence, Erosion, Breakdown and Renewal." In Larry Diamond, Juan Linz and Seymour Martin Lipset. (eds.), *Democracy in Developing Countries: Asia*. Boulder, Colorado: Lynne Rienner Publishers, 1989.

Díaz Herrera, Roberto. *Las vallas del silencio. Panamá: a los 18 años del golpe militar.* Panamá: Panamanian Defense Forces, 1986.

Diederich, Bernard. *Somoza and the legacy of US involvement in Central America.* London: Junction Books, 1982.

Dinges, John. *Our Man in Panama.* New York: Random House, 1990.

Dodd, Thomas. *Managing democracy in Central America: United States election supervision in Nicaragua, 1927–1933.* Miami: The University of Miami / North-South Center, 1992.

Dominguez, Jorge I. "The Caribbean Question: Why Has Liberal Democracy (Surprisingly) Flourished?" In Jorge I. Dominguez, Robert A. Pastor, and R. De Lisle Worrell (eds.), *Democracy in the Caribbean: Political, Economic and Social Perspectives.* Baltimore and London: The Johns Hopkins University Press, 1993.

Draper, Theodore. *A very thin line: the Iran-contra affairs.* New York: Hill and Wang, 1991.

Draper, Theodore. *The Dominican Revolt.* New York: Commentary, 1968.

Escobar Bethancourt, Rómulo. *Torrijos: colonia americana No.* Panamá: M. V. Publishing Co., 1981.

Everingham, Mark. *Revolution and the multiclass coalition in Nicaragua.* Pittsburgh: University of Pittsburgh Press, 1996.

Falk, Richard. *The Promise of World Order: Essays in Normative International Relations.* Brighton, Great Britain Wheatsheaf Books, 1987.

Farnsworth, David N. & James W. Mc Kenney, *US Panamanian Relations, 1903–1978.* Boulder, Colorado: Westwiew Press, 1983.

Gaddis, John Lewis. *Estados Unidos y los Orígenes de la Guerra Fría 1941–1947.* Buenos Aires: Grupo Editor Latinoamericano, 1989.

Gaddis, John Lewis. *The United States and the End of the Cold War Implications, Reconsiderations, Provocations.* New York and Oxford: Oxford University Press, 1992.

Galíndez, Jesús de. *The era of Trujillo: Dominican Dictator.* Santo Domingo: La Trinitaria, 1973.

Gambone, Michael D. *Eisenhower, Somoza, and the Cold War in Nicaragua, 1953–1961.* Wesport, CN: Praeger Publishers, 1997.

Gates, John M. "Problemas del desarrollo de la doctrina." *Military Review* (spanish american edition) vol. LXVIII, No. 8, August 1988, p. 7.

Gills, Barry, Joel Rocamora and Richard Wilson (eds.) *Low Intensity Democracy, London and Boulder.* Colorado: Pluto Press, 1993.

Gleijeses, Piero. *Shattered Hopes: The Guatemalan Revolution and the United States, 1944–1954.* Princeton: Princeton University Press, 1991.

Gleijeses, Piero. *The Dominican crisis: the 1965 Constitutionalist revolt and American intervention.* Baltimore: Johns Hopkins University Press, 1978.

Goertz, Gary and Solem, Jon. "Eastern Europe, 1945–1989." In Gary Goertz, *Contexts of International Politics.* Cambridge: Cambridge University Press, 1994.

Goertz, Gary. *Contexts of International Politics.* Cambridge: Cambridge University Press, 1994.

Goldrich, Daniel. *Sons of the Establishment: Elite Youth in Panama and Costa Rica.* Chicago, IL: Rand McNally and Co., 1966.

Goldwert, Marvin. *The Constabulary in the Dominican Republic and Nicaragua: Progeny and Legacy of United States intervention.* Gainesville: University of Florida Press, 1962.

Green, Daniel M. "Liberal moments and democracy's durability: Comparing global outbreaks of democracy—1918,1945,1989." *Studies in Comparative International Development,* (34: 1, Spring 1999), pp. 83–120.

Guerrero, Miguel. *El Golpe de Estado: Historia del Derrocamiento de Juan Bosch.* Santo Domingo: Editora Corripio, 1993.

Halloran, Richard. "US Troops to Go Slowly Into Panama." *The New York Times,* 12 May 1989, p. A8.

Denny, Harold Norman. *Dollars for Bullets: American rule in Nicaragua.* New York: L. MacKeagh, The Dial Press, 1929.

Hartlyn, Jonathan, Lars Schoultz and Augusto Varas (eds.) *The United States and Latin America in the 1990s.* Chapel Hill: University of North Carolina Press, 1992.

Herman, Edward S. and Frank Brodhead. *Demonstration elections: US-staged elections in the Dominican Republic, Vietnam, and El Salvador.* Boston: South End Press, 1984.

Herman, Margaret and Charles Kegley, "The Use of US Military intervention to Promote Democracy: Evaluating the Record." *International Interactions,* vol. 24, no. 2 (1998), pp. 91–114.

Herrera Zúñiga, Luis. *Relaciones internacionales y poder político en Nicaragua.* Mexico City: El Colegio de México, 1991.

Huntington, Samuel. "American ideals vs. American institutions." *Political Science Quarterly,* vol. 97, no. 1, (1982), p.27.

Hurrell, Andrew. "Explaining the resurgence of regionalism in world politics." *Review of International Studies,* vol. 21, 1995.

Institute for the Comparative Study of Electoral Systems (1966). *Nicaragua Election Factbook: February 5, 1967.* Washington, DC: Institute for the Comparative Study of Electoral Systems.

Jackson, Robert H. and James, Alan. "The Character of Independent Statehood." In Robert Jackson and Alan James (eds.), *States in a Changing World: A Contemporary Analysis.* Oxford: Clarendon Press, 1993.

Karl, Terry. "Imposing Consent? Electoralism vs. Democratisation in El Salvador." In Paul W. Drake and Eduardo Silva (eds.), *Elections and Democratisation in Latin America, 1980-1985.* San Diego, California: University of California, San Diego, 1986.

Keal, Paul. "On Influence and Spheres-of-influence." In Jan Triska, *Dominant Powers and Subordinate States: The United States in Latin America and the Soviet Union in Eastern Europe.* Durnham: Duke University Press, 1986.

Keal, Paul. *Unspoken Rules and Superpower Dominance.* London: MacMillan Press LTD., 1983.

Kempe, Frederick. *Divorcing the Dictator.* New York: G.P. Putnam's Sons, 1990.

Kirpatrick, Jeanne. "Dictatorship and Double Standards." *Commentary* No. 68 (November 1979), pp. 34–35.

Knut, Walter. *The regime of Anastasio Somoza, 1936–1956.* Chapel Hill and London: The University of North Carolina Press, 1993.

Krehm, William. "La era de un buen vecino." In *Democracias y Tiranias en el Caribe,* (Santa Fe de Bogota: Planeta, (1998) [1984c]), pp. 325–365.

LaFeber, Walter. *Inevitable Revolutions: The United States in Central America.* New York and London: WW. Norton & Company, 1983.

Latin American Studies Association Delegation to Observe the Nicaraguan General Election of 4 November 1984. "The electoral process in Nicaragua: domestic and international influences." Pittsburgh: LASA, 19 November 1984.

Leis, Raúl. *Radiografía de los partidos.* Panamá: Centro de Capacitación Social, 1984.

Lipset, Seymour Martin. *Political Man: The Social Bases of Politics,* expanded edition. Baltimore: The John Hopkins University Press, 1981.

Lipset, Seymour Martin. "The Centrality of Political Culture," *Journal of Democracy* 1 (Fall 1990), pp. 88-91.

Lipset, Seymour Martin. Some Social Requisites of Democracy," *American Political Science Review,* Vol. 53, 1959, pp. 69-105.

Lopez, George A. and Stohl, Michael (eds.). *Liberalization and Redemocratisation in Latin America.* Westport, Connecticut: Greenwood Press, 1987.

Lowenthal, Abraham. "The United States and Latin American Democracy: Learning from History." In Abraham Lowenthal (ed.), *Exporting Democracy: The United States and Latin America.* Baltimore and London: The Johns Hopkins University Press, 1991.

Lowenthal, Abraham. *Exporting Democracy: The United States and Latin America.* Baltimore and London: The Johns Hopkins University Press, 1991.

Lowenthal, Abraham. *The Dominican intervention.* Cambridge, Mass: Harvard University Press, 1972.

MacRenato, Ternot. "Somoza Seizure of Power, 1926–1939," Ph.D. Dissertation, University of California, San Diego, 1991.

Major, John. *Prize possession: the United States and the Panama Canal, 1903–1979.* Cambridge: Cambridge University Press, 1993.

Martínez, José de Jesús. *Mi General Torrijos.* La Habana: Casa de las Américas, 1988.

McIntosh, Charles D. "Life with the generalissimo." *American Heritage.* November 1997.

Meernik, James. "United States Military Intervention and the Promotion of Democracy." *Journal of Peace Research,* vol. 33, no. 4 (1996), pp. 391–402.

Michael Burton, Richard Gunther, and John Higley, "Elites and Democratic Consolidation in Latin America and Southern Europe: An Overview." In John Higley and Richard Gunther (eds.) *Elites and Democratic Consolidation in Latin America and Southern Europe.* Cambridge and Melbourne: Cambridge University Press, 1992.

Millet, Richard. *Guardians of the Dynasty: A History of the US created Guardia Nacional and the Somoza Family.* United States: Orbis Books, 1977.

Moreno, José A. *Barrios in Arms: Revolution in Santo Domingo.* Pittsburgh: University of Pittsburgh Press, 1970.

Morley, Morris H. *Washington, Somoza and the Sandinistas: State and Regime in US Policy Toward Nicaragua, 1969–1981*. Cambridge: Cambridge University Press, 1994.

Morrison, Delesseps S. *Latin American Mission: An adventure in Hemisphere Diplomacy*. New York: Simon and Schuster, 1965.

Muñoz, Heraldo. "Chile: The Limits of Success." In Abraham Lowenthal (ed.), *Exporting Democracy: The US and Latin America*. Baltimore, MD: The Johns Hopkins University Press, 1991.

Nohlen, Dieter (ed.) *Enciclopedia Electoral Latinoamericana y del Caribe*. San José: Instituto Interamericano de Derechos Humanos, 1993.

Noriega, Manuel and Peter Eisner. *The Memoirs of Manuel Noriega*. New York: Random House, 1997.

O'Donnell, Guillermo; Schmitter, Philip C. and Whitehead, Laurence. *Transitions from Authoritarian Rule*. Baltimore: John Hopkins University Press, 1986.

Palmer Jr. Bruce. *Intervention in the Caribbean: The Dominican Crisis of 1965*. The University Press of Kentucky, 1989.

Palmer, General Bruce. *Intervention in the Caribbean: The Dominican Crisis of 1965*. Lexington, Kentucky: The University Press of Kentucky, 1989.

Parkinson, Fred. "Latin America." In Robert Jackson and Alan James (eds.), *States in a Changing World: A Contemporary Analysis*. Oxford: Clarendon Press, 1993.

Pastor, Robert A. "The Lessons and the Legacy of Omar Torrijos." In *Whirlpool: US Foreign Policy Towards Latin America and the Caribbean*. Princeton: Princeton University Press, 1993.

Pastor, Robert A. "The United States and Central America Interlocking Debates." In Peter B. Evans, Harold K. Jacobson, and Robert Putnam (eds.), *Double-Edged Diplomacy: International Bargaining and Domestic Politics*. Berkeley, Los Angeles, London: University of California Press, 1993.

Pastor, Robert A. "Promoting Democracy Pushing on the Pendulum," in *Whirlpool: US Foreign Policy Toward Latin America and the Caribbean*. Princeton: Princeton University Press, 1992.

Pastor, Robert A. *Condemned to repetition: The United States and Nicaragua*. Pittsburgh: The University of Pittsburgh Press, 1987.

Pearcy, Thomas L. *We Answer Only to God: Politics and the Military in Panama, 1903–1947*. Albuquerque: University of New Mexico Press, 1998.

Peceny, Mark. "Forcing them to be free," *Political Research Quarterly*, vol. 52, no. 3 (September 1999), pp. 549–582.

Peceny, Mark. *Democracy at the Point of Bayonets*. University Park: Pennsylvania University Press, 1999.

Pezzullo Larence. Association for Diplomatic Studies, Foreign Affairs Oral History Program, Lawinger Library. Georgetown University, 24 February 1989.

Pinder, John. "The European Community and Democracy in Central and Eastern Europe." In Geoffrey Pridham, Eric Herring, and George Sanford (eds.), *Building Democracy? The International Dimension of Democratisation in Eastern Europe*. London: Leicester University Press, 1994.

Pridham, Geoffrey and Vanhanen, Tatu (eds.). *Democratisation in Eastern Europe: Domestic and International Perspectives*. London and New York: Routledge, 1994.

Pridham, Geoffrey. "International Influences and Democratic Transition: Problems of Theory and Practice in Linkage Politics." In Geoffrey Pridham (ed.), *Encouraging Democracy: The International Context of Regime Transition in Southern Europe*. London: Leicester University Press, 1991.

Pridham, Geoffrey. "Comparative Perspectives on the New Mediterranean Democracies: A Model of Regime Transition?" In Geoffrey Pridham (ed.), *The New Mediterranean Democracies: Regime Transition in Spain, Greece and Portugal*. London: Frank Cass and Co., 1984.

Przeworski, Adam. *Democracy and the Market: Political and Economic Reform in Eastern Europe and Latin America*. New York: Cambridge University Press, 1991.

Remmer, Karen L. "Democratization in Latin America." In Robert O. Slater, Barry M. Schutz, and Steven R. Dorr (eds.), *Global Transformation and the Third World*. Boulder and London: Lynne Rienner Publishers and Adamantine Press, 1993.

Remmer, Karen L. "Democratisation in Latin America." In Slater, Schutz, and Dorr (1993), *op. cit.*, pp. 97–98.

Ricord, Humberto. *Los clanes de la oligarquía panameña y el golpe militar de 1968*. Panama: undefined publisher, 1983.

Ritter, Jorge. *Los secretos de la Nunciatura*. Bogotá: Editorial Oveja Negra, 1990.

Robinson, William. *Promoting Polyarchy: Globalization, U.S. Intervention and Hegemony*. Cambridge: Cambridge University Press, 1996.

Rodriguez Stein, Rosa Emilia. "Collective Action in Peripheral Nations A comparative analysis of Five Central American countries." Ph.D. Dissertation, University of Arizona, 1989.

Roorda, Eric Paul. *The Dictator Next Door: The Good Neighbor Policy and the Trujillo Regime in the Dominican Republic, 1930–1945*. Durnham and London: Duke University Press, 1998.

Roosevelt, Theodore. *The Autobiography of Theodore Roosevelt*, (New York: Charles Scribner's Sons, 1919.

Ropp, Steve. *Panamanian Politics: From Guarded Nation to National Guard*. New York: Praeger Publishers, 1982.

Rosenau, James. "Pre-theories and theories of foreign policy." In R. B. Farrell (ed.), *Approaches to Comparative and International Politics*. Evanston, Illinois Northwestern University Press, 1966.

Rosenau, James. "Toward the Study of National-International Linkages." In James Rosenau (ed.), *Linkage Politics: Essays on the Convergence of National and International Systems*. New York and London: The Free Press and Collier-Macmillan, 1969.

Rosenthal, Andrew. "US Considered Aid to Panama Rebels." *The New York Times*, 5 October 1989, p. 1A.

Rustow, Dankart. "Transitions to Democracy: Towards a Dynamic Model," *Comparative Politics* 2 (April 1970), pp. 358–361.

Ryan, David, *US-Sandinista diplomatic relations: voice of intolerance*. Basingstoke: Macmillan, 1995.

Salamín, Marcel. *El Salvador: sin piso ni techo*. Bogotá: Editorial La Oveja Negra, 1980.

Sanchez, Jose Manuel. "U.S. Intervention in the Caribbean, 1954–1965: Decision-making and the information input." Ph.D. Thesis, Columbia University, 1972.

Santa Fe Committee. "A New Interamerican Policy for the Eighties," Report dated in 1980.

Schmitter, Philippe. "Una introducción a las transiciones desde la dominación autoritaria en Europa meridional: Italia, Grecia, Portugal, España y Turquía." In Guillermo O'Donnell, Philippe C. Schmitter and Laurence Whitehead (eds.), *Transiciones desde un gobierno autoritario: Europa Meridional*, Vol. 1. Buenos Aires, Barcelona, Mexico: Paidós, 1989 [1986].

Schoultz, Lars. *Beneath the United States: A History of U.S. Policy toward Latin America*. Cambridge: Harvard University Press, 1998.

Schwartz, Benjamin C. *American Counterinsurgency Doctrine and El Salvador: The Frustrations of Reform and the Illusions of Nation Building*. Santa Monica, California: Rand, 1991.

Semidei, Manuela. "Panama, les Etats-Unis et la Zone du canal." *Problemes D'Amerique Latine*, vol. XXIX (29 November 1973), p. 8.

Shifter, Jacobo. *Costa Rica, 1948: Análisis de documentos confidenciales del Departamento de Estado*. San José, Costa Rica: Editorial Universitaria Centroamericana, 1982.

Simensen, Jarle. "Democracy and globalization: Nineteen eighty-nine and the "Third Wave." *Journal of World History*, (10: 2, Fall 1999), pp. 391–411.

Slater, Jerome. *Intervention and negotiation: the United States and the Dominican revolution*. New York : Harper & Row, 1970.

Smith, Tony. *America's Mission: The United States and the Worldwide Struggle for Democracy*. Princeton: Princeton University Press, 1994.

Soler Torrijos, Giancarlo. "No hemos tenido el apoyo adecuado de Washington para el proceso de Contadora. Entrevista a James Carter." *Diálogo Social*, (September 1986), p. 47.

Soler, Ricaurte (comp.) *Pensamiento político en Panamá en los siglos XIX y XX*. Panamá: Biblioteca de la Librería Cultural Panameña, 1988.

Soler, Ricaurte. "Panamá: la autonomía universitaria de 1968 a 1978." *Tareas*, (April–September 1981), p. 71.

Stimson, Henry L. *American Policy in Nicaragua*, New York: Charles Scribner's Sons, 1927.

Tocqueville, Alexis de. *Democracy in America*. New York and London: Harper and Row, 1969.

Tong, Yanqi. "Economic Reform and Political Change in Reforming Socialist Societies: The Cases of China and Hungary," Ph.D. Dissertation, The Johns Hopkins University, 1992.

Tovias, Alfred (1984). "The International Context of Democratic Transition." In Pridham, *The New Mediterranean Democracies*, pp. 158-171.

Triska, Jan (ed.). *Dominant Powers and Subordinate States: The United States in Latin America and the Soviet Union in Eastern Europe*. Durnham: Duke University Press, 1986.

Tsingos, Bassilios. "Underwriting Democracy, Not Exporting It." M.Phil. Thesis, Oxford University, 1994.

Urrutia, Ricardo. "Panamá: Las crecientes tensiones con Estados Unidos." In Heraldo Muñoz (comp.) *Las políticas exteriores de América Latina y el Caribe: continuidad en la crisis.* Buenos Aires: Grupo Editor Latinoamericano, 1986.

Vanhanen, Tatu. "Introduction." In *Strategies of Democratisation.* Washington, Philadelphia and London: Crane Russak, 1992.

Vanhanen, Tatu. *The Process of Democratisation: A Comparative Study of 147 States, 1980-1988.* Washington, Philadelphia and London: Crane Russak, 1990.

Vega, Bernardo. *Eisenhower y Trujillo.* Santo Domingo: Fundación Cultural Dominicana, 1991.

Velásquez, Itzel. *El fin de la tregua: Crónica de la invasión norteamericana a Panamá.* México City: Editorial Diana, 1996.

Verney, Susannah. "To be or not to be within the European Community: the party debate and democratic consolidation in Greece." In Geoffrey Pridham (ed.), *Securing democracy: political parties and democratic consolidation in Southern Europe.* London and New York: Routledge, 1990.

Watson, Bruce and Peter Tsouras. *Operation Just Cause: the U.S Intervention in Panama.* Boulder, Colorado: Westview Press, 1991.

Weffort, Francisco. "New Democracies, Which Democracies?" Washington, DC: The Woodrow Wilson International Center for Scholars, Latin American Program's Working Paper Number 198, 1992.

Weiss, Thomas G. and James G. Blight (ed.) *The suffering grass: Superpowers and regional conflict in Southern Africa and the Caribbean.* Boulder and London: Lynne Rienner Publishers, 1992.

Whitehead, Laurence (ed.) *The international dimension of democratisation: Europe and the Americas.* Oxford: Oxford University Press, 1997.

Whitehead, Laurence. "East-Central Europe in Comparative Perspective." In Pridham, Herring, and Sanford (eds.), *Building Democracy? The International Dimension of Democratisation in Eastern Europe,* pp. 32–59.

Whitehead, Laurence. "International Aspects of Democratisation." In Guillermo O'Donnell, Philippe C. Schmitter and Laurence Whitehead (eds.), *Transitions from Authoritarian Rule: Comparative Perspectives,* Vol. 3. Baltimore and London: The Johns Hopkins University Press, 1986.

Whitehead, Laurence. "The Imposition of Democracy." In Abraham Lowenthal (ed.), *Exporting Democracy: The United States and Latin America,* (Baltimore and London: The Johns Hopkins University Press, 1991), pp. 356-382.

Whitehead, Laurence. "Geography and democratic destiny," *Journal of Democracy,* January 1999, pp. 74–79.

Whitehead, Laurence. *Economic Liberalization and Democratisation: Exploration of the Linkages.* New York: Pergamon Press, 1993.

Woerner, General Fred. "The Strategic Imperatives for the United States in Latin America." *Military Review* vol. LXIX, no. 2r3 (February 1989), p. 22.

Woodward, Bob. *The Commanders.* New York: Simon & Schuster, 1991.

Woodward, Bob. *Veil: The Secret Wars of the CIA.* New York: Simon & Schuster Inc, 1987.

Zakaria, Fareed. *From wealth to power: The unusual origins of America's world role.* Princeton, New Jersey: Princeton University Press, 1998.

Secondary documents:
Newspaper articles, no author

"Anuncia Torrijos al Pueblo: Guerra contra el desempleo y la pobreza." *La Estrella de Panamá,* 2 November 1977, p. 1.

"Belicismo de Reagan nos amenaza." *La Prensa.* Managua, 1 December 1980.

"Coyuntura: se inicia la recta final." *Envío* 6 (74, August 1987), p. 6.

"Desde Washington se le dio la alerta a Noriega." *La Prensa* (Panama City), 11 January 1990, p. 2-A.

"Drug Arrests Disrupt CIA Operation." *The New York Times.* 14 January 1990.

"Esquipulas II: Gran paso hacia la paz." *Envío* 6 (75, September 1987), p. 1.

"Esquipulas III: Jaque a la guerra." *Envío* 7 (80, February 1988), p. 4.

"Fracasó el Bloqueo Económico y Político a Panamá: W. Crowe." *Excelsior,* 17 October 1989, pp. 2-A, 27-A.

"La guerra retrocede: crisis de la política USA." *Envío* 8 (96, August 1989), p. 13–14.

"La inestabilidad en Panamá no permite negociar: Linares." *La Jornada,* 21 June 1992, p. 42.

"La recta final de las elecciones." *Envío* 4 (41, November 1984), p. 4-b.

"México y la resolución de la OEA sobre Panamá." *El Día,* (México, D.F.), 25 May 1989.

"No estamos hablando sobre bases después del año 2000." *Canal de Panamá Hoy,* (CELA's bimonthly bulletin, December 1992).

"Ofensiva de Panamá para evitar el aislamiento político." *Excelsior,* 28 October 1989, pp. 2-A, 21A.

"Panama likes democracy but wants something else too." *The Economist.* 2-8 February 1991, p. 39.

"Panamá, el Senado de los Estados Unidos y América Latina", *La Prensa* (Panama City), 9 April 1987, p. 3.

"Panamá: intervención y soberanía." *Coyuntura Centroamericana* no. 6–7, February–March 1988, p. 21.

"Reagan persiste: se dificultan los diálogos." *Envío* 7 (79, January 1988), p. 2.

"Royo: situación 'muy seria' si Reagan gana," *La Prensa.* Managua, 8 October 1980.

"Socialcristianos ante el triunfo de Reagan," *La Prensa.* Managua, 12 November 1980.

"Una propuesta que desarma: análisis de coyuntura del 5 de mayo al 6 de junio de 1986." *Envío* 5 (60, June 1986), pp. 1a–2a.

"El proceso electoral avanza entre grandes dificultades: Análisis de coyuntura del 5 de febrero al 5 de marzo." *Envío* 3 (33, March 1984), p. 3-a.

"Panama: Prospects for Relations with the US." Defense Intelligence Agency's Secret National Intelligence Estimate Number 84-68, dated 28 August 1968.

"Powell first US Black President?" *Star & Herald,* 22 August, 1990, p. 1.

Newspaper articles, with author:

Chamorro Barrios, Pedro Joaquín. "EEUU repite: el bloqueo posible," *La Prensa.* Managua, 23 November 1981.

Chamorro Barrios, Pedro Joaquín. "Los problemas de los nicaragüenses los resolveremos los nicaragüenses," *La Prensa.* Managua, 12 November 1981.

Engelberg, Stephen. "C.I.A. funnels Aid to Noriega's Elections Foes." *The New York Times*, 23 April 1989, p. 11A.

Engelberg, Stephen. "US Officials Say Senators Balked at Noriega Ouster." *The New York Times*, 24 April1989, pp. 1A, 11A.

Figueroa, Vilma E. "Implican a cuatro oficiales de E.U. en complot contra Guillermo Endara." *La Prensa.* 26 April, 1992, p. 1A.

Gordon, Michael. "Panama Alerted to Attack, General Says." *The New York Times*, 27 February, 1990, p. 15A.

Lira, Carmen. "Panamá: el rostro oculto de una invasión", Supplement of the Mexican daily *La Jornada*, 24 September 1992, p. 2

Martínez, Fernando. "Refuta Endara la acusación." *La Jornada.* 30 July 1991.

Martínez, Fernando. "Preocupa al Congreso de EU la inestabilidad panameña." *La Jornada*, 19 April, 1991, p. 29.

McClintock, John. "Comenzaron a presionar a Panamá E.U. y sus principales aliados de América Latina." *Excelsior*, 29 October 1989, pp. 36A, 38A.

Oppenheimer, Andres. "Participant: Secret Pact Made Over Inaugural Sit." *Miami Herald*, 27 December 1989, p. 1.

Pear, Robert A. "Canal pacts: U.S. Looking at Dire Results." *The New York Times*, 10 May1989, p. 11.

Interviews

Interview with Guillermo Manuel Ungo, leader of the Revolutionary Democratic Front of El Salvador (FDR), 23 December 1986.

Interview with Fernando Manfredo, 27 September 1995.

Interview with former PRD President Berta Torrijos de Arosemena, July 1995; this piece of information was confirmed with other interviews.

Interview with former President Manuel Solís Palma, September 1995.

Interview with former President Ricardo De la Espriella, September 1995.

Interview with Marcel Salamín, former Torrijos' advisor, April 2001;

Interview with President Francisco Rodríguez, August 1995.

Interview with Roberto Díaz Herrera, July 1995.

www.ingramcontent.com/pod-product-compliance
Lightning Source LLC
Chambersburg PA
CBHW022357280326
41935CB00007B/213